Cities and the European Union
Mechanisms and Modes of Europeanisation

Samuele Dossi

To Lorena, Sergio and Maria Elena,
for their endless love and understanding.

ecprPRESS

First published by the ECPR Press in 2017

The ECPR Press is the publishing imprint of the European Consortium for Political Research (ECPR), a scholarly association, which supports and encourages the training, research and cross-national co-operation of political scientists in institutions throughout Europe and beyond.

ECPR Press
Harbour House
Hythe Quay
Colchester
CO2 8JF
United Kingdom

Typeset by Lapiz Digital Services

Printed and bound by Lightning Source

British Library Cataloguing in Publication Data

A catalogue record for this book is available from the British Library

HARDBACK ISBN: 978-1-785521-58-4
PAPERBACK ISBN: 978-1-786611-09-3

www.ecpr.eu/ecprpress

Schools of Democracy: How Ordinary Citizens (Sometimes) Become Competent in Participatory Budgeting Institutions
(ISBN: 9781907301186) Julien Talpin
Transnational Policy Innovation: The OECD and the Diffusion of Regulatory Impact Analysis
(ISBN: 9781907301254) Fabrizio De Francesco
Urban Foreign Policy and Domestic Dilemmas: Insights from Swiss and EU City-regions
(ISBN: 9781907301070) Nico van der Heiden
Why Aren't They There? The Political Representation of Women, Ethnic Groups and Issue Positions in Legislatures
(ISBN: 9780955820397) Didier Ruedin
Widen the Market, Narrow the Competition: Banker Interests and the Making of a European Capital Market
(ISBN: 9781907301087) Daniel Mügge

Please visit www.ecpr.eu/ecprpress for information about new publications.

Table of Contents

List of Figures and Tables

List of Figures and Tables

List of Abbreviations

ACR+	Association of Cities and Regions for recycling and sustainable resource management
AMIAT	Azienda Multiservizi Igiene Ambientale Torino (Turin Multiservices Company for Ambient Hygiene)
ANCI	Associazione Nazionale Comuni Italiani (National Association of Italian municipalities)
ARPA	Agenzia Regionale per la Protezione dell'Ambiente (Regional Agency for Environmental protection)
ATA	Agenzia Territoriale per la Casa - Torino (Territorial Housing Agency Turin)
ATO	Ambiti Territoriali Ottimali (Optimal Territorial Areas)
CAFE	Clean Air for Europe programme
CEB	Council of Europe Development Bank
CEMR	Conseil Européen des Municipalités et Régions (European Council of Municipalities and Regions)
CF	Cohesion Fund
CIPs	Community Initiative Programmes
CoM	Covenant of Mayors programme
CONAI	Consorzio Nazionale Imballaggi (National Packaging Consortium)
CPR	Common Provision Regulation for the European Structural Investment Funds
DCPP	Dipartimento per il Coordinamento delle Politiche Comunitarie (Department for the Coordination of Communitarian Policies)
DG	Directorate General (at the European Commission)
DG Clima	Directorate General for Climate Action
DG Energy	Directorate General for Energy
DG Regio	Directorate General for Regional Policy
DICOTER	Direzione Generale per il Coordinamento Territoriale (General Directorate for the Territorial Coordination)
EAGGF	European Agricultural Guidance and Guarantee Fund
EAP	Environmental Action Programme
ECCP	European Climate Change Programme
EEA	European Environmental Agency
EEEF	European Energy Efficiency Facility
EIA	Environmental Impact Assessment

ELENA	European Local Energy Assistance
EMAS	Eco-Management Audit Scheme
EPI	Environmental policy Integration
ERDF	European Regional Development Fund
ESF	European Social Fund
ESIF	European Structural and Investment Funds
EU	European Union
EU - CEP	European Union Climate and Energy Package
GHG	Green House Gasses
GPP	Green Public Procurement
GTT	Gruppo Trasporti Torinese (Turin Transport Group)
IEE	Intelligent Energy Europe Programme
IREN	Iren Energy Society
ISPRA	Istituto Superiore per la Protezione e la Ricerca Ambientale (Italian National Institute for Environmental Protection and Research)
ISTAT	Istituto Nazionale di Statistica (National Institute of Statistics)
JRC	Joint Research Centre
MATTM	Ministero dell'Ambiente e della Tutela del Territorio e del Mare (Ministry for Environment and for the Protection of Territory and the Sea)
MLG	Multi-Level Governance
NEPI	New Environmental Policy Instruments
OECD	Organisation for Economic Co-operation and Development
PPA	Public Policy Analysis
PRU	Programma di Rigenerazione Urbana (Urban Recovery Programs)
PUMS	Piano Urbano della Mobilità Sostenibile (Urban Plan for Sustainable Mobility)
PWD	Packaging Waste Directive
SDS	Sustainable Development Strategy
SEA	Single European Act
SEAS	Strategic Environmental Assessment
SEAP	Sustainable Energy Action Plan
SGI	Services of General Interest
SMAT	Società Metropolitana Acque Torinesi (Turin Metropolitan Water Company)
SSCI	Social Sciences Citation Index
TAPE	Turin Action Plan for Energy
TARSU	Tassa Rifiuti Solidi Urbani (Urban Solid Waste Tax)
TEU	Treaty on the European Union

ToA	Treaty of Amsterdam
TRM	Trattamento Rifiuti Metropolitani (Metropolitan Waste Treatment)
UNFCCC	United Nation Framework Convention on Climate Change
UPPs	Urban Pilot Projects
WCED	World Commission on Environment and Development
ZTL	Zona a Traffico Limitato (Limited Traffic Zone)

Acknowledgements

I would like to thank everyone in the College of Social Sciences and International Studies at Exeter University for their continuous support, advice and encouragement during my years as PhD student in the Department. I am also grateful to people at the Centre d'études européennes at Sciences Po Paris, especially to Prof. Patrick Le Galès for his precious advice and great knowledge about cities and urban matters. I would also like to thank Professor Nolan McCarty – Woodrow Wilson School at Princeton University – for his precious advice and support when only few people seemed to believe in the ideas at the bases of my research. Finally and foremost, I am infinitely indebted to Professor Claudio M. Radaelli, my only veritable *maestro*. Words alone cannot express all of my gratitude to him. He is certainly the greatest professional I have ever known.

Acknowledgment

Preface

This volume draws on an original research I conducted during the period 2008–2012 when carrying out a PhD degree in European Studies at the University of Exeter, under the supervision of Professor C.M. Radaelli. The main drive motivating this book – as much as the research on which it is based – is the belief that the analysis of public policy, independently of the level of territoriality at which it is performed, should foremost consider as determinants of change the set of variables that are proper of the policy problem under consideration. This is for instance the nature of preferences at actors' disposal, their resources, the structuring of their interaction and the pay-offs of the overall interactive process. A second thrust of motivation behind the entire research is a personal interest in the urban dimension of the European Union, in particular for the way the process of European integration and the progressive – although asymmetrical – structuring of a EU-wide policy arena contribute to transform the design and making of public policies in the cities of Europe.

In contrast to an established approach, based on EU instruments formally addressing cities and urban areas, this volume sets out to explore an alternative, more encompassing view. In particular, it draws on the 'sharp public policy analysis tools' advocated by Carter and Smith to generate an initial catalogue of mechanisms and arenas to consider four ideal-typical modes. These modes – NOT the policies legally defined as EU initiatives for the cities – are the theoretical places wherein the Europeanisation effects can be traced, by examining public policies and their instruments across time. This research endeavour contributes – we argue – to revitalise the literature on modes (or arenas) of policy, thus those scholarships assuming that the structuring of politics depends on the type of confrontation and strategic interaction producing around specific policy issues.

Another ambition of this volume is to demonstrate that when assessing the nature of the process of Europeanisation in the case of urban governance researchers need to look at *different policy areas* involving cities across Europe. However, this step has been somewhat hindered by the implicit shortcomings of the Multi-Level Governance (MLG) approach (Marks, et al. 1996). The tabloid version of MLG, which appears in studies of Europeanisation of sub-national systems, reduces Europeanisation to the interplay between hierarchically ordered levels of governance, where sub-national levels and central States are maintained as competing or adversarial, due to the attempt of lower levels to evade 'central control'. Thus, sub-national actors and institutions are usually treated as constituting a unique and static layer of governance (Carter and Smith, 2008: 265-266).

At an even more abstract level, there is debate on the agenda for the 'normalisation' and 'sociologisation' of European Studies – the basic idea being that we should have the same concepts to study different political systems, so the EU empirical pieces should fall in the theoretical places that can be used also outside the EU (Hassenteufel and Surel, 2000).

This agenda ties in with the motivation to 'revitalise' the logic of social action. This understanding of Europeanisation, however, also connects with strategic interaction, the importance of considering 'micro-sociological' aspects, as well as the importance of referring to social mechanisms and the modes of interaction guiding actors within different systems of territoriality. Actors *use* the opportunities offered by the European Union, but at the same time they are transformed by these relations (Jacqout and Woll, 2008). However, the approach taken in this book, accounts both for the goals of rational actors as well as for the social and institutional environments in which they are embedded. This brings us to lessen the theoretical dividing between the approaches of rational choice and social-constructivism.

Chapter One

Introduction

This analysis explains how the public policy of the European Union (EU) affects cities. To achieve this objective, the volume draws on an approach developed over the last fifteen years or so in political science and sociology, called 'Europeanisation'. The latter provides an integrated approach to appraise and explain these developments. For us, Europeanisation is first and foremost a process that shapes, and in some cases redefines, the relationships between institutional orders and levels of governance. The focus on institutional orders brings us into a political sociology literature that has crossed roads with Europeanisation and has shown its strength in the analysis of local and regional public policies (Carter and Smith, 2008; Carter and Pasquier, 2010).

Specifically, this project identifies the modes through which EU public policy has an impact on cities, explains the mechanisms that shape Europeanisation processes and how change (or lack thereof) emerges. An important aim in this work is to appraise how the type of strategic interaction determines the character of Europeanisation. Accordingly, we will look at public policy systems as constellations of actors who interact in different domains characterised by a given set of problems, levels of uncertainty, pay-offs and policy instruments. The volume contributes to the literatures on Europeanisation, policy instruments, regulatory policy and urban governance.

Having introduced the theoretical ambition of the analysis, we now turn to the substantive topic. The late twentieth century has witnessed the rise of *cities* and *regions* as important spaces for regulation and as actors in the context of national and global politics and economy. As observed by a leading author in this field, 'Instead of a homogeneous world order, we are faced with a resurgence of regionalist movements, minority nationalisms, and the *renaissance of cities as global actors*' (Keating, 2001)[1]. After losing their central role to advantage of the Central State, cities are now re-establishing their status in the economy and polity of Europe (John, 2001; Goldsmith, 2003; Le Galés, 2002). Hence, the process is one of *re-territorialisation*, rather than de-territorialisation (Brenner, 1999; 2004).

Cities are centres for the accumulation and production of wealth, functioning at time as bulwark against the effects of market forces, at time as places of social and political inequalities. Therefore, socio-economic development increasingly assumes a regional and local focus, where processes of strategic and integrated planning are deployed in the attempt to improve the international role of cities and to tackle urban revitalisation, social exclusion and environmental protection

---

1.   In Scott, A. (Ed.), *Global City-Regions: Trends, Theory, Policy*, Oxford: Oxford University Press.

(Dente, 2010). These trends are backed by the general restructuring of the relations between governments and administrations within different systems of territoriality. This is a consequence of institutional developments both in the international policy making – with the creation of differentiated regulatory authorities and entities of coordination – and within the national borders, where various processes of redistribution of territorial powers entails a renewed role for regional and local authorities.

The rise of the EU as a political system has been accompanied by a transfer of *regulatory authority* downwards to subnational territories, that is regions and *cities*, and in some circumstances up-wards in favour of supranational territorial configurations (Bagnasco and Le Galés, 2000; Keating, 2001; Kazepov, 2005; Lefevre, 1998; Le Galés, 1998; 2002).

In this new 'political economy', the concept of *regulation* denotes relations between actors and the nature of conflicts around authoritative decisions (Le Galés, 1999). Subnational authorities are arenas for *political regulation*, defined as 'the range of institutions, networks, directives, actors, bodies of regulations, norms and customs – political, social and administrative, public or private, written or unwritten – which contribute to stability, direction and the capacity to run things' (Le Galés, 1998: 484)[2]. Cities and regions have emerged as an important level for the regulation of interests, groups and institutions.

In the EU, cities have now to deal with a 'constantly changing and often different set of challenges, opportunities and constraints as they seek to manage the turbulent environment in which they operate' (Goldsmith, 2003: 115). Within this changing framework, issues of *public governance* have gained importance, particularly at the level of regulation of urban and city areas. The EU policy is a non-trivial factor pushing cities (and regions) to adapt their *institutional* structure and capacity, to cope with the pressures and challenges generated (Goldsmith, 1993a; OECD, 2000).

Traditionally, the influence of the EU on cities has been assessed by looking at the impact of policy programmes belonging to the regional structural policy, since the establishment of the European Regional Development Fund (ERDF) in 1975. During the past two decades, following the Single European Act and the new wave of reforms in 1988, the EU has played an increasing role seeking to shape both regional and urban development. For the purposes of this work, the process culminated with the establishment of the Cohesion Fund in the Treaty on European Union (1993) and the launch of a series of 'community initiatives', partly financed by the structural funds, followed by a second launch in 1994, which sets up a further initiative specifically addressed to urban areas, named URBAN.

Four principles guide the action of the European Commission towards the subnational dimension. These are concentration, programming, additionality and partnership. The latter especially allowed the European Commission to initiate an intense dialogue with city representatives, thus broadening partnerships beyond

---

2. Cited in Wright, V. (1996) 'Introduction', in V. Wright and S. Cassese (eds.) *La récomposition de lEtat en Europe*, Paris: La Decouverte.

national and regional authorities, and institutionalised groups. This encouraged regions and cities to open representative offices in Brussels and to organise themselves collectively, by means of networks and interests groups.

The principle of partnership has been further on fostered by the publication of the White Paper on European Governance by the European Commission in 2001, which places considerable emphasis on the role of partnership between all stakeholders affected by a common policy issue.

As mentioned, the involvement of cities in the policy making of the EU is supposed to take place mainly within the structural policy (John, 2001) and the specific initiatives it entails for the 2007–13 programming period as well as within those policy sectors envisaged by the EU Lisbon Agenda - now Europe 2020 (European Commission, 2007). The dismissal of specific programmes addressed to cities after 2007 and their incorporation into wider regional policies confronts European cities with new challenges, thus opening up further questions as to the place and role of cities and urban actors within the EU. At the same time, though, the development of an urban policy of the European Union seems to still be far from an effective fulfilment.

The Lisbon Strategy brought European cities at the forefront of the EU-led policy making and urban territories become the centre for the regulation and promotion of crosscutting integrated policies. Cities are also a key component of the attempts to create new loci of legitimacy for the EU and to learn by learning through experimental governance at the local level, often in connection to the rise of new modes of governance like the open method of coordination (Héritier and Rhodes, 2011).

Building on these elements, the volume is organised as follows. Part I (*Contextualising Europeanisation of Cities*) will appraise the literature in the context-areas of this research, so as to uncover the main concepts as well as to highlight the trajectories undertaken by the contributions of scholars thus far. Therefore, Chapter Two (*Territorial Governance and Regulation in Europe*) will deal with the political economy of cities and urban areas in Europe by seeking to draw on the main theories of urban politics, to propose some alternative interpretations to link them with the broader field of European Studies.

The 'local dimension' of the EU will be considered by analysing the main stages through which its 'urban policy' actually developed as well as by accounting for those EU policy instruments and initiatives that are more likely to have an impact on urban areas. The role and the involvement of the European Commission in 'urban policy' or in urban-related policy issues will also be analysed.

Chapter Three *(Europeanisation: Concepts and Agendas for Research)* specifically deals with Europeanisation, which is the approach chosen to study the potential EU impacts – in terms of change, rather than transformation – on domestic territorial systems. In particular, an attempt will be made to point out the main methodological implications that the use of this approach to the study of European politics yields when applied to specific cases or policy areas. The review of the Europeanisation literature will outline the main research agendas proposed thus far, so as to eventually pinpoint the gaps that would instead need fulfilment.

In turn, Chapter Four (*Mechanisms and Modes of Europeanisation*) makes sense of different arenas for Europeanisation of urban politics, mechanisms and instruments by adopting a conceptual perspective informed by theoretical policy analysis. Specifically, the chapter presents the mechanisms through which EU-led policy instruments and initiatives are likely to impact urban systems. The aim of this chapter is to sort out Europeanisation mechanisms by starting from the ideal-types of ideational arenas (or *fora* in the tradition of French political science), distribution and regulation, to be then sorting out a typology of Europeanisation modes at the bases of the empirical analysis. Following that, Chapter Five *(Research Design and Methodological Issues)* presents the research design on which the empirical assessment of Europeanisation of cities will be grounded and some main methodological implication for the analysis.

Part II of the volume *(Assessing the Encounter Between Cities and the European Union)* will empirically account for the theory developed in the previous sections.

Four distinct chapters – Six to Nine – will each present the case of an EU policy instrument, from its promotion at the EU level, to the implementation stage in the city of Turin.

Therefore, the analysis of the Covenant of Mayors programme for CO_2 emission control and energy saving, wants to exemplify ideation as a mode of policy (Chapter Six). The regulatory mode of policy will be assessed through the analysis of the EU policy for waste management, by considering in particular the implementation of the EU directive 1994/60 on packaging and packaging waste (Chapter Seven). In turn, modes of coordination will be presented through the case of the EU policy for air quality control and the development of EU directive 1999/30 (Chapter Eight). The fourth empirical chapter will instead make sense of the mode of distribution by assessing the community initiative URBAN II for urban regeneration (Chapter Nine).

In the final part – *Theory Development and Perspectives* – the overall argument will be conceptualised with the purpose of *drawing the implications of case findings for theory* (Chapter Ten). After developing an analytical framework for the analysis of Europeanisation, specifically accounting for the Europeanisation of cities and urban areas, and building on the assessment of empirical cases analysis, this last part aims to draw the implications of case finding to actually develop a theory for the analysis of Europeanisation at the urban level. EU policy instruments will be systematically compared on the bases of their development and transformative impact in the urban context chosen to test our expectations.

A final chapter (Eleven) – based on recent developments in the EU policy-making elements of the new programming period 2014–20 of the EU Cohesion policy – will present suggestions on how the result of the research can be used by the European Commission, the member states and sub-national governments in tackling the policy problems they face.

PART I

CONTEXTUALISING EUROPEANISATION OF CITIES

In this section we identify the policy actions of the EU that bear the potential to bring about change within urban systems of governance. We draw on theoretical policy analysis to propose an innovative understanding of the relationship between cities and the EU policy making. We propose a framework for the empirical analysis of urban Europeanisation based on social mechanisms and modes of policy. The presentation of the methodological design of the research and of the case selection concludes Part I.

Chapter Two

Territorial Governance and Regulation in Europe

2.1 Introduction

Typically, European cities have been analysed according to the tenets of urban politics. Accordingly, the focus has been on the institutional structure of local governments, and the power relations amongst formal actors, including resource dependencies between formal institutional structures and private actors. However, the role of the EU is seldom examined in the field of urban politics. In urban sociology and territorial regulation, the tendency is to think about the EU as a political and geographical context within which several dynamics affecting cities occur. The studies explicitly assessing the role of cities within the European Union policy making have fallen short of offering a satisfactory wide picture of the mutual relationship between urban systems and the EU. Instead, these have mainly focused on the involvement of local government in the structural programmes promoted by the EU within its regional policy, thus neglecting other relevant dimensions.

However, we need to widen our horizon, by considering formal and informal channels of Europeanisation, connected to the policy instruments of the structural funds but also other sources of EU-induced change.

2.2 Contextualising *governance* within urban systems

Governance has become a very popular concept in the EU, mainly with regard to European Studies. It is impossible to review the large literature on this concept (Kooiman, 1993; Schultze, 2003). For us, it is sufficient to observe that governance refers to a 'new way' of governing that goes beyond solely formal institutions. Thus, governance signifies 'a change in the meaning of government, referring to a new process of governing, or a changed condition of ordered rules; or the new method by which society is governed' (Rhodes, 1996: 652–653). Thinking of the EU, governance can be seen as 'the production of authoritative decisions, which are not produced by a single hierarchical structure...but instead arise from the interaction of a plethora of public and private, collective and individual actors' (Christiansen and Piattoni, 2004: 6).

The European Union has progressively emerged as part of a reconfigured pattern of European governance characterised by the evolution of institutional arrangements and processes implying a shift towards the greater role of more autonomous or semi-autonomous agencies, and forms of 'self-regulation' underpinning partnership models (Wallace and Wallace, 2000). The EU policy process has often been described as *multi-level governance*. This picture, we argue, applies more within some policy areas than within others (i.e. EU-financed programmes) and during certain phases of the 'policy cycle' (i.e. implementation). The multi-level governance approach conceives of the European Union policy making as no longer monopolised by national states, and policy decision no longer as the aggregate outcome of several national preferences to a lowest common denominator.

The increasing involvement of sub-national authorities in the EU-wide policy making that followed the further completion of the single market and the reform of structural funds in 1988 inspired multi-level governance thinking in European Studies. The key idea is that decision-making competences are, though to varying degrees, shared by multiple actors at different levels and the nature of decision making into the boundaries of the states is now 'collective' (Hooghe, 1996; Hooghe and Marks, 2001; Marks, 1992; Marks, *et al.*, 1996).

Particularly in the policy area of structural funds, the governance approach emphasises the emergence of networks, whereby sub-national governments interact both with the EU and cross-nationally. Further, it points to the dialogue of the Commission with sub-national authorities and their interaction with the supranational level (Hooghe and Marks, 2001: 12).

Within the picture offered by multi-level governance in relation with city and urban systems, Europeanisation would occur because of the greater awareness of local authorities and other organisations of the importance of EU policies and funding opportunities. From the 'bottom-up' perspective of the process, this array of activities reinforces the trend to governance because of their potential to foster new or stronger partnership arrangements across local organisations. In relation to that, the governance approach facilitates investigations of the whole policy process – throughout all its phases. It points out the importance of variation by sectors and to the role of a wide range of actors in policy making. By endorsing a governance approach to Europeanisation, especially at the urban-city level, it is possible to assess the top-down, bottom-up, vertical and horizontal channels of relations, rather than exclusively focusing on hierarchically channelled relationships.

So-called new modes of governance have widened the EU approach to governance, with a focus on 'benchmarking, the dissemination of best practices, mutual learning and peer pressures, intended...not only to deliver policy outcomes, but also to act as a process for improving policy formation' (Hodson and Maher, 2001: 375). Due to a lack of knowledge, 'the centre' has to concede room for manoeuvre to regions and localities. One group of stakeholders explicitly targeted over the last decade by the European Commission is *cities*. Cities, 'instead of being mere policy takers are increasingly qualifying as *policy makers*, which is clearly sign for more *participative governance* in the EU' (Schultze, 2003: 123).

2.3 The 'urban policy' of the EU

What is the urban policy of the EU, exactly? Let us start from two important documents: *Towards an Urban Agenda in the European Union* (European Commission, 1997b) and *Sustainable Urban Development in the European Union: a Framework for Action* (European Commission, 1998). Through these two documents, the European Commission recognised the existence of a specific 'urban dimension'.

Four main reasons were pointed out to justify why the 'city-dimension' requires special attention within the overall EU system. Urban areas in Europe deserve specific consideration due to the high percentage of people currently living therein – almost 80 per cent of the total European population – and are considered as the dynamo of the European economy. Besides that, initiatives were to be undertaken in consideration of the growing rate of social exclusion in urban areas and the fact that cities have traditionally been centres of social and cultural life (European Commission, 1997b: 4–6; 1998: 2–5). By taking into account the large-scale problems affecting cities within the EU, the Commission claimed that 'whilst urban authorities cannot be the sole agencies to act on these large issues, they should be fully involved in the policies related to these matters, as there can be no effective solution on the ground without their active participation' (European Commission, 1997b).

Despite the strong emphasis put on problems affecting cities and on the need to tackle them through the promotion of specific initiatives, the Commission specified in turn that 'it does not intend to ask for additional power at the European level, merely to assess the extent to which existing policies affect urban areas and to examine the...possibilities for improving urban development and for increasing the effectiveness of existing community interventions in urban areas' (European Commission, 1997b).

The 'policy objectives' outlined in the 1997 communication were later integrated into wider 'policy ideas' in the 1998 action framework. These are named in terms of strengthening the economic prosperity and employment in towns and cities, the promotion of equality, social inclusion and regeneration in urban areas, the protection and improvement of the urban environment, contributing to good governance and local empowerment (European Commission, 1998: 5–6). In 1997 the Commission argued for the promotion of services of public interest and urban development. It envisaged a change towards strengthening the contribution of structural funds and the participation of cities in the preparation and implementation of regional development programmes. The Commission also argued for the promotion of the exchange of experiences between cities, throughout the creation of urban and city networks (European Commission, 1997b: 13–14).

For the programming period 2007–13 the Commission – through its *Community Strategic Guidelines on Cohesion* – expressed the formal intention to strengthen the place of urban issues by fully integrating actions in this field into the overarching structure of the renewed objective of the structural funds (European Commission 2006b). Within the new structure, urban-related programmes became part of the

Table 2.1: Stages of EU regional policy and its urban dimension

	EU regional policy	Urban dimension in the EU policy
Stage 1 1975–1988	Regional policy as a tool to reach economic integration.	Not existing, neither implicitly nor explicitly.
Stage 2 1989–1993	First reform of the structural funds and creation of the cohesion fund.	The urban pilot projects represent the first attempt of the EC to have an explicit urban policy.
Stage 3 1994–1999	Second reform of the structural funds and doubling of their financial allocation.	The EC pushes towards the development of an urban policy, but the divergence existing between the actors still prevented its institutionalisation. Two programmes specifically targeted to cities are financed by the structural funds: UPP II and the CI URBAN.
Stage 4 2000–2006	Third reform of the structural funds and reduction of the priority objectives from seven to three.	Besides URBAN II and the Urban Audit II, also a relevant part of the Objectives 1 and 2 of the SF is meant for cities.
Stage 5 2007–2013	Further simplification of the cohesion policy which now counts three main priorities and three financial instruments.	Community initiatives are not renewed and urban-related programmes are embedded in the mainstream regional programmes
Stage 6 2014–2020	Further harmonisation of funding mechanisms and stronger focus on result orientation	Urban areas are addressed within mainstream programmes through mechanisms of community-led local development and integrated territorial investments.

Source: elaboration from Euricur (2004): 47.

mainstream regional programmes under the new objectives 1 and 2. Consequently, regional authorities were responsible for the programming and management of 'urban programmes'. Similar prominence on the potentials of urban-focused action was sketched in the *Communication from the Commission on cohesion policy and cities* (European Commission, 2006a). The communication laid down recommendations on a broad set of fields, ranging from transport services, environment and culture, territorial partnerships, employability, governance, exchange of experiences and the development of financial engineering.

Similar emphasis on the potential of urban-focused action is sketched in the *Communication from the Commission on cohesion policy and cities* (European Commission, 2006b). Besides proposing the strengthening of the urban dimension and concentrating resources to avoid them being spread too thinly, the communication laid down concrete recommendations to the cities and the actors involved in urban development, covering transport services, environment and culture, to territorial partnerships, employability, governance, exchange of experiences and the development of financial engineering.

At the same time, the European Commission argued that cities, as relevant partners, should be consulted and participate in the 'preparation, implementation, monitoring and evaluation of the operational programmes in accordance with national rules and practices' (European Commission, 2006b). Actions relating to sustainable urban development – the document added – may be part of the thematic and territorial priorities identified in the National Strategic Reference Frameworks, to be presented by member states to ensure the coherence of the funds intervention with the Commission Strategic Guidelines.

Nonetheless, the mainstreaming of community initiatives in 2007–13 led to stronger sectoral focus, perhaps partly weakening the community involvement compared to the context of the previous URBAN Community Initiative (European Commission, 2008). In turn, as established by Art. 11 of the regulation laying down general provisions, relevant partners – local, regional and urban authorities as well as economic and social partners – must be consulted and participate in the 'preparation, implementation, monitoring and evaluation of the operational programmes in accordance with national rules and practice'[1].

Within the provisions of the European Regional Development Funds – whose financial assistance will cover part of all three objectives – the thematic priorities associated with urban issues mostly deal with supporting sustainable integrated regional and local economic development and employment – *convergence objective* – where priority for assistance is addressed towards research and technological development, promoting innovation society, aid for structures providing local services to create new jobs, environmental issues including the rehabilitation of the physical environment, integrated strategies for clean transport, the improvement of energy efficiency, education and the fostering of social infrastructures. Under the *regional competitiveness and employment objective*, assistance spaces out between multiple 'policy areas', with a particular focus on supporting initiatives aimed at boosting innovation and the knowledge economy, promoting investments for the environmental ameliorations and access to transport and telecommunications services of general economic interest. In particular, Art. 8 of the ERDF regulation, allows regions to support integrated urban development projects based on participative strategies in urban areas.

The *European territorial cooperation objective*, albeit endowed with the smallest financial provision (2.52 per cent of the funds), offers most of the potential for the action of cities. Previously covered by the INTERREG Community Initiative, it aims in particular to forge the link between the projects drawn up under territorial cooperation and those supported within operational programmes.

Several programmes with potential urban focus are foreseen within the three programmatic parts through which the objective is organised – cross border

---

1. Council regulation (EC) No 1083/2006 of July 2006 laying down general provisions on the European Regional Development Funds, the European Social Fund and the Cohesion Fund and repealing regulation (EC) No 1260/1999, OJ L 210/25 of 31.7.2006.

cooperation, transnational cooperation and interregional cooperation. In particular, the interregional cooperation component provides for four additional programmes. URBACT II urban network support programme, which follows the URBACT programme carried out during the 2000–06 period, is designed to support cities in developing innovative and sustainable solutions to integrate economic, social and environmental dimensions. This is pursued through exchanging and sharing good practices and learning dynamics. URBACT, in particular is structured in a way that involves all parties having a stake in the city, namely policy professionals, policy makers and representatives of both different domains of the society. For the 2007–13 period, URBACT comprised forty-four projects, involving 255 cities and more than 5000 participants in twenty-nine countries[2].

The INTERREG IVC interregional cooperation programme on the other hand aims to support cooperation between regional and local authorities in order to facilitate the exchange of experiences and best practices. The programme, in particular, focuses on the priority axis of innovation and knowledge society and environment and risk prevention. The ESPON 2013 (European Spatial Observatory Network) study programme supports policy development and intends to set up a European scientific community in the field of territorial development by boosting general knowledge about territorial structures, trends and policy impacts across the European Union. Besides that, the INTERACT II programme provides expertise for the management of all territorial cooperation programmes to improve on their implementation. In turn, URBACT II and INTERREG IVC programmes are part of the 'Regions for Economic Change' initiative, which aims to strengthen networking and exchange of experience, mainly owing to the further extension of the scope of eligibility for the URBACT II programme[3].

As regards the financial engineering of programmes, the managing authorities in each member state are enabled to finance public-private partnership thereby ensuring a more flexible management of the allocated funds; contextually financial expenditures are foreseen to support financial instruments for enterprises, such as venture capital funds, guarantee funds and loan funds. To support the organisation and the appropriate functioning of these instruments, the Commission, together with the European Investment Bank (EIB) and the Council of Europe Development Bank, launched the JASPERS, JEREMIE and JESSICA Initiatives[4].

Such priorities are further integrated by those allowed by the European Social Fund under both the 'convergence' and the 'competitiveness and employment' objectives; these are designed to support the enhancement of conditions for workers

---

2. For a more detailed overview on the activities and projects managed within URBACT programme, reference is made to www.urbact.eu (accessed 10 November 2016).

3. For a complete analysis of the operational programmes co-financed by the European Regional Development Fund (2007–13) see European Commission (2008) 'Fostering the Urban dimension. Analysis of the Operational programmes co-financed by the European Regional Development Fund (2007–13)', Brussels, Commission of the European Communities.

4. JASPERS: Joint Assistance in Supporting Projects in European Regions; JEREMIE: Joint European Resources for Micro to Medium Enterprises; JESSICA: Joint European Support for Sustainable Investment in City Areas.

and enterprises, strengthening the access to employability and reinforcing social inclusion and human capital. The Cohesion Fund, planned to finance programmes for convergence, provides assistance as regards the environment and the trans-European Networks, where clean urban transport is the leading investment priority.

Quite differently from other programming periods though, there was an urban dimension in the 2007–13 period. Within the Lisbon Strategy, initiatives and regulatory devices addressed to cities are explicitly delineated. Furthermore, other initiatives underpin policy instruments with an indirect impact for urban areas (European Commission 2006b). Under the Lisbon growth and jobs strategy, we find the application of internal market and competitions policy, the European employment and social policy, the urban dimension of the environmental policy, the European R&D and the transport policy, energy policy and information and communication policy.

The urban dimension is to a lesser extent touched upon by initiatives carried out within other policy areas, whose instruments remain predominantly national. In spite of that, *urban components* are at stake in some parts of the justice, freedom and security policy, in particular as regards migration control and crime prevention, in the European rural development policy, where small towns fall in the definition of rural areas and finally in some of the provisions of the EU external policy where this calls for transnational cooperation between urban areas.

To the former group we may ascribe the application of internal market and competitions policy, the European employment and social policy, the urban dimension of the environmental policy, the European R&D and the transport policy, energy policy and information and communication policy as to the part concerned by the Seventh Framework for Research, technological development and demonstration activities (FP7).

In particular, it is worth mentioning the regulatory framework of the internal market and competition policy, which conform the provision of certain Services of General Interest (SGI) by urban authorities and the regulation of public procurement[5] and public private-partnerships[6] for the supply of certain SGI as well as the (informal) regulation of state aid for regeneration purposes in urban areas. As regards the employment policy, the ESF supports reforms to strengthen urban governance and management through the promotion initiatives in the context of the European Employment Strategy (and its related Social Agenda 2005–10) and operationalised via the Open Method of Coordination. In particular, actions are possible under the financing of the European Globalisation Adjustment Fund[7] within the framework of the PROGRESS programme for Employment and

---

5. Directive 2004/17/EC of the European Parliament and of the Council of 31 March 2004 coordinating the procurement procedures of entities operating in the water, energy, transport and postal services sectors; Directive 2004/18/CE on the coordination of procedures for the award of public works contracts, public supply contracts and public service contracts.

6. COM (2004) 327; Communication from the Commission on Public-Private Partnerships and Community Law on Public Procurement and Concessions, COM (2005) 569 final.

7. Regulation (EC) No 1927/2006.

Social Solidarity aimed at boosting mutual learning, exchange of information and the diffusion of good practices. Within the 6th Environmental Action Programme, a Thematic Strategy on Urban Environment provides guidance for an integrated and focused approach using existing policy instruments and initiatives, by mostly building on the LIFE + programme whose thematic priorities related to urban areas deal with combating climate change, favouring environment and health safety in urban areas and fostering the sustainable use of resources.

Within the Seventh Framework Programme for Research, development and demonstration activities are envisaged so as to crosscut several policy areas such as ICT, energy, environment, transport and socio-economic sciences and humanities. In particular, under the CIVITAS plus Initiative, the Commission is co-financing projects, which address energy and transport issues, whilst the CONCERTO Initiative in the field of renewable energy sources is thought to provide a platform for the exchange of ideas and experiences. Other actions with an urban target are carried out within the EU policy for enterprises (mainly addressed to SMEs), the culture policy, the European youth policy, the education and training policy and the EU policy for active European citizenship, all widely interested by programmes and initiatives implemented in the context of the employment and social policy.

2.4 From government to *governance* within urban systems?

Theories of urban governance emphasise outcomes over formal political processes and stress public-private interaction over formal policy implementation. Despite persisting national differences (Jordan *et al.*, 2005), the shift from urban government to urban governance (Rhodes, 1996) seems fit to portray the overall situation of many European countries, especially those that are members of the European Union.

In this connection, the *partnership approach* to governance (Stoker, 1998, Pierre, 1998a) captures the character of the changing urban landscape, underpinning dynamics of economic urban regeneration and social cohesion. Over the last two decades, the European Commission has promoted partnership arrangements, both vertically – between different tiers of government – and horizontally – between different types of actors. The implementation of this approach has nonetheless varied considerably according to different urban and national contexts (Cento Bull and Jones, 2006). Especially at the urban level, 'if we are speaking of *governance* it's precisely because the government, whether centralised or local, is no longer capable of governing alone and now has to come to terms with and co-produce with other stakeholders and participants' (Jaquier, 2005: 374).

In cities across European countries, the EU action takes place alongside a background of multiple domestic institutional constraints. Local actors have to carry out their 'policy action' by dealing with pre-existing domestic institutional arrangements and constraints, while simultaneously reacting and accomplishing European programmes (Cento Bull and Jones, 2006, Marshall, 2005). The increasing participation of cities in EU programmes has proceeded alongside with the development of a wide array of *local regeneration partnerships*, which, often in the form of public-private partnerships (hereinafter PPPs), have the potential to become broadly institutionalised, although started according to the guidelines and funding of the European Union.

'...thus, at both metropolitan and neighbourhood level, the *download* of European norms of partnerships has facilitated participatory modes of working that spur on the transition from *urban government to urban governance'* (Marshall, 2005: 679, *italics added*).

Although public-private partnership is now a well-established form of public-private interaction in urban policy, PPPs differ through time and urban regeneration projects depending on the actors involved and how power is distributed among actors. Public-private partnerships in urban systems can be seen as 'institutionalised forms of cooperation between government and one or more private partners in a project with common interests via a distribution of decision rights, costs and risks' (Van Boxemeer and Van Beckoven, 2005: 3).

Understanding governance is very much about understanding the roles of institutions operating in a certain context. Therefore, within a governance framework of analysis, government and institutions have to be treated as a variable rather than a parameter whose influence and powers are considered as given (Pierre, 1998b). Thus, within the changing urban policy environment, PPPs should be better considered as *institutions*. Public-private partnerships at the urban level do have important institutional and structural properties; a partnership arrangement relies upon rules as well as on a certain number of shared values among participants and some common policy goals, acting as symbolic and utilitarian components of the relationship.

2.5 Concluding remarks

Europeanisation at the local-urban level is linked to networks and the creation of new forms of governance. The clustering of economic activities in solely specific areas of Europe and the consequent disparities arising, make it necessary for urban-local authorities to work by means of 'networked-based ways', as they need to develop strategies useful to respond to these economic concentrations (Benington, 1994; Goldsmith, 1993b).

Local authorities, and particularly cities, are not simply receptors of norms and rules downloaded from the upper tier of the EU, but also 'active users and shapers' of these EU-policy norms, in order to elaborate them by means of processes of *policy learning, policy transfer* and *networking*. Thus, processes of 'cognitive Europeanisation' (Pasquier, 2005: 296) are at stake, whereby 'knowledge about policies, administrative arrangements, institutions in one time and/or place is used in the development of policies, administrative arrangements and institutions in another time and/or place' (Dolowitz and Marsh, 2000: 344).

Evidence from urban-local Europeanisation is more marked in certain policy areas than in others, in particular where the European Union shows a major degree of institutionalisation and where, as a consequence, local authorities may act more freely from the constraints traditionally imposed by the state. This is actually the case with cohesion and structural policy.

Here, the small dimension of EU bureaucracy compared to that of member states, and the lack of information characterising EU institutions, have favoured the involvement of sub-national and sub-regional authorities and the development of innovative policy solutions. Amongst them, *European programme partnership*, with local authorities playing a role during different stages of the policy process, *representative organisations* functioning as formal bodies for representation (AER; CEMR; CLRAE; IULA)[8], and *representative offices* set up in Brussels by regions and cities.

The participation of sub-national bodies in *trans-national networks* is often connected to specific policy sectors. Some of them are directly sponsored by the European Commission in order to connect the participants in specific initiatives, like under the RECITE programme launched in 1991. Others, more 'bottom-up' in nature, arose from the spontaneous initiative of groups of cities sharing common characteristics or pursuing similar objectives. This is the case of EUROCITIES, founded in 1986 at the initiative of Rotterdam to connect medium/large cities across Europe. These activities have sometimes led to developments at the EU level, like on occasion of the *Committee of the Regions and Local Authorities* establishment in 1994.

Europeanisation within cities and urban areas affects institutions, individuals and organisations as well as the relations between 'the city' as a system of governance and other systems differently involved over the same policy matters. In this connection, the various 'components' of the city polity may adapt, resist, or change (Goldsmith and Klausen, 1997); in any case, the city as a whole reacts to the processes following EU action.

Urban governance conserves specific characteristics that distinguish it from the broader study of 'sub-national governance'. It is then problematic as well as challenging to isolate the process of Europeanisation in urban-city areas from its manifestation at other 'sub-territorial' levels. What follows is that 'urban and metropolitan Europeanisation requires an analytical paradigm that enables researchers to test the salience of EU influences on local institutions and actors' (Marshall, 2005: 669).

Assessing the Europeanisation of local-urban systems means to take into analytical account not only the transferred policies, the learnt practices and the selected alternatives, but also to assess the role of and interrelations occurring between individual and collective actors/institutions involved in the policy-game within such localities.

'…the European turn experienced by urban institutions and actors is a unique process which can be only examined by combining elements of the Europeanisation approach with a nuanced understanding of urban governance, local dynamics, and domestic contextual factors' (Marshall, 2005: 672).

---

8.   Assembly of European Regions; Council of European Municipalities and Regions; Conference of Local and Regional Authorities; International Union of Local Authorities.

Chapter Three

Europeanisation: Concepts and Agendas for Research

3.1 Introduction

Over the last fifteen years, an important analytical debate about the potential impacts of the European integration process on the territorial and administrative units constituting the European polity has arisen. The shift of analytical focus brought scholars to question the influence of the European Union in terms of its institutional transformation, policy change and ideational construction within its member states and other sub-national layers of government and organisation (Goldsmith, 1993a; Marshall, 2005; Zerbinati, 2004).

Traditionally, research in the field of European Studies was mainly concerned with analysing member states responses to the construction of the European polity, meaning the process and outcomes of European integration. Therefore, a bottom-up outlook was the privileged analytical perspective of these studies (Börzel, 2003).

In this connection, the academic debate evolved around two main theoretical paradigms, diverging on the interpretation of the role of member states and European institutions. On one hand, *intergovernmentalist* approaches, mainly rooted in *neo-realist theories of international relations*, which consider the European Community as an international organisation, rather than a supranational organisation endowed with autonomous functions and a relatively recognisable sphere of political sovereignty. Far from evolving towards a coherent supranational institutional system, the European Union will remain an integrated system, or a confederation within which each member state will maintain its institutional and political sovereignty (Moravcsik, 1991; 1998). On the other hand, *neofunctionalist* approaches focus on domestic actors, keen on promoting their interests at the European level. The main concept in these theorisations is 'political community', that is the creation at the supranational level of a system-coherent 'political authority' lying upon a system of supranational institutions triggered by the shift of loyalty from the central authority of nation states to the supranational arena (Haas, 1958; Sandholtz and Stone Sweet, 1998).

In conjunction with the sudden acceleration of the European integration process by the end of the 1980s, during the '90s research interests within European Studies partly moved towards the analysis of the member states responses to the impact of European process and institutions, thus assuming a more marked top-down perspective (Börzel, 2003; Börzel and Risse, 2003).

Therefore, to cope with the renewed perspective, traditional paradigms were partially revisited. According to liberal-intergovernmentalists, the power of control of nation States would be enhanced as the process of integration advances (Moravcsik, 1993; 1999; Milward, 1992), due to the well-defined preferences with which national leaders are maintained to enter EU negotiations. Later, neo-functionalist theories instead suggested that the process of integration would have provided domestic actors with the necessary resources, influences and political channels to circumvent – at least to some extent – the power constraints of their respective nation States (Hooghe and Marks, 1997; Marks, 1993; Marks, *et al.*, 1996a).

Building on this last approach, proponents of *multi-level governance* interpreted the European polity as a nested system of governmental levels, which interact on the base of formalised and non-formalised structures (Hooghe and Marks, 2001; Marks, 1993; 1992; Marks, *et al.*, 1996b; Scharpf, 1994). In this connection, the process at stake does not strengthen or weaken member states in an exclusive manner – thus following the logic of a zero-sum game – instead, it contributes to transform their structures and the power relationships between their constitutive parts (Kohler-Koch and Eising, 1999; Rhodes, 1996; 1997).

More recently, in the attempt to overcome the analytical drawbacks of this debate as well as to bypass the scarce dynamism of the two main competing paradigms, scholars have focused their analyses on specific public policies and on the relationship between the actors taking part in the different phases of the policy process (Majone, 1994; Wallace and Wallace, 2000). Amongst this new branch of studies, emerged the analysis on the Europeanisation of domestic structures of politics and policy. Studies on Europeanisation seek to understand the relationships between the European and the 'domestic' politics, by underling interactions between actors and institutions involved in a specific policy area, and the transformations eventually occurring in both the institutional setting and the policy making (Green Cowles, *et al.*, 2001; Héritier, *et al.*, 2001; Featherstone and Radaelli, 2003).

Studies of Europeanisation have been rather prolific over the last ten years. As showed by those few analyses on the diffusion of academic studies on Europeanisation since the early 1980s, the number of scientific articles dealing with Europeanisation has constantly increased compared to the overall production within social sciences (Exadaktylos and Radaelli, 2009).

Within this approach, the theoretical effort is not addressed to puzzles concerning powers distribution, instead 'the theoretical effort in Europeanisation as a research agenda is all about bringing domestic politics back into our understanding of European integration' (Radaelli, 2004: 3). The new research agenda of Europeanisation attempts to better assess the potency of EU-initiated policies within domestic systems of governance, as well as to seize the potential influences – in terms of both opportunities and constraints – on national and sub-national politics (Graziano and Vink, 2007).

3.2 Europeanisation: definition and the problems of establishing causality

A general dividing line can be drawn between scholarships that consider Europeanisation as an overall top-down process ranging from the EU level down to the domestic one, and those endorsing more bottom-up oriented definitions, underpinning a circular account of the Europeanisation process (Lenschow, 2005b). In this connection, advocates of the 'top-down' perspective tend to consider Europeanisation as the *explanans* (or the independent variable), whereas 'bottom-up' accounts have been more inclined to consider Europeanisation as the factor to be explained and eventually as the dependent variable of the analysis.

By analysing the institutional transformation of France, Ladrech defines Europeanisation as an 'incremental process reorienting the direction and shape of politics to the degree that EC political and economic dynamics become part of the organizational logic of national politics and policy-making' (Ladrech, 1994: 69). This definition of Europeanisation emphasises dynamics of domestic adaptation to the European logic as well as the role played by processes of learning and policy change.

Börzel's definition focuses on the potential impact of the EU policy making on the national institution and policy arenas. Europeanisation is thus referred to as the 'process whereby domestic policy areas become increasingly subject to European policy making' (Börzel, 1999: 574). However, this understanding leaves open questions about how policy arenas at the domestic level are likely to be influenced by the European-wide dynamic.

From a clear institutionalist standpoint, J. P. Olsen argues that 'the most standard institutional response to novelty is to find a routine in the existing repertoire of routines that can be used' (Olsen, 2002: 932). Bulmer and Burch define Europeanisation as 'the extent to which EC/EU requirements and policies have affected the determination of member states' policy agendas and goals' (Bulmer and Burch, 1998: 607). Also in these cases the analytical focus is mainly on the vertical, 'top-down' channels of influence.

In the empirical attempt to gauge the scope of Europeanisation in different national contexts, Green Cowles and her colleagues define Europeanisation as 'the emergence and development at the European level of distinct structures of governance, that is, of political, legal and social institutions associated with political problem solving, that formalize interactions amongst the actors, and of policy networks specializing in the creation of authoritative European rules' (Green Cowles, *et al.*, 2001: 1). According to their conceptualisation, Europeanisation has led to a distinct and identifiable change in the domestic institutional structure of member states. Domestic structures are here assumed as the dependent variable of the entire process, whose most significant component is institutions, both formal and informal. As such, even this definition does not contribute to fully demarcate the specific 'interest area' of Europeanisation as a field for empirical enquiry (Radaelli, 2004). Similarly, Knill and Lehmkuhl's definition stresses the EU action, wherein the process of integration is conceived as the independent variable. By differentiating between mechanisms of Europeanisation, they point out three forms of 'integration'. These are 'positive integration', associated with the prescription of institutional models, 'negative integration', implying the alteration of the domestic opportunity structure, and finally 'framing integration', that is associated with the alteration of the beliefs and expectations of domestic actors (Knill and Lehmkuhl, 1999).

To fill the conceptual gap, scholars redirected analytical attention towards the compound nature of the Europeanisation process. In this vein, Europeanisation has been defined as 'a complex process whereby national and sub-national institutions, political actors, and citizens adapt to, and seek to shape, the trajectory of European Integration in general, and EU policies in particular...the result is usually some convergence in policy outcomes, but of a kind that is neither widespread nor uniform' (Bomberg and Peterson, 2000: 7). For these scholars, patterns of causality are not easily distinguishable and the process assumes a multidimensional fashion of development.

Therefore, according to Radaelli, Europeanisation is more likely to be understood as 'a process of construction, diffusion and institutionalisation of formal and informal rules, procedures, policy paradigms, styles, 'ways of doing things' and shared beliefs and norms which are first defined and consolidated in the EU policy process, and then incorporated in the logic of domestic discourse, political structures and public policies' (Radaelli, 2003: 30).

The process of Europeanisation may be associated with either continuity or change and potentially variable and contingent outcomes. Thus, 'Europeanisation as an analytical focus stresses key changes in contemporary politics, it highlights the adaptation of institutional settings in the broadest sense at different political levels in response to the dynamics of integration, the emergence of new, cross-national policy networks and communities, the nature of policy imitation and transfer between States and sub-national authorities. Furthermore, Europeanisation points out the restructuring of the strategic opportunities available to domestic actors, as EU commitments, having a differential impact on such actors, may serve as a source of leverage' (Featherstone, 2003: 19).

When dealing with the concept of Europeanisation and with the processes it underpins, some problematic methodological implications stand out. Within Europeanisation, the distinction between structure and agency is not an easy task, as well as clearly distinguishing between dependent and independent variables. Thus, to be profitably assessed, Europeanisation needs to be seen '...as a problem, not a solution, as something that needs to be explained' (Radaelli, 2004: 4). It is important to focus on 'whether and how the term can be useful for understanding the dynamic of the evolving European polity' (Olsen, 2002: 922); Europeanisation has to be treated not as an end-state, but instead as a procedural device useful to explain changes and changing dynamics at various levels of government and policy making.

A possible analytical risk consists in attributing causality to the action of the EU – and to the EU-wide policy making – whereas changes may be the resultant of alternative dynamics and processes, such as purely domestic variables, global factors or the action of other macro-regional organisations acting within the European soil. Therefore, even when attempting to explain the potential transformative effect of the EU policy action, it is of crucial importance to account for alternative hypothesis or 'rival mechanisms'; this in turn allows to highlight those factors, other than Europeanisation, that may have brought along changes within domestic systems (Exadaktylos and Radaelli, 2012).

To conclude on this point, we contend that *Europeanisation is an interactive process wherein domestic systems of governance are in time changed by the diffusion of ideational construct, legal and social norms, regulations and instruments. These are first identified, negotiated, contested and agreed upon within the EU-wide arenas, and eventually used by domestic actors to shape their institutional orders.*

Emphasis is placed on the concept of *institutional orders*. These are systems of intertwined policy sectors and territorial regulation characterised by the interactive mediations 'between sectoral regulation, usage of territory and the reproduction of the EU polity' (Carter and Smith, 2008: 266). Institutional orders are to be preferred to the traditional 'levels' portrayal of the European policy insomuch as analytical attention is redirected towards matters of power distribution, conflict and bargaining over resources as well as competitive dynamics within processes of territorial regulation.

3.3 Europeanisation the urban way

By acting through networks and other arrangements, cities can account for 'soft outcomes' (Schultze, 2003: 136) such as shaping and setting important parameters for the debate between institutions, influencing the policy agenda as regard urban issues, and getting their proposal into key documents useful for policy implementation.

European institutions involve cities as stakeholders in the policy process, especially in some policy areas and within specific programmes, such as URBAN Community Initiative during the period 1994–2006. 'Europeanisation and sub-national mobilisation have thus *unlocked* cities from the often rather hierarchical constraints of the national system by allowing them to build trans-national coalitions, which suggest a careful re-labelling of cities as *policy makers*, at least for the urban dimension of the Structural Funds, but possibly also for other policy areas' (Schultze, 2003: 137).

Within the field of European Studies, academic research on the relations between cities and the EU has been practically confined to the Structural and Cohesion Policy (Marshall, 2005; Zerbinati, 2004), or to those policy programmes clearly holding the heading *urban* on their tin (Cento Bull and Jones, 2006; Halpern, 2005; Tofarides, 2003), thus neglecting other dimensions where the encounter between Europe and urban systems is, theoretically at least, likely to yield transformative effects. The emphasis is often on in-depth analysis of changes occurred within the institutional structure of local government, triggered by the involvement of the city in specific initiatives for urban regeneration – URBAN CI – or more extended programmes for regional development, where cities administrations act in synergy with upper levels of government.

Therefore, this narrow focus may bias any possible generalisation on the extent and scope conditions of the Europeanisation of urban areas. These studies conceive Europeanisation mainly as a two-fold process of downloading new institutional models and uploading via policy networks and lobbying activities (Marshall, 2003; 2005). The process of Europeanisation of cities and urban areas is eventually described – rather than measured or causally explained – and the influence of the action of the European Union partly prejudged due to scarce accuracy paid to the causal mechanisms likely to trigger change within urban systems.

The dependent variables of these analyses are often identified with the institutional arrangements of local government and eventually with the organisational structure put in place for the management and implementation of the EU programme under examination. The main flaw though, is the absence of a clear research design and reference to causal conditions eventually leading to change. This, in turn, makes it particularly difficult to disentangle the effects of the EU action – and thus to characterise or measure the process of Europeanisation – from rival explanation based on alternative dynamics, such as for instance domestic processes of reform or international phenomena of policy diffusion.

An exception is provided by Zerbinati's comparative analysis of Europeanisation in Italy and England where attention is accorded to both direct and indirect pathways for EU influence on local authorities. But also in this study the analysis is confined solely to the structural funds; this view is too narrow to generalise about the influence of the EU on urban systems. Somewhat different is the approach employed by Kern and Bulkeley in their study of transnational municipal networks in the context of local climate change policy.

The character of local policy networks in the field of climate change – they argue – is influenced by the process of Europeanisation, thus assumed more as an *explanans* rather than the phenomenon to be explained. They portray municipal networks somehow as devices at the disposal of cities to circumvent the power of the central State (Kern and Bulkeley, 2009). Their study therefore examines the structure of a specific set of municipal networks, rather than exploring the encounter between cities and the EU.

Turning to the field of urban studies, the EU is factored in as an intervening variable within a process where Europe is reduced to a mere functional context for the action of cities (Goldsmith, 1993b; Kubler and Le Galès, 2002; Piliutyte, 2007). The EU is therefore considered somewhat equal to other international governance contexts where due to an enlarged opportunity structure, cities and regions are confronted with new channels to exercise 'para-diplomatic' activities beyond the control of the central government. Sometimes the action of the EU is explicitly addressed and an attempt is made to grasp the Europeanisation of cities and urban areas; nonetheless the analysis is limited to accounting for the transnational activity of cities within network structures (Kubler and Piliutyte, 2007).

In these cases the analysis focuses on the intergovernmental relations between urban systems and other levels of governments within the hierarchically structured European polity – where cities are perceived as a lower level seeking to supersede the filtering power exercised by regional and central authorities. This kind of analysis, in turn, pays little attention, if any, to the policy action of the EU in terms of change of urban systems of governance. It neglects elements of research design and causation concerning Europeanisation at the level of cities and local authorities[1].

Urban policies, we submit, at both the domestic level and in the context of the European Union have instead to be considered as part of broader domains of public policies and their analysis should be therefore carried out accordingly. As claimed by Le Galès, 'in analytical terms, it has been a common mistake to analyse urban policy as independent from changes in public policy in general' (Le Galès, 2007: 13). This is particularly the case when the attempt is to assess the systems-actors interplay in the context of the EU policy making.

Therefore, the literature suffers from an overall lack of theoretically informed approaches to EU-related urban policies grounded on specific assumptions, which in turn has reinforced the tendency to preserve the dividing between European studies and urban studies within the discipline of political science.

3.4 Concluding remarks

The academic debate surrounding Europeanisation remains lively and prone to produce competing understanding (Haverland, 2007; Radaelli and Exadaktylos, 2009b). This, in turn, proves both the true potential for Europeanisation to yield new theories within other major disciplines (i.e. comparative politics and international relations) and the controversial nature of the concept. The existence of a distinctive EU system of interaction and the 'encounter' between the EU and domestic systems/actors are considered necessary factors for changes to occur within domestic systems, therefore as a necessary element for Europeanisation to happen.

Research on Europeanisation has led scholars to propose different mechanisms through which EU action – and in turn its impact on domestic systems – develops. Thus, explanations have been differently grounded in mechanisms of direct EU pressure, institutional compliance or regulatory competition. Most recently, to overcome the shortcoming of the 'goodness of fit' argument, analytical attention has been paid to mechanisms of learning via facilitated coordination (Bulmer and Radaelli, 2005) and discourses legitimisation (Schmidt, 2002b; 2007; Schmidt and Radaelli, 2002). Yet, consideration has been given to more general mechanisms of socialisation in the form of ideational transfer, exchange of knowledge and policy benchmarking (Radaelli, 2008).

---

1. For a review of research design issues in the field of Europeanisation see Exadaktylos, T. and Radaelli, C. M. (2009) 'Research Design in European Studies: The Case of Europeanisation', *Journal of Common Market Studies* 47(3): 507–30.

Nonetheless, studies of Europeanisation grounded in mechanism-based explanations, fall short to reach satisfactory accounts of the connection between causes and effects of Europeanisation. In turn, they do fail to highlight the causal relations underpinning the procedural mechanisms through which the relation between Europe and domestic systems transmits. Attempts of measuring the process and its potential effects have been rather scarce in number, and often pivoted on matters of implementation or transposition of EU directives and regulations within domestic systems (Franchino, 2005b; Gilardi, 2005; Giuliani, 2003; Levi-Faur, 2004).

Empirical research on Europeanisation has mainly focused on changes occurring within national structures of policy and politics, where institutional compliance – or lack of it – and pressures for adaptation are more likely to yield the transformation of existing arrangements.

When the level of analysis is centred on sub-national systems, notably regional authorities, Europeanisation is generally assessed by considering structural programmes for regional development financed under the various funds enacting the Regional policy of the European Union. In these cases, Europeanisation is usually thought as the diffusion of regional action beyond the borders of the State or as the action of regional networks at the EU level in an attempt to boost specific instances, instead of common policy requests (Jeffery, 2000; 1996; Jones and Keating, 1995; Pasquier, 2005; Piattoni and Smyrl, 1998). Instead, when the analysis focuses more prominently on institutional domestic structures, yet, it tends to almost exclusively point out change directly attributable to the implementation of specific structural programmes.

Local authorities – cities in particular – have almost been disregarded as a possible level of analysis to appraise the potential impact of the EU action. The 'encounter between cities and the EU' can be thought both in terms of direct promotion of policies and – indirectly – as a model to draw on to legitimise discourses towards reforms, yet again as a system of forums where cities can interact to exchange policy practices and new ideas.

In those few cases where the relation between urban systems and the European policy making has been assessed through the Europeanisation approach, attention is generally paid to the political sphere and in particular to the role of local leaders and to their political legitimacy, both locally and towards the central government (Borraz and John, 2004; John, 2000; Goldsmith and Larsen, 2004). Extended theoretical accounts supported by empirical evidence of the process of Europeanisation within urban areas have seldom been offered hitherto. Analytical paucity, in this case, can be attributed to several reasons.

One of the reasons for the lack of analyses is that this issue-area falls in between dominant research domains, sub disciplines and research traditions. On one side, research on the EU is mainly based on theoretical approaches from IR and comparative politics, whereas urban studies usually confine the analysis within the state borders, thus partially neglecting the 'foreign relations' of cities and moreover the role of city policy actors within the EU policy making. Another reason has to do with the presumptive scarcity of empirical evidence as to the direct influence of the European action within urban systems.

This, in turn, has led to analyses focusing mainly on the promotion and implementation of the structural and cohesion policy of the EU in the localities. Finally – and most challenging – there is the issue of research design. Within a context area where the potential cases to be selected are in the vicinity of thousands, it appears more difficult to draw conclusions that can be generalised for 200,000 local authorities than doing the same based on the situation in twenty-seven member states.

Chapter Four

Mechanisms and Modes of Europeanisation

4.1 Introduction

Not only do cities access the policy arena at the EU level, they also exert influence and partial control over policy outcomes. European institutions involve cities as stakeholders in the policy process, especially in some policy areas and within specific programmes. Therefore, the new set of opportunities offered by the intervention of the EU at the urban level suggests a cautious re-labelling of cities as policy makers, at least for the urban dimension of the Structural Funds, but possibly also for other policy areas.

The decision to terminate specific programmes addressed to cities after 2007 and to incorporate them into wider regional policies has opened up questions as to the place and role of cities and urban actors within the EU. At the same time, though, the development of an urban policy of the European Union seems to be still far from an effective fulfilment.

Nonetheless, the Lisbon Strategy brings European cities at the forefront of the EU-led policy making and urban territories become centres for regulation and the promotion of crosscutting integrated policies. Finally, cities are also a key component of the attempts to create new loci of legitimacy for the EU and to learn through experimental governance and via the Open Method of Coordination by tapping the benefits of local knowledge (Sabel and Zeitlin, 2008; Zeitlin and Trubek, 2003).

When researchers try to identify the policies of the EU affecting the urban political domains, they look for those EU programmes with 'cities' on the tin, that is, the policies formally identified by the EU as targeting cities. This is a major pitfall since the identification of the units of policy analysis is a task of the researcher, and often formal-legalistic definitions are incomplete. To illustrate, no serious researcher would think of studying the welfare policies of the EU by running a word-search on the official websites or legislative datasets looking for 'welfare'. Instead, they would most likely start from a theoretical definition of 'welfare', think about its applications to the EU domains, and then identify empirical manifestations of the conceptual constructs suggested by literature. This is the aim of this chapter. This is particularly relevant, because most of the literature on cities has followed a kind of formal or legalistic approach.

The chapter sorts out Europeanisation mechanisms by starting from the identification of ideal-types of arenas – or '*fora*' in the tradition of French political science (Jobert, 2003). The arenas can be ideational, distributive or regulatory.

In turn, mechanisms have a differential impact on the domestic (city) domains of policy (i.e. actors, instruments, resources, styles and cognitive structures of policies) and eventually on the political structures of urban areas (administrative, representative and cognitive/normative). Throughout the chapter, the framework of Europeanisation will be used to reveal causal mechanisms and the scope conditions at the bases of the encounter between cities and the EU wide policy-making arenas.

4.2 For a public policy analysis of cities Europeanisation

The process of European integration is accompanied by the creation of a growing bulk of legislation, rules and policy initiative that, with different degrees of influence, may impact on European cities. Additionally, the EU official rhetoric often portrays cities as 'powerful agents of legitimisation' (Le Galès, 2007) by designating cities and urban areas as 'target population' (Schneider and Ingram, 1993) where to re-address new citizenship discourses.

The idea of 'Europe of cities' is also one of the components of the European polity in this legitimising discourse. In turn, this is giving urban systems and other actors within their boundaries, new legitimacy and resources to act within the various systems of governance characterising the policy making of the European Union.

In this connection, urban policies are the resultant of policy making within multiple territorial and administrative units. When 'new urban policies' are introduced, regardless of the source of their promotion, they are likely to ensue from a mixture of new provisions and existing long lasting traditions in promoting public policy. Therefore, innovation and change within urban policies are generally incremental processes following path dependant dynamics. Policy novelty is most often an addition to existing programmes, which are now reassembled and reframed. The 'urban experiment' of the EU is the resultant of different state traditions in promoting and managing issues of economic development, social protection and environmental regeneration at the local level (Le Galès, 2007).

The high variety of responses thus far offered by cities involved in EU-led urban programmes clearly shows how Europeanisation is one amongst other core aspects of governance at the urban level. Therefore, urban-city Europeanisation as a research agenda needs to be considered as a compound process whose analysis has to take into account other transforming dynamics, such as domestic and international processes.

Therefore, the concepts of participation and power deserve greater analytical attention. Participation is not a panacea for the effective involvement of actors in policy making. Yet, even in connection to participation, past policy arrangements have to be taken into account as well as the long-standing inequalities in the distribution of powers within different administrative systems and between groups of actors. Participation is context-centred and specific (Jones, 2003). Participation, either into networks or in other more traditional forms, underpins power relationships and normative constraints. Participating, in turn, does not necessarily imply the possibility to shift existing power relations towards accruing self-benefits. Therefore, it is useful to approach the policy-polity relation with a theory of power distribution and assignment of authority able to account for the distribution of gains from the process of Europeanisation and the dynamic of conflict management within different policy domains.

In turn, each of the aforementioned processes is likely to underpin different logics of action, as well as mechanisms through which these logics transmit. Thus, the Europeanisation of cities is associated to broader processes of socialisation through discourse formation and refinement, as well as via changes in the set of preferences within different groups and policy networks. When Europeanisation is related to EU action through the promotion of specific programmes for urban regeneration it is more likely to translate via processes of bargaining and negotiation, implying at times complex dynamics of compensation and conflict resolution within different policy arenas. Additionally – also in the case of urban systems – EU action increasingly transmits by means of regulatory provisions generating impacts on the pre-existing regulatory systems within cities. Thus, new sets of regulations boost mutual learning processes between actors and institutions towards efficiency in the pursuit of renewed policy objectives.

Therefore, to assess the nature of the process of Europeanisation in the case of urban governance, researchers need to look at different policy areas involving cities across Europe.

However, this step has been somewhat hindered by the implicit shortcomings of the Multi-Level Governance approach (Marks, *et al.* 1996). The tabloid version of MLG, which appears in studies of Europeanisation of subnational systems, reduces Europeanisation to the interplay between hierarchically ordered levels of governance, where subnational levels and central States are maintained as competing or adversarial, due to the attempt of lower levels to evade 'central control'. Thus, subnational actors and institutions are usually treated as constituting a unique and static layer of governance (Carter and Smith, 2008: 265–266).

To partially overcome these drawbacks, this appraisal draws on an approach grounded in public policy analysis (Carter and Smith, 2008). In particular, we will focus on the different European policy arenas – orders – within which actors and institutions relate interchangeably in order to attain specific policy goals. Processes of interest formation, strategic decision making and regulatory competition taking place over time in the context of policy orders have the potential to influence the character of Europeanisation and eventually the features of domestic politics within different domains. Policy arenas, as well as the institutional and individual actors therein involved, have to be conceived as constituting dynamic systems, where cities are sometimes EU-level actors, sometimes the recipients of the Commission's programmes, yet the places where EU regulatory measures and provisions are actually implemented. Either way, they are not pigeonholed in the lower layer of governance by definition (Carter and Smith, 2008).

The analysis of cities Europeanisation offers room to apply the 'sharp public policy analysis tools' evoked by Carter and Smith by accounting for the nature and use of *policy instruments*, an approach that has been rarely used until now in the studies of cities in the EU. Focusing on policy instruments as well as on the mechanisms through which these instruments are likely to be promoted, and reacted to, allows to move beyond functionalist approaches by at the same time integrating the understanding of the new forms of networked governance (Rhodes, 1997) with the mechanisms for the control and direction of behaviour (Hood, 1998).

4.3 Policy instruments and the 'new' tools of public intervention

Discussion on policy instrumentation – instruments – has gained renovated vigour in so far as the internationalisation of the economy and dynamics of regional institutionalisation have shown the partial inefficacy of some governmental tools traditionally employed for public intervention.

A policy instruments perspective may be advantageous when the overall attempt is to seize the pace of influence and transformation of the EU policy making on the functioning of urban systems of governance as well as on the interplay between actors in the EU-wide policy arenas. Looking at the policy instrumentation governments are endowed with – in this case the European Union – reveals particularly convenient within a realm – *urban policy* – where the EU does not have a specific and formal competence and where interactions between 'cities' and the EU are likely to take place within multiple policy areas and at different stages of the policy process.

Therefore, a policy instruments perspective in the analysis of Europeanisation may simplify the task of accounting for the high number of activities carried out by the EU policy machinery. Additionally, unpacking the set of instruments promoted by the EU provides insights into the long-term purposes of 'the legislator' as well as on the degree of fulfilment the promotion of tools will eventually reach. Hence, instrument-based accounts 'can provide some antidote to the all-too-common assumption in government affairs that things could not possibly be handled in any other way than they are at present' (Hood, 1983: 9).

Policy instruments: definitions and classifications

Policy programmes – and public policies more in general – are performed through multiple instruments, which in turn embed specific sets of policy tools.

Despite the technicality of the decisions leading to the choice of instruments to carry out a specific policy strategy, the process of tools selection is inherently political. This is especially true when the policy making takes place within multiple territorial and policy arenas. Specific instruments give some actors – and in turn some of the ideas these actors seek to promote – a certain degree of advantage in establishing how policies will be carried out, thus contributing to promote certain sets of interests and preferences over others. The choice of tools is also profoundly affected by cultural norms and ideological tendencies. Once in place, instruments contribute to frame public attitudes towards the state, or the governmental body – such as the EU – in charge of their initial promotion (Lascoumes and Le Galès, 2007).

Instruments for policy action have been variously defined and classified. In this connection, *one-sided analysis* focus on specific fields of policy, whereas *cross-sided analysis*, attempt to look at the whole range of instruments used by governments across the entire spectrum of public action. This has opened the way for more comprehensive analyses of governmental activity in response to earlier systematisations of public policy performed in the form of typologies (Hood and Margetts, 2007).

Instruments of public action can be defined as 'an identifiable method through which collective action is structured to address a public problem' (Salamon, 2002a: 19) or likewise, as 'the set of techniques by which governmental authorities wield power in attempting to ensure support and effect or prevent social change' (Vedung, 1998: 21). Thus, policy instruments, or tools, are clearly identifiable on the bases of common features, but can vary in their design. In this case, tools are maintained as means to structure relationships and courses of actions, thus assuming the character of institutionalised forms. As a result, policy instruments may be conceived as 'institutions' (Peters, 1999; Pierson, 1993; 2000; Powell and Di Maggio, 1991) embedding specific criteria for the selection of actors, for role attribution and for the establishment of the rules of interaction. Yet, instruments are identified as devices structuring collective actions to solve public problems, hence implying the involvement of actors other than the sole governmental bodies (Salamon, 2002a: 20).

Distinction is made between policy instruments and other devices for public intervention, such as techniques and tools. In this vein instruments are interpreted as types of social institutions; techniques would represent concrete devices through which instruments are operationalised. The latter – tools – are instead defined as micro devices within a technique (Lascoumes and Le Galès, 2007)[1]. Additionally, policy action may be analytically framed by disentangling between instruments or tools, and more comprehensive policy initiatives whereby different combinations of policy instruments are brought into practice. In this case, instruments are distinguished from programmes – which embody the tools to apply in different circumstances – and policies, which are instead collections of programmes targeted at addressing general objectives within similar fields. In turn, a single policy may employ a single tool – instrument – or instead a range of tools. Salamon further distinguished between the *internal* instruments used by governments to handle 'in-office' operations, and *external* tools, which by contrast are used to affect target portions of the society (Salamon, 2002b).

---

1. For instance, census taking may be conceived as an instrument as well as statutory regulation or taxation, whereas statistical nomenclature or specific types of laws and decrees are techniques for their operationalisation. The specific categories for statistical representation, peculiar types of obligation and the eventual presence of sanction are instead to be considered as the tools through which techniques are put into practice.

Policy instruments can also be classified according to their constitutive elements, including *type of goods, delivery vehicle, delivery system* and *sets of rules* defining the relations within the delivery system. In turn, each instrument would be characterised by descriptive criteria for its evaluation in terms of *efficiency, effectiveness, equity, manageability* and *policy feasibility*, as well as on the bases of various dimensions useful for their analytical grouping –*coerciveness, directness, automaticity* and *visibility* (Salamon, 2002b).

Other analyses have more prominently focused on the behavioural assumptions guiding the process of instruments selection. Schneider and Ingram differentiate between five categories on the bases of the behaviours that policy programmes seek to modify. Thus, policy instruments may be grouped in *authority tools, incentive tools, capacity tools, symbolic or hortatory tools* and *learning tools*, In particular, a focus on the behavioural dimension of policy tools would favour the comparative analysis of the relationship between policy instruments and policy participation by target populations across policy types (Schneider and Ingram, 1990).

Here, we endorse a definition according to which a *public policy instrument* is a 'device that is both technical and social, that organises specific relations between the state and those it is addressed to, according to the representations and meanings it carries. It is a particular type of institution, a technical device with the generic purpose of carrying a concrete concept of the politics/society relationship, and sustained by a concept of regulation' (Lascoumes and Le Galès, 2007: 4).

The process of instruments selection is made of political choices, in turn underpinning specific relations between actors and institutions involved in their choice. For the purpose of this research, policy instruments are strategies that produce their own effects, regardless of the final result they are meant to trigger; they are policy apparatus embedding specific forms of knowledge as to the exercise of social control.

Additionally, policy instruments are political constructs (Schneider and Ingram, 1993) resulting from conflict over definitions of problems. Instruments may be conceived as institutional forms framing the interactions and behaviours of actors and organisations; they affect relations of power, by at the same time privileging certain actors and some interests over others (Lascoumes and Le Galès, 2007).

Changing instruments of urban policy

Urban policies and programmes, at the level of both national and local government – and more recently under the initiative of the European Union – were thought and then re-designed in order to face what is generally labelled the 'urban crisis' (Le Galès, 2007), which caused the partial decline of the most industrialised regions of Western Europe.

In particular, the economic crisis hitting Europe during the 1970s entailed side-processes of de-industrialisation, marginalisation of the working class, the appearance of new forms of poverty, increasing unemployment, the partial restructuring of the labour market and the increasing recourse to forms of privatisation in the provision of services and utilities within urban and metropolitan areas.

In an attempt to tackle the problematic implications of the economic and industrial decline faced by many cities, urban policies were partially refocused. Hence, preference was given to policy programmes characterised by multi-instrumental provisions, integrated nature – whereby a specific programme covers various policy areas – and by an increasing appeal to horizontal methods for management and implementation.

In the context of the European Union, the traditional prerogatives of the state administrations diminished within a number of issue areas, wherein the action of other international and macro-regional institutional bodies has contextually expanded, thus exposing public policy to the intertwined influence of multiple regulators. The agreement on the free movement of goods and people, in particular, has enabled enterprises to venture new and wider markets, and social actors to gain increasing capacities to access public goods and political legitimisation beyond the state borders.

This renewed policy environment and the dynamics characterising the interplay between actors have led to the search for a new analytical framework able to seize the novelties of the changing policy scenario. According to the advocates of the *new governance* paradigm for instance, the policy making would increasingly be collaborative and based on the action of a range of third parties, alongside the government, for the provision of public services and the pursuing of public purposes (Salamon, 2002a).

The policy making is therefore pictured as relying to a greater extent on partnership arrangements between public and private actors, whereas in classical public administration accounts the parties are usually considered as competing for the provision of public services. Therefore, 'New Governance' policy environments are thought as responding to a renewed approach to public management, in which process of command and control – characterising the traditional management approach – are replaced by processes of negotiation and persuasion during the phases of negotiation and implementation of policies and programmes. Contextually, analytical emphasis shifts from management skills and the control of large bureaucratic organisation, to those skills enabling the involvement of an enlarged set of actors and partners within network assets, as well as to favour coordination to attain common policy goals in situations of high interdependence (Salamon, 2002a: 9–11).

In this connection, policy instruments are conceived as linking devices between different policy areas and programmes, rather than devices for the development of 'less politicised' arrangements, nonetheless fostering, at times, mechanisms aimed at the control and direction of behaviours (Hood, 1998).

Social mechanisms and the value of mechanistic explanation

A focus on mechanisms allows to highlight the constellation of *entities* and *activities* that are interconnected to one another, thus bringing about specific types of outcomes (Hedström, 2005; Hedström and Swedberg, 1996; Machamer, *et al.*, 2000). Social mechanisms constitute powerful tools to attain causal explanations of the phenomena under analysis.

Specifically, mechanism-based explanations, as opposed to statistical explanations and covering-law explanations, allow to better distinguish between causality and coincidental association, by at the same time increasing the understanding of the potential reasons triggering the observed event or process (Hedström and Swedberg, 1996). Yet, differently from other types of explanations, accounts based on social mechanisms bring the added value of revealing the processes underpinning the relationships under analysis (Bunge, 1967; 2004).

Sorting out the potential generative mechanisms for change facilitates the task of specifying the causal agents at the foundation of the observed relationship between the entities under analysis. Causal agents correspond to individual actors; social mechanisms therefore refer to the causes and potential consequences of individuals' actions. In the context of sociological theories – which generally aim at explaining social outcomes – individuals constitute the entities and their actions and interactions represent the activities responsible for the occurrence of the social phenomena to be explained. In turn, the different ways entities are linked together – *structures of interaction* – influence the character and nature of the social outcome at stake. Therefore, activities, as different interrelations of entities, are the actual producers of change, 'they are constitutive of the transformations that yield new States of affairs or new products' (Machamer, *et al.*, 2000: 4).

Mechanistic-type explanations must be attentive to the interaction between causal mechanisms and the context in which they operate. In turn, this calls for adapting concepts and measurements of the variables under analysis to the specific circumstances in which they are applied and where they occur (Falleti and Lynch, 2009)[2]. Therefore, causation is to be retrieved, not only in the attributes of the unit of analysis, but also in the mechanisms framing the interplay between different structures of interaction.

Amongst other definitions, mechanisms can be defined as 'precise, abstract, and action-based explanation, which shows how the occurrence of a triggering event regularly generates the type of outcome to be explained' (Hedström and Swedberg, 1996). A causal mechanism is a 'series of events governed by law-like regularities that lead from the *explanans* to the *explanandum*' (Little, 1991: 14). As such, the mechanisms in operation are not always directly observable, their existence is likely instead to be conjectured by means of hypotheses and imagination corroborated by available data (Bunge, 2004). In this respect, mechanisms represent simplified assumptions referring to subsets of potentially important events having the potential of accounting for what happened; mechanisms find their theoretical and analytical value in their capacity to 'produce interesting hypothesis or explanations at the higher level' (Stinchombe, 1991: 27).

---

2. Similar arguments have been emphasised by other scholars such as in Adcock, A. and Collier, B. (2001) 'Measurement validity: a shared standard for quantitative and qualitative research', *American Political Science Review* 95(3): 529–546.

In this connection, causal mechanisms – and social mechanisms in this case – can be conceptualised as factor-links connecting independent variables and dependent variables.

Differently from explanations based on probability statements, which usually entail a direct link between the presence of a certain input and the occurrence of outcomes ($I{\rightarrow}O$), in this case the occurrence of a certain outcome, if a certain input is present, is the resultant of the mediation of specific mechanisms ($I{\rightarrow}M{\rightarrow}O$).

Mechanisms are *relational concepts* (Abbott, 2007). They describe and make sense of the interactions taking place among the units of analysis. Therefore, mechanisms bear a different ontological position compared to variables. Social mechanisms reveal different relations between actors, different modes through which individuals frame their beliefs and expectations. Yet, they reveal how institutions may resist to, or instead curve change and how different policy measures are likely to transmit, and to affect target populations. Causal mechanisms do not operate in a deterministic manner. If a certain – pre-conjectured – mechanism operates, it is not certain it will systematically produce the same outcome of interest, as instead argued by other accounts (Mahoney, 2001).

A detailed characterisation of hypothetical mechanisms of Europeanisation helps to reduce theoretical fragmentation thus highlighting possible structural resemblances between processes. Furthermore – by connecting entities with activities in terms of the potential outcome they are supposed to regularly bring about – mechanisms increase the possibility to sort out the causal relationships between a certain cause and its effects (Hedström, 2005).

Therefore, when we say 'mechanisms of Europeanisation' we refer to theoretically justified patterns of interaction that may bring about Europeanisation. We do not prejudge the degree of Europeanisation that may eventually occur. We do not even make the assumption that, since there is a theoretically-derived mechanism that produces Europeanisation, the mechanisms will operate. Indeed empirically, one may find constraining or countervailing mechanisms. Thus, we leave the matter of 'how much Europeanisation' out of this conceptual exercise.

We contend that when considering the range of programmes and policy initiatives promoted by the European Union – either those directly addressed to cities and urban areas, or those promoted in the context of wider actions having nonetheless the potential to influence the management of public policies within urban systems of policy making – analytical attention should focus more narrowly on the commonalities and differences of policies on the basis of the set of instruments deployed among different areas.

In turn, policy instruments underpin different sets of mechanisms for their transmission. A well-known mechanism of Europeanisation is the *goodness of fit* (Börzel, 1999; Green Cowles, *et al.*, 2001). Bringing forwards the discussion, Knill and Lehmkuhl contend that the range of mechanisms is broader (Knill and Lehmkuhl, 2002). Their set of mechanisms includes Europeanisation by explicit adaptational pressures – *institutional compliance* – considered as the principal mechanisms characterising those policy areas of 'positive integration' (Scharpf, 1999), *regulatory competition* and *framing* domestic beliefs and expectations.

Additionally, there are situations in which the action of the European Union can affect national policy systems even in the absence of clear EU directives of regulation. It is actually the case of those areas of *facilitated coordination*. Here, the key actors are domestic governments (Bulmer and Radaelli, 2005), and mechanisms of *learning* and *discourses legitimisation* trigger transformations within the EU as an arena for the exchange of best practices and ideas. Some of the *modi operandi* typical of the open method of coordination become particularly relevant in the case of subnational authorities. The lack of resources and the need for information often characterising the action of cities within the EU-wide policy making, may favour collective forms of action and dynamics of policy learning and processes of diffusion of best practices between local authorities.

4.4 The approach: policy modes and mechanisms of Europeanisation

Building on the previous discussion, in this section we devise a series of potential mechanisms for the Europeanisation of urban areas as associated to different modes – domains – of policy, through which the 'encounter between cities and the EU' is supposed to occur. This is an exercise based on simple deduction and classification, but useful to explore causality[3]. To understand how causality works, we have to consider causal mechanisms of change and mechanisms of transmission.

To overcome the limitations of current literature, instead of looking at legal/ formal definitions of urban policy, we proceeded from a much wider scanning of the ways in which EU policy affects urban policy and politics. Specifically, we have drawn on the literature on policy types (Anderson, 1997; Gormley, 1986; Lowi, 1964, 1972; Spitzer, 1987; Van Horn, *et al.*, 2001) and the literature on mechanisms of Europeanisation (Eberlein and Radaelli, 2010; Knill and Lehmkuhl, 2002), as well as on the discussion on the logic of choice and the logic of appropriateness (March and Olsen, 1998). Table 4.1 illustrates this framework.

Table 4.1: Mechanisms of Europeanisation of cities and urban areas

	Mechanisms of change	Mechanisms of transmission
Mechanisms of ideation	*socialisation* *legitimising discourses* *reflexivity-social learning* *deliberation and framing* *proceduralisation*	• Communication • Benchmarking • Policy learning/transfer • Networking • Promotion of new paradigms and tools of governance

---

3. For a similar catalogue-like approach see Knill, C. and Lehmkuhl, D. (2002) 'The national impact of European Union regulatory policy: Three Europeanisation mechanisms', *European Journal of Political Research* 41: 255–80.

Table 4.1 (*Continued*)

		Mechanisms of change	Mechanisms of transmission
Mechanisms	*of regulation*	*Pareto efficiency* *regulation* *collibration*	• Regulatory competition • Regulatory compliance
Mechanisms	*of coordination*	*coordination* *cooperation*	• Self-regulation • Cooperative learning • Targets compliance (Standardisation)
Mechanisms	*of distribution*	*strategic bargaining* *negotiation*	• Institutional framing • Programming • Targets compliance • Territorial rescaling

Nonetheless, researchers willing to explore the dynamics of Europeanisation, that is, how the EU affects or does not affect the local systems of policy and politics, need more than a catalogue based on abstract causal mechanisms.

Thus, we develop, in turn, the argument that there are four different modes of Europeanisation. As a consequence, to grasp the essence of a single instrument or a given EU initiative, one has to establish which mode is prevailing in the policy logic of that instrument or initiative. We will define the modes in a moment. It is therefore useful to elicit from the previous discussions the core variables that explain change. The previous sections seem to suggest that the two core variables concern the status of actors' preferences and the nature of strategic interaction. The variables we tease out of the discussion in literature can be outlined as follows.

The first (a) – *preferences* – concerns the initial arrangements of preferences. Preferences can be endogenous – and thus subject to change due to processes of learning and socialisation in situations where actors' behaviours are mainly guided by a logic of appropriateness – or exogenous – therefore leaving actors with a restricted space of manoeuvre within dynamics of bargaining dictated by a logic of choice.

According to the latter logic – *expected consequences* – actors are likely to choose among alternatives by accounting for the possible consequences that these choices are likely to have on individual or a collective set of objectives. In turn, decisions are usually the outcome of processes of negotiation in situations characterised by rational actors pursuing personal preferences and possible gains from coordinated action. Situations where actors are mainly guided by a logic of appropriateness are instead characterised by rules that associate specific identities to certain situational patterns; in this case the attainment of prefigured goals may be seen as identity-based and less dependent on interests, yet again, more guided by the selection of certain rules of conduct by individual rational expectations (March and Olsen, 1998).

The implications of these two logics rest on different ontological and epistemological assumptions and on diverse theoretical explanations underpinning different techniques for conflict management – respectively *aggregation* and *transformation*. Our analysis will privilege, nonetheless, a 'both/and' line of reasoning, rather than the traditional exclusive 'either/or' frame. This implies that both appropriateness and consequence may be at work; analytical priority will be therefore given to assess the scope conditions and the modalities characterising the logic of actors' behaviours within different policy domains.

The other dimension (b) – *nature of strategic interaction* – deals with the distribution of payoffs from Europeanisation, meaning the relative or absolute advantages that actors and institutions may draw from their involvement in the EU-steered policy game. In turn, this dimension can be displayed on a continuum where one pole is represented by zero-sum games – where either the values at stake are mainly social values therefore hardly negotiable, or the process of interaction is likely to generate winners and losers from Europeanisation (Thatcher, 2004). The other pole is positioned within the Pareto frontier. In this case the overall goal is not to defend a specific initial position, but to reach Pareto optimality, thus protecting efficiency.

The combination of (a) and (b) thus originates a four-dimensional space. We can therefore develop a typology for the modes of Europeanisation, which chimes with current theorisation on the EU modes of governance (Borras and Jacobsson, 2004; Eberlein and Kerwer, 2004; Héritier and Rhodes, 2011; Treib, *et al.* 2005).

Table 4.2: The space of modes of Europeanisation

		Distribution of payoffs from Europeanisation	
		ZERO SUM GAMES **Winners and losers from Europeanisation**	PARETO OPTIMALITY **Europeanisation on the Pareto frontier**
Logic of preferences	ENDOGENOUS **Preferences can change** *Appropriateness*	*Social Values* (1) **IDEATION**	*Efficiency* (2) **REGULATION**
	EXOGENOUS **Preferences are given** *Choice*	(4) **DISTRIBUTION**	(3) **COORDINATION**

The four modes as presented in the typology partly overlap with types of policy well known in literature. In particular, modes of regulation are similar to Lowi's *regulatory arenas* (Lowi, 1964; 1972) and may reveal some of the defining properties that feature in the sub-types of regulatory policies suggested by Gormley in terms of 'hearing room', 'operating room', 'street level' and 'board room' politics (Gormley, 1986; Van Horn, *et al.*, 2001).

Thick-learning/reflexivity can be identified as interactive attributes of ideation, which is to consider as a distinctive mode only for typological and analytical purposes. Ideational components, in fact, are characteristic of different domains of policy as well as diverse phases of the policy process. Thus, for instance, regulative arenas are grounded in rulemaking practices: their logic of change is based on Pareto-efficiency and market-preserving mechanisms. In part, this overlaps with ideational mechanisms since Pareto-efficiency is one of the legitimising discourses of the EU (Majone, 1992).

Modes of ideation

Cell 1 better describes situations characterised by endogenous distribution of preferences and a tendency for interactions to lead to zero-sum games. Therefore, within *ideational* arenas, the main research question is about the scope conditions for reflexivity (via discourse or sustained interaction, as well as thick socialisation and/or frame reflection). Reflexivity dynamics carry the strongest potential to transform zero-sum games and situations of stalemate within the decision making over specific policy issues into possible cooperative arrangements (Lenoble and Maesshalck, 2006).

Dynamics of interaction characterising *ideation domains* of policy find their foundation in those ontologies and models predicting the possibility of change within preference sets due to different processes of socialisation and discursive interaction between individual and institutional actors (Adler, 1997; 2002; Checkel, 1998; Ruggie, 1998), as well as on the social construction of the European polity stressing the importance of language, ideas and inter-subjectivity (Checkel, 2005; Christiansen, *et al.*, 1999; 2001) and the political role of legitimising discourses (Schmidt, 2008; Schmidt and Radaelli, 2004). Constructivism mainly 'concerns the issue of human consciousness: the role it plays in international relations, and the implications for the logic and method of social enquiry of taking it seriously' (Ruggie, 1998: 33), where the constitutive blocks of the international reality are both ideational and material. Ideational factors, whose meaning and significance are related to time and place, in turn, have normative as well as instrumental dimensions and express the intentions of collective and individual actors.

Within ideational domains, the preferences of political agents are endogenous, thus subject to change due to dynamics of social learning, socialisation, routine and normative diffusion (Checkel, 1999). Preferences may change due to general processes of *socialisation* or *social learning* both at the level of the European-wide policy making as well as within and between cities, when EU-policy instruments embedded in specific programmes or more extended policy initiatives are deployed in domestic systems. Drawing on sociological-institutionalist accounts, socialisation may be initially defined as 'a process of inducing actors into the norms and rules of a given community', thus implying that 'an agent switches from following a logic of consequences to a logic of appropriateness; this adoption is sustained over time and is quite independent from particular structure of material incentives or sanctions' (Checkel, 2005: 804).

Other key mechanisms through which conflicting preferences transform are *deliberation* or *arguing* (Elster, 1998). Deliberative approaches identify the importance of 'argumentative interaction for the coherence of a polity, its social acceptance and its normative acceptability' (Neyer, 2006: 779). According to the proponents of 'deliberative supranationalism' for instance, exchange of arguments in an evidence-based, issue-specific context, would lead actors to realise the potential externalities of their preferences for others, thus modifying these preferences accordingly (Joerges and Neyer, 1997; Neyer, 2006). In this case the EU assumes the character of a framework facilitating the 'public use of reason' (Gerstenberg, 1997: 351), where for deliberation to be effective two main conditions must apply: deliberation has to be an open process taking place in public spheres where actual participation has to be guaranteed (Neyer, 2006).

Another set of mechanisms suggests transformation of preferences following iterative and problem-driven dynamics, thus shifting the locus of change from the socialisation of individual actors to alterations through proceduralisation (Eberlein and Radaelli, 2010). One of these mechanisms is *framing*, defined as 'the process of selecting, emphasising and organising aspects of complex issues according to an overriding evaluative or analytical criterion' (Daviter, 2007; Schon and Rein, 1994). In their study on conflict management strategies within regulatory policy areas, Radaelli and Eberlein propose *proceduralisation* as a further mechanism through which actors may interrelate thus changing their preferences within the ideational policy arena. In this case, actors find it easier to agree on the process through which outcomes will be defined and on the instrument that will be used to define desirable goals instead of directly agreeing on the policy targets to be achieved (Eberlein and Radaelli, 2010).

The transmission of ideational/discursive policy programmes and instruments is likely to take place within cross-sectional 'fora' for discussion through mechanisms relying on patterns of *communication, benchmarking, policy learning* as well as on the promotion of *new policy paradigms* and *new tools of governance* agreed within the EU policy arena. The tools are afterwards eventually experimented in the localities, which progressively become targets of renewed legitimisation for the policy action of the EU and loci to experiment innovative and 'more participative' modalities for the management of policy programmes and initiatives.

Regulatory modes

Cell 2, on the other hand, captures situations of non-fixed preferences where the overall objective of interaction around policies is to attain procedural efficiency. Therefore, regulation as a mode of governance typifies this domain.

Domains where *regulation* is the characteristic mode of interaction have a rank of values at stake that is not disputed and eventually composed by actors. Although the set of preferences within this domain can be initially considered as variably both endogenous – thus subject to change through technocratic argumentation – and exogenous – where instead actors eventually realise the advantages that may stem from coordinating their reciprocal positions – here, the defining logic of policy action is its tension towards preserving *efficiency* over equity. Two main sets of procedural mechanisms can be maintained herewith in operation that is *regulation* and *efficiency* (Majone, 1994). Legitimacy is sought through administrative procedures (Majone, 1996).

In the case of regulatory policies, the role played by the EU can be thought as one version of *collibration*, defined as 'an intervention by government to use the social energy created by the tension between two or more social groupings habitually locked in opposition to one another to achieve a policy objective by altering the conditions of engagement without destroying the tension – unless deliberately' (Dunsire, 1993: 12).

Regulatory arenas respond to various theories of rational policy analysis. Also in the context of the EU, the growing demand for accountability has led to the diffusion of analytic and quantitative techniques to assist in resources allocation and the policy making process (Carley, 1980). Different techniques for cost-benefit analysis, environmental impact assessment, social impact assessment, the use of social indicators and various types of methods for evaluation are particularly relevant in the case of regulatory policies in the EU.

The functioning of regulatory arenas is often identified with Pareto-efficiency. Regulatory regimes attempt to reach policy efficiency through differentiated positioning of actors within the Pareto frontier, as showed by several explanations of international policy coordination (Krasner, 1991). In this case mechanisms of transmission cover *regulatory competition* and *regulatory compliance*. Competition is more likely to apply when the regulatory action of the EU limits the range of alternative policy solutions available at the local level (e.g. via negative integration). Regulatory compliance is more likely to characterise those actions promoting more stringent regulatory clauses thereby aiming at replacing existing arrangements with new sets of regulatory institutions agreed within the EU policy arena.

EU action in urban areas within regulatory domains mainly proceeds through the mediation of national policy channels, which is through general provisions to be domestically applied at the level of each member state of the EU. For this reason, the distinction between regulatory competition and compliance is not always possible and the two mechanisms are instead more likely to deploy in entangled ways.

Modes of coordination

Cell 3 – *coordination* – portrays arenas characterised by the fixed distribution of preferences, where nonetheless, there are gains from cooperation to be exploited. Coordination as a specific mode of interaction has been partly overlooked. Its nature remains rather under-theorised. Despite presenting similar features to 'regulation' as a mode of interactions, for our purposes – at least in the phase of theoretical elaboration – *coordination* can be maintained as a specific and theoretically grounded mode of policy. In the case of *coordination* the set of preferences available to actors is exogenous and, as in the case of regulation, the rank of values at stake is not disputed and eventually composed by actors.

Two prevailing sets of mechanisms are herewith in operation in terms of action *coordination* and *cooperation*. Examples in this sense are represented by the promotion and affirmation of various EU measures aimed at promoting *better regulation*. In this case, the instruments in which the better regulation agenda is grounded are 'soft' in character and there are advantages from the partial coordination of reciprocal actions and the exchange of ideas over policy alternatives. Preferences are not necessarily subject to change and change is conditional upon advantages gained from the process of learning through cooperation; this, in turn, may lead to reforms to be undertaken domestically.

The transmission of programmes and instruments that conform to modes of coordination entails various mechanisms of *self-regulation, cooperative learning* and *target compliance* (standardisation) within domains where the European legislator eventually set target rules, without instead acting through 'command and control' modalities foreseeing compliance to strict procedures or the common adoption of specific policy provisions. As showed by several studies of international regimes and standardisation, the specificities of coordination as a mode of interaction can be better understood by endorsing the tenets of game-theoretic models (Scharpf, 1997; Snidal, 1985).

In particular, dynamics of coordination entail that 'no centralised enforcement is necessary, because neither the state has incentive to depart from an established convention' (Snidal, 1985: 932); furthermore, central authorities in situations of coordination problems are 'less concerned with enforcement than with codification and elaboration of an existing or latent convention and with providing information and communication' (Snidal, 1985: 932).

Modes of distribution

Cell 4 features situations where preferences are fixed and interaction is modelled by zero sum games. Extended processes of bargaining are the only way forward in terms of composing preferences, often via conflict management through side payments or by using a kind of 'veil of ambiguity' to settle on long-term solutions that are amenable to short-term bargaining (Eberlein and Radaelli, 2010).

The theoretical foundation of *distributive arenas* is the rational choice paradigm of fixed and conflicting preferences that need to be aggregated – or transformed – within different issues and over time. Preferences aggregation can be systematised through the two variants of *issue based aggregation* – which constitute the traditional focus of negotiation processes – and *arena-based aggregation*, where instead interaction deploys through sophisticated ways for the compensation and negotiation of interests and in which conflict is generally addressed via the institutional adjustment of arenas (Eberlein and Radaelli, 2009).

In this connection, interaction over policy issues can take the general form of *bargaining* and *negotiation* (Keohane, 1984: 12). When related to the dynamic of construction of the European polity, cooperation arrangements are locked in institutional choice as explained by intergovernmental accounts of European integration (Moravcsik, 1993; 1998). An illustration is the negotiation of structural funds, where local representatives are often involved in the phase of domestic consultation, and only in 'second instance' at the supranational level when dynamics of *grand bargaining* can be considered completed (Pollack 1997; Sandholtz, 1992). Another way to conceive interaction within distributive arenas is to think of it as a series of nested games (Tsebelis, 1990) taking place within different arenas of governance, where actors' suboptimal strategy in one game can be part of a strategy to maximise payoffs when all arenas are taken into account. This, in turn, may imply the shifting of arenas, thus moving to a different decisional and actor set (Héritier and Lehmkuhl, 2008), instead of strategies for the creation of sub systemic arenas where partial positive-sum games may be reached within an overall situation of disagreement (Radaelli and Kraemer, 2008). Cities-EU interactions may conform to mechanisms of 'two-level games' (Buchs, 2008; Putnam, 1988). Drawing on Buchs, we can hypothesise that cities attempt to influence the EU agenda on urban-sensitive issues to obtain additional *justification* for previously planned but unpopular – or financially unfeasible – reforms at home (Buchs, 2008).

Cities can alternatively seek to *upload*, through bargaining, domestic policy approaches so as to reduce costs when implementing EU-led policy programmes; finally *ignorance* applies to situations where the policy issue at stake does not contain legally binding provisions and agreements at the EU level will not have negative repercussions within domestic systems of policy making.

A second set of mechanisms is associated with all those policy initiatives aiming to support the endorsement of specific models for economic and social development, territorial integration as well as the alignment to certain institutional arrangements for the management and implementation of programmes, whose tenets are agreed upon at the EU level. This is mainly the case for those areas of policy having a distributive nature, where EU structural action aims to promote regional and local development and territorial economic harmonisation through specific funds providing financial assistance for cross-sectoral initiatives.

Therefore, different mechanisms of transmission can be identified in terms of *institutional framing, programming* (it is especially the case for the structural policy of the EU), *targets compliance* and *territorial rescaling* (cities-regions; cities-central state, cities-urban areas). These, in turn, underpin dynamics of institutional rescaling within urban systems and processes leading to the 'institutionalisation of weak ties' (Granovetter, 1973) following the application of new modalities and arrangements for the management of policies.

This characterisation of modes of Europeanisation has the merit of reducing theoretical fragmentation. It also sheds light on similarities between Europeanisation and wider characterisations of modes of governance. Indeed, an advantage of Table 4.2 is that each of the cells of the typology can be associated with modes of interaction well known to the literature on governance and policy coordination. A second advantage consists of the fact that policy instruments can be observed dynamically.

4.5 Modes of Europeanisation and policy instruments

Not only do policy domains characterise for different procedural dynamics of interaction between actors and mechanisms for the transmission of EU-related policies in the localities, but they can also be distinguished on the basis of sets of policy instruments to be associated to single areas of policy within each domain.

Our argument on this occasion is that different sets of policy instruments contribute to determine the character of different policy domains through which the process of Europeanisation of urban politics is expected to have effects. In turn, EU policy instruments can be sorted out according to ideational-reflexive, bargaining-distributive, regulatory and coordination modes. Policy instruments can be observed dynamically; depending on how they are implemented at the local level, they can move from one cell to another thus, revealing alternative modes of interaction as well as the mechanisms for their transmission.

To sum up then, this analysis suggests some different mechanisms at work, and enables us to situate existing EU policy programmes and instruments which are likely to have an impact effect on urban systems of governance in a coherent framework. In a second phase, EU policy instrumentation substantiated in specific programmes, initiatives and regulations – as potential catalysts for Europeanisation of politics within cities and urban areas – can be compared throughout their development on the basis of the theoretically grounded typology for the modes of Europeanisation. Having outlined four distinct *Modes of Europeanisation* allows for the dynamic analysis of policy instruments associated with specific policy initiatives or programmes within each of the cells. Instruments and policy programmes, although initially coupled with one domain or another, are expected to move across cells.

This builds on the assumption that EU policy instruments, differently substantiated into policy programmes and regulations can be initially conceived as mainly ideational, regulatory, of coordination or distributive, and organised accordingly. When, however, we use the classification to select a specific policy programme for empirical research, the dynamic analysis of the process of Europeanisation may well show that instruments reveal different modes of interaction and therefore change 'cell' in the typology.

Examples of cell 1 in our typology are the series of 'fora' for discussion and exchange of policy ideas, such as URBACT II[4] support programme, the CIVITAS[5] forum in the field of transport or by the CONCERTO[6] initiative for the exchange of ideas in the field of energy efficiency, yet the Covenant of Mayors[7] aimed at promoting sustainable energy at the local level. These instruments can be considered as preponderantly ideational, thus conforming to logics of learning and reflexivity. However they have the potential to trigger

---

4. http://www.urbact.eu

5. http://www.civitas-initiative.org

6. http://www.concertoplus.eu

7. http://www.eumayors.eu

alternative logics – bargaining and regulation – especially if they are endowed with financial provisions and/or eventually rules of implementation. Further, inherently regulative instruments typical of cell 2, such as the EU rules on public procurement and services of general interest[8], the water framework directive[9], the waste framework directive[10] and the directive on ambient air quality and cleaner air[11] are often evolving in their ideational elements, which may eventually substantiate into a forum for discussion and learning between actors involved in implementation (and therefore may move to cell 1 – learning and reflexivity). Yet another example are instruments with a distributive nature – mostly substantiated in structural programmes – which despite reflecting modes of interaction in line with cell 3, are sometimes transforming into modes of learning and reflexivity typical of cell 1. The Community Initiative URBAN II during the 2000–06 period, the LIFE + Programme for the environment and the various financial instruments part of the cohesion policy (ERDF and Cohesion Fund) exemplify these types of instruments. As shown by Eberlein and Radaelli (2010) the walls separating choice and appropriateness are rather porous.

---

8. Directive 2004/17/EC of the European Parliament and of the Council of 31 March 2004 coordinating the procurement procedures of entities operating in the water, energy, transport and postal services sectors, OJL 134/1 of 30.4.2004.

9. Directive 2000/60/EC, OJ L 327/1 of 22.12.2000.

10. Directive 2006/12/EC of the European Parliament and of the Council of 5 April 2006 on waste.

11. Directive 2008/50/EC of the European Parliament and of the Council of 21 May 2008 on ambient air quality and cleaner air for Europe.

Chapter Five

Research Design and Methodological Issues

5.1 Introduction

Despite the limited (and not legally provisioned) competences of the EU legislator to intervene in urban areas, the 'encounter' between the EU policy making and urban systems can take place through different channels and in the contexts of multiple policy domains. Therefore, we recognise the possibility for EU action to influence urban systems – and in particular their policy making structures – also in the context of policy domains that are not directly consecrated by the EU legislator to cities and urban areas.

Throughout the research, the main purpose is to qualify *how* urban systems of governance interact within the EU policy making in relation to the various components of the policy sectors considered to carry out the analysis. Specifically, interactions will be analysed in accordance with the typology for modes of Europeanisation (Table 4.2) and with reference to different *policy instruments*.

This analysis wants to single out the causal mechanisms structuring the encounter between cities and the EU. Whether specific mechanisms of Europeanisation are detected, the aim is to assess the character assumed by Europeanisation and to highlight the scope conditions for the Europeanisation of different arenas of politics at the urban level.

Therefore, the research questions guiding the analysis are the following:

- *How does the European Union influence urban politics and policies? Therefore, what are the modalities through which the encounter between cities and the European Union can be structured?*
- *In the case influence can be detected, what are the mechanisms that structure the interaction between actors and the process of Europeanisation, thus eventually triggering change within urban systems of governance?*
- *Do policy instruments and programmes perform according to specific modes of interaction, or do they trigger unforeseen contingencies instead?*
- *Yet again, does the nature of strategic interaction determine the character of the Europeanisation of urban systems of governance?*

This research has an *explorative* nature. The paucity of empirical evidence and theoretical accounts in the research area of this study suggests to opt for a research strategy centred on the exploration of few case studies and aimed more at describing and understanding social *interaction* and possible *transformations*, than to explain and test causal hypotheses, which lean on uncertain foundations

(Nørgaard, 2008). In turn, causal explanations also require a certain degree of interpretation and description; especially those causal explanations concerning intentional and strategic actions. As claimed by Weber: 'we must understand human behaviour and the subjective meaning actors ascribe to it in order to proceed and account for the causes of a specific type of behaviour, its course and effects' (Weber, 1993: 29–36).

The relevance of the 'time factor'

The study of Europeanisation is mainly concerned with the process following the response of domestic systems – cities in our case – to pressures originating within the EU policy making and the *usage* domestic actors make of Europe (Radaelli, 2004). In turn, Europeanisation can be detected when the logic of domestic political actors changes following a 'reference-shift', whereby elements of EU policy making become a cognitive and normative frame for actors in domestic systems (Muller, 1995; Surel, 2000).

Drawing on the tenets of implementation theory (Winter, 2003), the enactment of EU policies is accompanied by redistributive consequences – although these can be considered weak in the classic sense (Majone, 1996). In fact, the policies promoted by the EU also entail the allocation and reallocation of resources, thus implying the mobilisation of actors and interest groups within domestic systems (Martinsen, 2007).

In this connection, public policies on the whole can be defined according to their temporality and associated degree of change (Hoeffler, *et al.*, 2010). The relevance of the time dimension in the analysis of the public action informs studies in the neo-institutionalist tradition (Hall and Taylor, 1997; Skocpol, 1992). In fact, political institutions may channel change within specific and 'path dependant' trajectories, often in opposition to agency-centred approaches, which tend to understate the importance of history and the transformation of actors' preferences over time (Pierson, 2004). The inclusion of time-based variables may help to complement the analysis of institutional configurations with the consideration of developments situated in time sequences, so as to demonstrate the importance of *temporality* in promoting structural and institutional change (Bonoli, 2007).

Time becomes a crucial factor in the analysis of Europeanisation. This is especially the case when the analysis focuses on policy areas where the intervention of the European legislator does not comply with direct patterns of implementation and it is consistent over time. The Europeanisation of a policy area is not a 'one off'; it deploys over time through multiple interactions between domestic systems and the EU.

5.2 Methodology and research design

An important methodological issue concerns causality. This calls into question the importance of *research design* when attempting to assess the impacts of the EU upon domestic systems. Baseline-type of enquiry relying on 'top-down' accounts run the risk – we argue – of reducing Europeanisation solely to the analysis of the impact of EU decisions on the domestic institutional system, thus drawing the parallel 'European action/direct effects', by considering the domestic effects of independent variables defined at the EU level.

Other approaches stress the importance of rooting Europeanisation in the *context* of its eventual manifestation, and of explicitly treating the issue of causality (Radaelli, 2003). In this connection, those claiming for a *bottom-up* or *inside-out* perspective through process-tracing based on temporal causal sequences, aim to assess *whether, when* and eventually *how* the action of the EU policy making has effectively brought about change within each of the components of the domestic system. By adopting such a strategy, the qualification of the EU impact is not uni-directional – meaning solely the 'reaction' to the European legislator – instead an attempt is made to consider alternative modalities through which Europe is often 'used' by domestic actors and institutions (Radaelli 2004).

Therefore, Europe – as a system to be 'encountered' by domestic actors and institutions – can, at times, become a constraining model to which domestic systems should adapt, other times it represents a set of resources, opportunities to re-define and re-orient discourses and political action at the domestic level (Radaelli and Pasquier, 2007: 37–38). EU-level variables are maintained as exogenous to the context of analysis, thus, EU policy and politics are not considered as the independent variables. In fact, to produce Europeanisation effects, EU-level interactions need to become a yardstick for political action within domestic systems by means of both socialisation effects and policies that progressively alter the logic of domestic political action.

In turn, the empirical analysis starts from the set of actors, problems, rules, styles, ideas and outcomes at the domestic level at a given time – T0 – to then *process-trace* the domestic system of interaction over a certain lag of time. The research attempts to identify those critical junctures or turning points that cause major changes to take place under the form of ideational transformations, alterations of the structure of actors, yet as the re-definition of problems (Radaelli and Pasquier, 2007).

Following that, each juncture has to be causally assessed in order to establish the causal nature of change, in particular to assess whether the transformation was domestic in nature or exogenously triggered instead, thus caused by variables such as the EU or global processes. To make inference from the contribution of exogenous variables, the research needs to proceed *backwards-up* from the domestic to the EU level, to control patterns and establish the nature of causal influence on domestic structures. EU variables have to be then further considered, so as to establish their actual importance within the domestic system. They can in fact be facilitators or bond instead, and at times they can be a source of learning for domestic actors, yet factors bringing to the possible alteration of the domestic structure of opportunities; 'causality is then examined *in vivo* by looking at temporal causal sequences' (Exadaktylos and Radaelli, 2009).

Other types of research design can be opted for when carrying out research on Europeanisation. Choosing amongst alternative research designs should not reflect any assumption in terms of the nature of Europeanisation, which can be interpreted as a society-actors driven process or a top-down steering mechanism (Radaelli and Pasquier, 2006). A distinctive EU system of interaction is a necessary condition for Europeanisation to occur, and all research design perspectives acknowledge that. At the same time though, socialisation and the formulation of European policies, as well as eventual adaptational pressure stemming from the EU are not considered sufficient conditions in bottom-up design accounts, where the establishment of EU policies is neither a necessary nor a sufficient condition for Europeanisation.

Analytic process tracing

For the purpose of this work, the analysis via the process tracing of single cases allows to better unravel and eventually test the mechanisms structuring the encounter between cities and the EU so as to reveal possible causal processes within the same case (George and McKeown, 1985). Additionally, the process-tracing method fruitfully adapts to different theoretical frameworks (i.e. social constructivism and rational choice), by at the same time allowing to explore and explain the decisional process through which some initial conditions translate into certain outcomes later on in time (George and Bennet, 2005).

Therefore, the objective is to formulate, and eventually test 'middle-range' theoretical propositions able to avoid the intrinsic pitfalls of 'a-theoretical descriptive narratives', without pretending on the other hand to lead towards the formulation of 'universal law of human behaviour that hold across all time and places' (George and Bennet, 2005).

The overall purpose becomes instead to discover and observe the *causal mechanisms* connecting dependent and independent variables in each of the particular contexts considered, so as to test theories in situations characterised by complex effects of interaction and multiple causality, wherein the task of explaining outcomes in terms of a reduced number of independent variables is rather difficult (Hall, 2003). Process-tracing analysis is a particularly suitable method for studies where the main objective is to give a certain degree of historical relevance to the formal theories beneath the analysis, thus giving importance to elements such as stories, accounts and contexts.

The tracing of processes underpinning the cases under analysis is performed via the *narrative assessment* of the selected policy instruments. Thus, narratives aim to underline processes and stories behind events, so to make processes the 'fundamental building blocks of sociological analysis' (Abbott, 1992: 428). The overall meaning of a narrative resides in the intertwined function of present and past contexts, therefore in the interactions producing around a certain set of issues.

Nonetheless, analytic narratives do not reduce to deductive histories. Rational choice models rely on deductive components, but the analysis is *de facto* carried out via inductive methods that aim to highlight the role of actors, their preferences and the structure of the environment. Deductive reasoning is then used to study behaviours and actions within the context of the devised theoretical framework.

Fundamental importance is attributed to the processes and to temporal sequences of actions happening within 'constraining or enabling structures', where instead, 'normal methods parse social reality into fixed entities with variable qualities. They attribute causality to the variables – hypostatized social characteristics – rather than to agents; variables do things, not social actors' (Abbott, 1992: 428).

An example – amongst others[1]– is offered by the work of Bates and his colleagues, whose *analytic narratives* combine analytical tools of economics and political science – rational choice theory and game theory – with the narrative form commonly used in history (Bates, *et al.*, 1998). By focusing on concrete historical cases, where the main interest is to explore the choices of individuals who are embedded in specific settings, their analysis proceeds by tracing the 'sequence of action, decisions and responses that generate events and outcomes'. The approach of *analytic narratives*, although informed by deductive reasoning, seeks to account for *outcomes* via the identification and exploration of the mechanisms 'behind' them. This, in turn is made by considering *time* and *place* and by locating and tracing the processes that generate the outcome of interest. By isolating and unpacking such mechanisms, analytic narratives offer structural accounts paying attention to the identification of 'the *actors*, the *decision points* they faced, the *choices* they made, the *paths* taken and shunned, and the manner in which their choices generated events and outcomes' (Bates *et al.*, 1998: 13–14).

Relevant for the construction of narratives informed by a rational choice approach is the consideration of structural contexts, namely the 'broader structural arrangements that represent the contextual component of social action' and that are treated as dynamic targets enduring 'throughout a given event sequence' (Pedriana, 2005: 356). The contextual framework then provides the theoretical link between historical processes and the social actors that guide their development.

In particular, the analysis proceeds by first modelling a portion of the critical dynamics of interest coherently with the hypotheses and ideas governing the overall research. Following that, through the narrative, a single case is used to test the hypotheses and to eventually generate new hypotheses that can be generalised. As such, the method of analytic narratives is used to develop and test theory-driven models, thereby employing 'theory to gain deeper insight into the complex working of the real world' (Bates, *et al.* 2000).

Design and strategy of research

Policy instruments are initially associated with the four modes of Europeanisation previously outlined. We then use techniques like *analytic processing* to verify whether instruments actually perform according to the 'mode' to which they have been initially paired, or if they trigger contingencies that have not been theoretically/deductively foreseen. Unlike 'modes', that cannot be empirically observed, instruments can be empirically assessed as they 'develop' during the

---

1.   An overview on the narrative tradition of analysis can be found in Abbott, 1992.

policy process, starting from their launch at the EU level, through their negotiation, their combination into broader policy initiatives and then their implementation, in this case in the policy making within urban systems of governance.

Therefore, four policy instruments are initially selected – as associated with the four modes of Europeanisation – and empirically assessed in order to verify whether they actually perform according to the 'mode' to which they have been initially paired, or if they trigger contingencies that have not been theoretically/deductively foreseen.

To explore mechanisms, one may not need more than one city, since comparison is made between domains of policy, where variation is expected to occur. The analysis of each of the four modes proceeds along two steps.

During a first phase, the *top-down* analysis will focus on the key points that have produced change at the EU level and observe how the urban system(s) considered reacted to them. Contextually, a similar analysis will be conducted at the national level in the state where our city of reference is located. This recognition will allow us to assess how the evolution of the instruments considered has been responded to, both at the national and urban level. In turn, this would make it possible to highlight 'critical junctures' – focal points – which eventually characterised this lapse of time. Therefore, analytical attention will focus on the key points that have produced change at the EU level, to be then observing how the urban system considered reacted to them. At the same time, a further assessment will be conducted at the level of the national state in order to verify how the instruments have been handled within national administrations and how urban systems (cities) have been addressed.

In a second phase, a *bottom-up* technique (of the type described by Radaelli and Pasquier, 2007) is employed. The subjects of interest during this phase are the policy-making structures regarding the interaction between the EU and the urban system considered for the analysis. In particular, we ask ourselves here whether these structures have been subject to modification during the lapse of time considered, and if it is the case, through which mechanisms such evolutions took place. This step aims at establishing whether opportunities, pressures and incentives originating at the EU level (and linked to the promotion of EU policy instruments), as defined in the first step, play any actual role and conform to the expectations arising from the policy modes. Therefore, once relevant changes for the domestic *urban* systems of interaction have been identified, the analysis traces back to the EU (and national) level, to verify how the EU variables have exercised causal influence on the domestic structures of policy in the city considered.

Through the process-tracing method, the main intent is to identify the casual mechanisms at play between the dependent variable and the various outcomes of the dependent variable. This means to establish *if*, *when* and eventually *how* the process of Europeanisation entails a variation within the policy structures of the interaction between Europe and the urban context considered.

Nonetheless, variation is not to be expected for each of the components and for each of the policy instruments analysed with the same degree of intensity. It is rather interesting, in fact, to observe the lack, rather than the presence of logical sequences between the variables considered. Due to the dynamicity of the process of Europeanisation as well as to the nature of EU policy instruments (within the policy areas taken into consideration), the analysis aims to assess when and where variations occur, the possible relation between the variables, and the role played by other dynamics or processes in this context of analysis.

5.3 Actor constellations and game representations

Drawing on Scharpf's interaction-oriented policy research programme, the purpose of our research is 'to identify the set of interactions that actually produces the policy outcomes that are to be explained' (Scharpf, 1997: 43), which are part of the Europeanisation of different arenas within urban systems. Since we are mainly concerned with the character of the encounter between the EU policy making and cities, what is relevant are the actions within different *institutional orders* (Carter and Smith, 2008), therefore the rules establishing competencies, right of participation and eventually prescriptions in the specific policy process taken into consideration.

In turn, *actors* – individual or collective – are characterised by their strategic action orientations that we defined in terms of – ideal typical – *modes of Europeanisation*. These are defined on the bases of the logic of preferences and the payoffs from Europeanisation; preferences over policy outcomes may be rather stable, or can be aggregated through processes of learning and socialisation according to the diverse nature of the policy issue at stake. Thus, what really matters is the assemblage – *constellation* – of actors involved in the policy interaction upon a specific policy issue. Yet, according to Scharpf, a constellation 'describes the players involved, their strategy options, the outcomes associated with strategy combinations (*in terms of payoffs*), and the preferences of the players over these outcomes' (Scharpf, 1997: 44).

Game theoretic representations assume – in the context of this research – the form of a combination between a 'specific actor constellation' forming in specific circumstances and in the course of a definite lapse of time, and a specific 'mode of interaction' that we associate with specific mechanisms. However, it is relevant to highlight how both aspects of the game – actor constellations and modes of interaction – can vary independently from one another, and both have explanatory power.

Game-theoretic representations allow describing and eventually comparing different constellations. In the context of our research, this allows to eventually gain leverage in terms of the potential generalisation of the model and to discover regularities in the deployment of specific causal mechanisms of Europeanisation.

As recalled by Radaelli in his study of coordination in international tax policy 'the games real actors can play inevitably are complex, yet it is useful to draw upon the insight provided by game-theoretic models for understanding the structure of strategic interaction and then move on to consider the more dynamic aspects of the

Figure 5.1: Interaction-oriented policy research: the domains

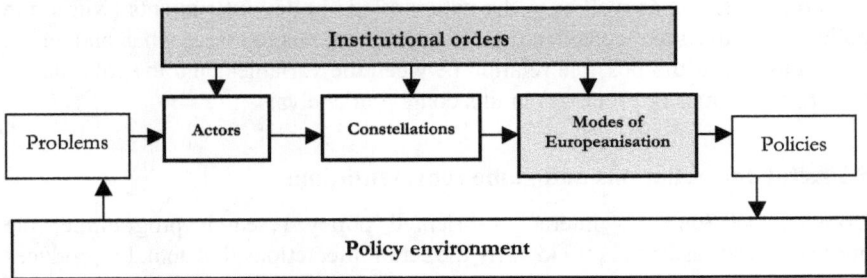

Source: adapted from Scharpf 1997: 44

policy process with the aid of *new institutional theory*' (Radaelli, 1998: 15 *italics added*).

To paraphrase Scharpf 'what matters in the present context is that the explicit conceptualisation of actors' constellations provide the crucial link between substantive policy analysis and interaction-oriented policy research' (Scharpf, 1997: 45) with the overall intention of revitalising Lowi's call for a political theory that will treat 'policy' as an independent variable influencing the types of politics that will be encountered.

For the purpose of this research, we explore the analytical tools offered by game theory (McCain, 2009; McCarty and Meirowitz, 2007). To exemplify interactions within the modes of Europeanisation in our typology we refer to well-known game models with strong implications for the mechanisms we aim to unravel.

Thus, the modes of Europeanisation we presented can be theoretically paired with different *mixed-motive game* situations (or variable-sum games) 'in which the preferences of players are partly harmonious and partly in conflict' (Scharpf, 1997: 73)[2]. Despite presenting two-by-two games, it is common sense to recognise that most of the real-life situations and consequently what we encounter in empirical research often conform to multiple-actors interactions, with a potentially large repertoire of action as well as different outcomes to be expected (Scharpf, 1990, 1997).

As suggested by Scharpf, the possibility for strategic interaction to occur depends on the deployment of one or the other of two mechanisms – *decoupling* and *aggregation* – to be used by both actors and the analyst for simplification purposes (Scharpf, 1991). Whether *decoupling* would imply treating many of the interdependencies object of the strategic interaction as part of a given environment

---

2.   Scharpf distinguishes *mixed-motive games* from the simple situations of *pure conflict* (zero-sum or constant sum) games in which one side must lose what the other side gains and situations of *pure coordination*, in which all actors can maximise their own payoffs by agreeing on concerted strategies. In particular, he differentiates amongst four 'archetypal' constellations well known in game-theoretical studies in terms of 'Assurance', 'Battle of Sexes', 'Prisoner Dilemma' and 'Chicken'.

'for the purpose of a particular policy interaction', the alternative mechanism, *aggregation*, entails aggregating and composing otherwise overly-complex actors' constellations (cities in the case of this research). Thus, the analyst, at least initially, deals with only few 'corporate actors', to eventually expand the number of actors considered inasmuch as the analysis advances. In this way, representation of oversimplified – two by two – games (as in our case) may not involve any loss of accuracy or information.

To conclude, 'game theoretic models provide the initial conceptual framework, but they must be supplemented by forms of analysis more sensitive to the contextual aspects of the policy process' (Radaelli, 1998: 2). The process-tracing of the issue under analysis may reveal, in fact, alternative or additional dynamics that contribute to improve our understanding of the games that real actors play.

5.4 Concluding remarks

This research can be ascribed to a tradition that seeks to analyse Europeanisation from a sociological perspective (Hassenteufel and Surel, 2000; Jacquot and Woll, 2004; Smith, 2000), notably as regards its attention to elements such as the 'microscopic analysis' and the territorial dimension of investigation (Pasquier and Weisbein, 2004; Sawicki, 2000; Smith, 1999). At the same time, it aims to account for the role of actors and the relevance of their interactions in order to comprehend the processes and the mechanisms structuring the encounter between the EU and domestic systems. Attention is directed at strategic interactions and the preferences of actors involved in the process of policy making; dynamics of conflict and power distribution are also regarded and reconsidered as important elements of the analysis.

From a theoretical perspective this calls for combining elements from different scholars in political science. Therefore, we draw on accounts endorsing an actor-centred perspective focusing on the role of intentional and rational individual actors that make reasoned choices given the likely choices of others and the contextual-institutional constraints they face, as postulated by *rational choice* scholars (Sheples, 1986; 2006). Additionally, attention is addressed at how rational actors generate collective outcomes and aggregate behaviours that are often socially sub-optimal and personally undesirable (Levi, 2007), without nonetheless, dismissing the importance of the institutional environment within which actors interact and frame their normative convictions, specifically by influencing the perceptions, preferences and capabilities of individuals (Scharpf, 1986).

Part II

ASSESSING THE ENCOUNTER BETWEEN
CITIES AND THE EUROPEAN UNION

Chapter Six

Europeanisation via Modes of Ideation: The Covenant of Mayors Programme for Energy Saving and Renewal

6.1 Introduction

The production of renewable energy sources features as a subject of particular concern for many Western governments. This is due to both the environmental problems linked to the use of traditional energy sources and to the necessity of reaching greater differentiation in patterns of energy use, because of the progressive depletion of traditional stocks.

The fight against climate change, and thus the promotion of alternative energy use is a top priority for the European Union. In this connection, the EU has launched a series of initiatives and set ambitious objectives to be attained in each member state. This is meant to provide incentives for alternative energy use, thus boosting the production of different kinds of renewable energy: thermo solar, solar photovoltaic, wind-power and natural biomasses. Therefore, the overall objectives to be reached by 2020 – known as the *'20-20-20'targets* – foresee the reduction of greenhouse gasses by 20 per cent[1], the reduction of energy consumption by 20 per cent[2] and above all an increase in the use of renewable energy sources by bringing it to 20 per cent of the total energy consumption.

Half of greenhouse gas emissions are produced by cities, and the main bulk of total energy is consumed within urban areas. Local authorities can play a key role in mitigating climate change; this is not only because local administrations are the closest to citizens, but above all for their potential to favour the relations between public and private interests and therefore the possible integration of sustainable energy into more general plans for local-territorial development. City governments are progressively realising the benefits of tapping the adverse effects of climate change through the promotion of local sustainability strategies. Despite the activism revealed by local administrations in Europe – 'one of the latest developments in the analytical and policy sphere of climate change' – coherent and necessary policy frameworks are still missing (Egenhofer, *et al.*, 2010).

---

1. The percentage of greenhouse gasses reduction is to be calculated by assuming 1990 as the baseline year for the calculation of emission.
2. For Italy the value has been fixed at 17 per cent.

An important step towards the full recognition and support for the role of cities in this policy domain was taken by the EU with the launch – amongst other initiatives – of the Covenant of Mayors in 2009, which gives European cities the opportunity to coherently put in place local sustainable energy policies through long period action plans.

The involvement of signatories translates into a series of concrete measures and projects, and in their commitment to report and being monitored during the implementation of the action plans. Despite its recent launch, the Covenant of Mayors initiative brought into focus the importance of supporting local action by contextually designing a structure of governance able to sustain and address long-term objectives and actions (Egenhofer, et al., 2010).

Considering the promotion and initial implementation of a voluntary-based initiative like the Covenant of Mayors with reference to a specific territory, allows us to point out some of the mechanisms structuring the relations between actors that trigger change and transformation within various arenas. In this connection, the process of Europeanisation is thought as unfolding following patterns of communication, benchmarking, policy learning and transfer, eventually leading to the promotion of new paradigms and tools of governance through a general dynamic of extended socialisation and reflexivity. Two main reasons motivate the choice of accounting for the Covenant of Mayors initiative as the instrument to exemplify ideation as a mode of Europeanisation.

On one hand, the voluntary nature of the programme, which implies – at least prospectively – a certain degree of dynamism and self-organisation of the cities that participate, thus the necessity to put in place an internal system of partnership to secure the acceptance of the candidature and the eventual realisation of the planned actions. On the other hand, the role of the EU and of the European Commission in particular, which in this case is confined to the initial promotion of the initiative and to the eventual funding of the planned actions in the localities, whereas management and monitoring are outsourced to an external structure. We contend that interactions developing in the context of the CoM thus far as well as within the urban system of Turin during the early phases of the initiative, chime with some properties of *cheap talk* game models and more generally the class of imperfect information games, like the *signalling game*.

6.2 Contrasting climate change in the European Union

The EU has long been at the forefront in combating climate change. As of the early 1990s, the European Union played a decisive role in international negotiations that led to agreements respectively on the United Nations treaties, the UN Framework Convention on Climate Change in 1992, and the Kyoto Protocol in 1997. By the mid-2000s the European Commission officially declared that tackling climate change would have been the main challenge for European Countries as well as the central thrust of EU action in the years to come (Oberthür and Pallemaerts, 2010).

In 2007, EU leaders agreed on a comprehensive package[3] of climate and energy policies aimed at transforming Europe into a highly energy-efficient, low carbon economy. Integrated measures were adopted to reduce emissions by 20 per cent from their 1990 levels by 2020, to centralise and strengthen the emission trading system[4], boosting the use of renewable energy, limiting emissions from new cars[5] and funding new carbon capture and storage facilities[6] (Jordan, *et al.*, 2010).

As argued by Jordan and his colleagues, some main reasons make the analysis of the EU's effort to govern climate change – and we contend also the analysis of the role of cities in this sense – a subject of particular interest. The EU is a rather significant emitter of greenhouse gases, with a total emission share of about 10.5 per cent in 2006[7] that still largely depends on the use of fossil fuels. At the same time though, the EU is an important player in the global governance of climate change and its leading role in this sense dates back to the early 1990s. Yet, the EU has been consistently acting within its member states through the promotion of a long series of initiatives and programmes that contributed to the progressive Europeanisation of diverse national and local policy domains (Jordan, *et al.*, 2010).

Whether the action of the European Union in the period prior to 1988 mainly evolved around scientific researches commissioned by the Directorate General Environment, the creation of a European Commission's inter-service group on 'greenhouse issues' – and the release of the first communication on climate change[8] – and the European Council's declaration in Rhodes bestowed a certain degree of political support on internal developments. Thus, EU action became more explicit through the exploration of specific policy options and instruments. Following this initial phase of 'agenda setting', more tangible initiatives were taken by member states in the post-1988 stage and in 1992 the Commission launched a first package of proposals concerning the areas of energy efficiency, renewable energies, CO_2 emission and fuels (Jordan and Rayner, 2010). This laid down the basis for the cohesive participation of the EU in the adoption of the United Nation Framework Convention on Climate Change.

---

3.   The EU climate and energy package sets emission reduction targets for several sectors, but the attainment of sector-specific targets often requires measures within other sectors.

4.   Directive 2003/87/EC of the European Parliament and of the Council of 13 October 2003 establishing a scheme for greenhouse gas emission allowance trading within the Community.

5.   Regulation (EC) No 443/2009 of the European Parliament and of the Council of 23 April 2009 setting emission performance standards for new passenger cars as part of the Communitys integrated approach to reduce CO 2 emissions from light-duty vehicles (23 April 2009).

6.   Directive 2009/31/EC of the European Parliament and of the Council of 23 April 2009 on the geological storage of carbon dioxide.

7.   Data are available in the European Environmental Agency Annual EC Greenhouse gas Inventory 19902006 and Inventory report 2008. EEA Technical Report6/2008. Copenhagen: EEA, cited in Jordan et al., 2010.

8.   The greenhouse effect and the Community. Communication to the Council. Commission Work Programme Concerning the Evaluation of Policy Options to deal with the 'Greenhouse Effect'. Draft Council Resolution on the Greenhouse Effect and the Community. COM (88) 656 final, 16 November 1988.

Despite the partial backlash following the rejection of the Maastricht Treaty in 1992 and a general climate of stalemate as to the adoption of climate change policies at the EU level, member states eventually managed to reach an agreement that allowed the EU to sign the Kyoto protocol as a unique actor. Through the European Climate Change Programme launched in 2000, the European Commission intended to develop new policies and measures by favouring the dialogue with an extensive range of groups and actors. Amongst the policies adopted, there was a voluntary agreement with car manufacturers secured in 1998 and a series of proposals which led to the adoption of the Emission Trading Directive[9] in 2003 (Oberthür and Kelly, 2008). A series of other initiatives were afterwards adopted to back the launch of the ECCP[10], and the action of the EU – with the re-launch of the ECCP in 2005 – ventured into new policy domains, such as carbon capture and transport. The new course of action was waved in a comprehensive Green Paper in 2007[11], in a report issued by the Commission during the same year[12] and in the launch of a new climate strategy[13] where four priority action areas – renewable energies, carbon capture and storage, bio-fuels, energy efficiency – were set up.

Yet, an overall package of proposals was launched in January 2008 under the title of *20 20 by 2020 – Europe's Climate Change Opportunity*. As previously stated, it is principally aimed at reducing emissions by 20 per cent and incrementing renewable energy by 20 per cent, before 2020. Nonetheless, the attainment of the objectives as fixed in the package will require embarking on a series of reforms – both nationally and at the EU level – to establish new mechanisms to cope with the requirements of the attached regulation as well as new forms of financial and technological support (Jordan, *et al.*, 2010: 11).

Cities can play a prominent part in the fight against climate change. The EU is gradually developing policies and instruments to favour the action of local authorities in this domain.

The EU Covenant of Mayors initiative as promoted by the European Commission represents a pioneering example in the attempt to combine actions and investments

---

9. Directive 2003/87/EC of the European Parliament and of the Council of 13 October 2003 establishing a scheme for greenhouse gas emission allowance trading within the community and amending Council Directive 96/61/EC.

10. Amongst these measures there are the Communication (COM 2001/580) on the ECCP claiming for new policies to be adopted, a decision to ratify the Kyoto protocol thus formalising the burden sharing agreement, Regulation (842/2006/EC) and Directive (2006/40/EC) limiting the emission of fluorinated gases, a directive setting minimum standards for the energy performance of buildings (2002/91/EC).

11. 'Adapting to climate change in Europe – options for EU action' (COM/2007/354 final).

12. Communication from the Commission, *Progress towards achieving the Kyoto objectives* (required under Decision 280/2004/EC of the European Parliament and of the Council concerning a mechanism for monitoring Community greenhouse gas emissions and for implementing the Kyoto Protocol).

13. *Limiting Global Climate Change to 2 Degrees Celsius – The way ahead for 2020 and beyond* (COM (2007)2) and *An Energy Policy for Europe* (COM (2007)1).

to reduce GHG emissions, thus tapping the regulatory and financial power of cities to engage in low-carbon investments (Egenhofer, *et al.*, 2010).

Embarking on low-carbon strategies may be more effective and acceptable at the local level than on the national or international scale, since actions can affect other tangible domains, such as the quality of life, social cohesion and the environment. In this connection, the role that cities can play is diversified, where local authorities can act as suppliers of services, consumers of energy and emitters, regulators and planners as well as leaders in promoting change through awareness campaigns and the diffusion of information (Egenhofer, *et al.*, 2010).

Archetypal game model: is the CoM just cheap talk?

Arenas where learning and reflexivity are the principal mechanisms of interaction may be exemplified through different games of *cheap talk* and more generally the class of imperfect information games – *signalling games* – involving interaction between a more informed agent, the sender (i.e. the EU, the European Commission in our case) and a less informed agent, the receiver (cities in the case of this research). In this case, the sender moves first (McCarty and Meirowitz, 2007). In this sense, the main difference between games of signalling and cheap talks lies in the fact that cheap talk is generally considered as communication between players, which does not directly affect the payoffs of the game, whereas in signalling, sending certain messages may be costly for the sender depending on the state of the world[14].

In a cheap talk game, messages have no *direct* impact on payoff functions. If the receiver ignores the message, the sender's payoff is unaffected. But if the receiver acts, then the sender might be affected. Usually, these are coordination games, where given the true state of the world that the sender knows, his preferred receiver-action is positively correlated with the receiver's preferred receiver-action (Rasmussen, 2007).

However, the sender's action might affect the payoffs for both parties by changing the receiver's action. There are cases, in fact, where the conveyed information is not exogenous private information and cheap talk is indeed used to coordinate action, without, nonetheless guaranteeing efficiency in games; even unlimited cheap talk does not necessarily lead to Pareto-efficient outcomes (Farrell, 1993; Farrell and Rabin, 1996).

Some conditions must hold for cheap talk to affect the outcomes of the game. In particular, the *receiver must care about the type of sender;* on the contrary only the receiver's action may affect his payoffs. Additional conditions relate to the fact that *different sender types must have different preferences* and to the necessity for the sender and the receiver to have *non-opposite preferences*.

Thus, 'cheap talk' can be an important feature of the interactive game played by actors, but it cannot be considered as a game in its own. In fact, cheap talk situations can be utilised at different stages within different types of game situations

---

14. For a formal modelling of the signalling game and dynamic games of incomplete information see McCarty and Meirowitz (2007), ch. 8.

(Ben-Pohrat, 2003). One example is the *free trade model*[15]. It can be considered as exemplificative of this policy, where reiterated communication and learning can transform an initial zero-sum situation into positive sum games (Ellingsen and Östling, 2010).

Our argument in this occasion is that interactions developing – within both EU arenas and arenas in the city taken into consideration – during the initial phases of the CoM programme and its implementation in the case of Turin conform to some of the properties of cheap-talk/signalling game models, without excluding other properties and alternative mechanisms to be in place, thus eventually leading to alternative outcomes.

6.3 The Covenant of Mayors programme

With the purpose of tapping the potential benefits of action at the local level within each of the domains mentioned above the European Commission launched the CoM programme. The main rationale behind the programme was to promote actions and eventually boost change within local territories by at the same time respecting the subsidiarity principle. Besides that, there was the intention to boost 'sustainable development business' through the CoM. The Covenant, as such, was not an initiative of the EU Commission, which instead acts as a platform to favour the feasibility of the overall initiative.

During the development of the programme, this should imply the actual involvement of 'all stakeholders' interested in the energy saving and renewal policy and process, therefore not solely central administrations, within a logic of 'impossibility to detach energy policy from the actual place where energy is consumed and produced'. Therefore, city mayors commit to going beyond the EU-CEP objectives in terms of CO_2 reduction through the implementation of Sustainable Action Plans (SEAP), which are prepared by the local authorities themselves.

The programme has now reached its 'delivery phase' with almost 3000 signatories[16] that committed to respect the EU's CO_2 reduction objective by 2020. Signatories are expected to submit their local Sustainable Energy Action Plans (SEAPs) following their accession and regular reporting on their progress. The CoM received the endorsement of the Committee of the Regions that gave its favourable opinion on the CoM in 2009. The first covenant was signed in the European Parliament in February 2009.

The covenant was preceded by the launch of thirty pilot projects in 2006, together with the *mise en place* of energy efficiency action plans and a general consultation process. When the CoM was launched in 2009, about 100 cities

---

15. The game is usually represented as a particular application of the Prisoners' Dilemma. The model depicts a situation where repeated interaction over an infinite number of periods would allow cooperation to be sustained by the reward of the good equilibrium and the sanction of the bad. For a formal modelling of the situation see McCarty and Meirowitz (2007), ch. 9.

16. The figure refers to September 2011.

signed the document of commitment. The increasing number of cities involved in the initiative contributed to increase its overall credibility, and for the time being its operational success. Through the CoM, one of the main intentions of the European Commission is to pursue the creation of a credible action asset by matching political commitment with concrete action. In this vein, the covenant functions as a benchmark for future initiatives within the same policy domain.

Participant authorities are due to submit their action plan within one year following the adhesion, where the strategic actions to reach the CO_2 reduction targets are outlined, so as to involve both public and private actors. The Covenant Office provides guidelines[17] for the compilation and implementation of SEAPs, which have been prepared following recommendations of the Joint Research Centre (JRC) of the European Commission. SEAPs have to include actions in the sectors of built environment, including new buildings and major refurbishment, municipal infrastructures (district heating, public lighting, smart grids, etc.), land use and urban planning, decentralised renewable energy sources, public and private transport policies and urban mobility, citizen and, in general, civil society participation, intelligent energy behaviour by citizens, consumers and businesses.

In this connection, the 'assessment procedure' of the submitted plans deploys following a three-step process. After a *quick check mechanism* based on the criteria set in the council decision on effort sharing[18] as well as on the compliance to the strategic axis of the programme – an *eligibility check* is performed. Finally, a *consistency check* is carried out and cities are informed. A parallel verification process is eventually undertaken towards those signatories, which are unlikely to respect the commitment to deliver an action plan. Those are warned through a three-step process and eventually their participation in the programme is 'frozen' till they actually present a feasible plan.

The European Commission does not act directly towards the signatory authorities, but its role is channelled via the action of a CoM Office[19]. In particular, the office provides technical and promotional assistance; it implements evaluation and monitoring tools and facilitates dynamics of information sharing between cities, the exchange of virtuous experiences and eventually the replication of

---

17. Guidelines are aimed at providing recommendations for the elaboration of SEAPs and for CO_2 baseline inventory. Building on baseline emission inventories, signatories can more accurately estimate the actual sources of emission and therefore the range of efficient actions to be implemented. Major information about the guidelines for the drafting of the SEAPs can be found at: http://www.eumayors.eu/actions/sustainable-energy-action-plans_en.html.

18. Decision (406/2009/EC) of the Council and the European Parliament of 23 April 2009 on the effort of member states to reduce their greenhouse gas emissions to meet the communitys greenhouse gas emission reduction commitments up to 2020.

19. The CoM Office is funded through the Intelligent Energy Europe Programme (http://ec.europa. eu/energy/intelligent/) and aims to facilitate networking activities within the covenant, support the promotion of the Covenant of Mayors, support liaison with other actors in the covenant and support liaison with other relevant EU initiatives and policies.

successful measures. The JRC backs the CoM Office by providing benchmark examples to streamline existing activities and networks in order to support the role of local authorities[20].

In turn, some institutional partners ensured their contribution to the covenant. This is necessary to assure a certain level of political support to the programme. Thus, the CoM found the full support of the EU Committee of the Regions, the European Parliament that hosted the first signature ceremony and the European Investment Bank, which furnishes technical assistance facilities for the definition and implementation of financial instruments in cities. Supporting structures[21] are instead deputed to provide guidance, financial and technical support to those municipalities willing to sign the covenant, but lacking the necessary skills and resources to prepare their own SEAPs.

The European Commission is creating specific financial mechanisms to sustain local authorities in carrying out the planned actions. Hitherto, three main financial instruments can be deployed to fund or incentive action within the context of the CoM.

The European Local Energy Assistance (ELENA) instrument aims to trigger further investments in the area of energy efficiency, renewable energy sources and sustainable urban transport. In turn, the facility is funded through different financial streams. The European Investment Bank guarantees the involvement of international financing institutions to finance projects with a budget superior to €50m. Financing is mainly meant to stimulate investments at the local level despite the general scenario of economic crisis, so as to also boost the 'spending capacity' of local authorities, thus eventually promoting a culture of action going beyond mere distribution. Furthermore, investments in the area of energy efficiency are supposed to generate new jobs as well as actual savings and income for cities and local administrations. ELENA-KfW, on the other hand, supports medium size investment initiatives of less than €50 million with a focus on carbon crediting via the involvement of commercial banks acting locally. In partnership with the Council of Europe Development Bank, ELENA-CEB provides assistance to develop investment projects in the field of social housing.

A second main instrument of financial support attached to the CoM is embedded in the Intelligent Energy Europe Programme (IEE), which aims to mobilise local economic instruments and to favour energy integrated plans and better economies of scale. The European Energy Efficiency Facility (EEEF) provides further financial leverage through the European Economic Recovery Programme and the EIB in order to provide equity, guarantees and debt products

---

20. Additionally, the JRC operates a technical helpdesk service in co-operation with the CoM Office, researches new methodologies and tools and assists in the selection of Benchmarks of Excellence.

21. Supporting Structures can be District administrations, Regional offices or networks of local authorities committing to improve the impact of the Covenant.

for public authorities[22]. The ELENA financial instrument has proven particularly successful thus far. Together with the overall success of the initiative, this led to the amendment of the ERDF regulation. Now, managing authorities will be able to use ERDF to create 'revolving funds'.

As to the implementation stage of the programme, it is important to underline how the main effort today consists in the elaboration of a common monitoring methodology, which will eventually lead to a system for the certification of emissions reduction, whose legal bases are already given by the 'effort sharing' regulation. This obliges member states to reduce emissions by an additional 10 per cent in the non-ETS sectors. Concerning a common methodology, there are on-going discussions between DG Clima and DG ENER responsible for the programme at the Commission, especially regarding the elaboration of sound mechanisms to boost initiatives for energy saving and renewal at the local level (i.e. cities).

The CoM office has received a new contract to cover actions for the upcoming two and half years, whereas the auxiliary role of the JRC has been prolonged for another three years. Relevant for the gist of our investigation in this sense, is the intention to set up a renewed system of coordination based on instruments for enhanced capacity building.

In particular, the effort will be addressed towards the elaboration of a portal for E-learning, where the signatory cities can take part in on-line seminars, benchmarking and policy learning based on an overall dynamic of decentralisation. The intent is therefore to boost networking and knowledge-diffusion between cities sharing similar needs. This, in turn, should boost a twofold dynamic. On one hand, cities and their networks are likely to increase their lobbying capacity towards national governments as well as to EU institutions; on the other hand, this should constitute a trigger to implement local actions based on the integrated approach.

Promising results have been showed thus far, especially due to the sound evidence given by cities' action. The expectation though, is to have greater feedback loops to other policy areas where local actors may actually play a decisive role. Nonetheless, some main weaknesses are recognised.

The partial incapacity to properly link the energy part of the initiative to other policy sectors seems to be the main hindrance towards the full achievement of the objectives as set by the proponents of the programme. The CoM has certainly been successful in raising awareness, ownership and generating interests in the localities, but the real challenge is now posed by the actual implementation of the plans. The

---

22. Additional financial sources can be tapped by local authorities taking part in the programme drawing on the different streams of the Structural and Cohesion Funds (ERDF, ESF, CF), JESSICA – Joint European Support for Sustainable Investment in City Areas – technical assistance, JASPERS – Joint Assistance to Support Projects in European Regions – that assists the twelve Central and Eastern member states in the preparation of major projects to be financed under the Structural and Cohesion Funds. Further support can be found in the cooperation programme INTERREG IV |(A, B and C) and through the European exchange and learning programme URBACT as well as in the Municipal Finance Facility and the Sustainable Energy Initiative.

main pitfall in this sense is the partial lack of capacity to act, which would require a legal mandate for cities and local authorities to take decisions and to regulate in the area of emission reduction[23]. Improvements are deemed necessary as to the processes of measurement, reporting and verification. Currently, in fact, emissions are reported through a non-harmonised system, made of different methodologies that hinder statistical comparison, and therefore prospective elaborations. This is closely related to the need to enhance mechanisms of consultation with cities, for the selection and evaluation of projects as well for the quality control of the plans so as to guarantee their overall feasibility.

In this connection, a precondition for the success of the programme, and for the overall attainment of its objectives is that local actions are acknowledged and attain major visibility in order to receive the support of citizens, potential funders, investors and local businesses. The CoM provides a valuable platform to wave, discuss and stimulate local government actions, but above all it contributes to construct a durable and effective political and financial framework that will eventually constitute the basis for a sound and integrated EU-wide policy (Egenhofer, *et al.*, 2010).

6.4 Exploring the mode: the Covenant of Mayors in Turin

Amongst the countries that committed to the Kyoto protocol, Italy lags behind *vis-à-vis* the other signatories and did not manage to attain the objectives set for 2010. Veritably, this occurred despite the political and normative measures introduced in order to harmonise the national situation with the strategies endorsed at the EU level, particularly as regards the promotion of renewable energies (Amatucci and Vestito, 2009). In turn, the delay accumulated by the country in relation to the Kyoto objectives hampers the achievement of the targets set by the *Burden Sharing System* of the EU[24]. This is a rather surprising negative performance, especially in the light of the role that Italy played since the early '80s for the promotion of renewable sources following the deployment of a National Energetic Plan in 1981.

As part of the decentralisation process undertaken in Italy, the provisions of the law decree 112/98[25] transferred to regions and local authorities – amongst others – competences in the field of energy, thus retaining for the central state the role of defining general national guidelines and the adoption of coordination acts for

---

23. In this connection, cities can legislate/regulate on just a small part of the emissions produced within their territories (~20 per cent of the total emissions), whereas the most part of them are regulated at the national level, under the provisions of the EU ETS (Egenhofer *et al.*, 2010).

24. Italy has been assigned an overall objective of greenhouse gasses reduction equivalent to 13 per cent for non-ETS sectors in relation to 2005 values. The national objective for the renewable energy share is 17 per cent of total consumption by 2020 according to a system based on pro-capita income. Nonetheless, pollutant emissions increased by 12 per cent in 2006 – baseline 1990 (Legambiente, 2008).

25. Law decree 31 March 1998, n. 112 'Conferimento di funzioni e compiti amministrativi dello Stato alle Regioni ed agli enti locali, in attuazione del capo I della L. 15 Marzo 1997, n.59', published in the Official Journal on the 21 April 1998, n. 92, S.O.

regional energetic planning. Regions are instead deputed to coordinate the action of local authorities in the field of energy saving. Local authorities are in charge of the functions relating to the development of programmes to boost renewable energy sources and energy saving, the control of thermic plants production and performance, yet granting authorisations for the establishment of new plants. In compliance with the provisions of directive 2001/77 of the EU[26], Italy adopted law decree 387/2003[27], which established national objectives for the use of renewable energy sources, as to both the production and consumption of electricity and the incentive mechanisms.

With the endorsement of a National Strategic Plan in 2007[28], Italy underlined the chief importance of promoting local development through boosting the production of renewable energy and favouring energy saving. These objectives will be therefore pursued via a strategy aimed at removing those ties still impeding the full diffusion of renewable energy sources by fully implementing regional operational programmes.

To date, the majority of Italian regions have approved their own energy plan as well as the Regional Environmental Energy Plans (as provisioned by Art. 5 of the law 10/91 on the 'norms for the actuation of the National Energy Plan, energy saving and development of renewable energy sources')[29]. Nonetheless, the division of competencies for energy matters remains a sensitive subject, since uncertainties persist in the relation between regions and the central administration, and between regional authorities and local governments, especially when granting authorisations for new energy plants[30].

Also in the Italian case though, local authorities – cities – can play a decisive role in boosting the production of renewable energies. Municipalities are *de facto* entitled of the territorial development policy, according to the regional guidelines. In this connection, cities issue regulations to favour the reduction of heating dispersion from buildings and the self-production of energy, by introducing for

---

26. Directive 2001/77/EC of the European Parliament and of the Council of 27 September 2001 on the promotion of electricity produced from renewable energy sources in the internal electricity market.

27. Law decree 29 December 2003, n. 387 'Attuazione della direttiva 2001/77/CE relativa alla promozione dell'energia elettrica prodotta da fonti energetiche rinnovabili nel mercato interno dell'elettricità', published in the Official Journal n. 25, 31 January 2004. In particular, the decree introduces important novelties as to inventive mechanisms via the so-called 'Green Certificates.

28. *Quadro Strategico Nazionale per la politica regionale di sviluppo 2007–2013*, Ministry for Economic Development, June 2007. Available at: http://www.dps.mef.gov.it/documentazione/QSN/docs/QSN2007-2013_giu_07.pdf.

29. Decree 1998, n. 112 lists the competences reserved to the Central State and the Regions in energy matters; it also establishes the exclusive obligation for the regions to introduce a Regional Energy Plan in respect of the guidelines as outlined in the National Energy Plan.

30. For a more comprehensive overview on these aspects, reference is made to: Amatucci, F. and Vestito, D. (2009) *Lo sviluppo di fonti energetiche innovative per la realizzazione di ambienti urbani sostenibili*, CITTALIA working paper 5/2009, pp. 33–36.

instance new planning criteria and the obligation for energetic certification[31]. Overall, energy saving is a relevant task for local authorities in Italy, which seek to orient their action towards the minimisation of wastage and the better rationalisation of energy use. This attempt necessarily needs to foresee useful actions to raise public awareness and eventually boost responsible behaviour through the active involvement of local actors in the territorial development.

Logic of action in Turin

In the context of the second edition of the EU sustainable energy week[32] – January 2008 – the city of Turin showed its will to join the CoM programme. The official subscription to the programme took place in February 2009, following the formal domestic approval through the endorsement of a council resolution during the session of the municipal council. Like the other signatories, Turin committed to elaborate and implement a SEAP – Turin Action Plan for Energy (TAPE) – with the intention of reducing CO_2 by 2020[33]. In particular, better energetic performance of existing buildings, a more diffused use of renewable energy sources, innovative transport policies as well as the extension of urban district heating have been set as the key objectives for the new energy strategy of the city, through the participation in the CoM.

Amongst the reasons for the city of Turin to take part in the CoM programme there is the intention to take advantage of the renewed role of the mayors in Italy, who now have more chances of decisional manoeuvre *vis-à-vis* the central administration. Despite the general climate of economic scarcity at the local level, the intent is to anchor existing projects and plans to a wider programme of intervention like the one provisioned under the aegis of EU support. Additionally, the practicality of the CoM programme was deemed as one of the main reasons for the city's participation as well as an occasion to harmonise and improve the relations between public and private subjects involved in the development of the city territory.

The methodology afterwards employed to work out the SEAP for the city saw the direct involvement of two main operational bodies: the *City of Turin* and the *Turin 'Politecnico' University*, whose relation was regulated through a specific three year protocol signed in October 2009. Amongst the subjects involved in the process of data collection and elaboration of emissions inventory – that then led to the choice of actions to insert in the SEAP – there were different sectors of the municipality, the Piedmont region, the province of Turin, AMIAT, GTT, IREN, SMAT, ATC and FINPIEMONTE. In particular, the regional administration

---

31. In particular, Art. 5 of the law 10/91, establishes that the General Regulatory Plans of municipalities with a population over 50000 inhabitants are due to endorse a Municipal Energy Plan.

32. http://www.eusew.eu/.

33. In particular, CO_2 emissions in Turin dropped by ~19 per cent during the period 1991(baseline)–2005. The TAPE foresees a further reduction for the 2005–20 period, that should contribute to an overall reduction by 40 per cent for the 1991–2020 period.

endorsed a programmatic relation on energy in 2009, thus setting ambitious targets for energy saving and use of renewable sources.

Apart from defining interventions in the energy field to be carried out in urban areas, the province of Turin is in charge of the environmental energy plan elaboration and of drafting the provincial energy report. Both of these activities are relevant for the actual redaction of emission inventories and the definition of actions to be undertaken. On this occasion, the province is acting as supporting structure for the CoM. It has been giving assistance to thirty-five municipalities – excluding Turin – within the provincial territory since February 2010. Not only does this activity translate in the 'promotion' of the programme in the localities, but also in monitoring and proposal through 'integrated packages'.

The Turin Action Plan for Energy was elaborated following the Commission guidelines. As such, it includes the inventory of the CO_2 emission relative to 1992 and the record for 2005. In this connection, the action plan elaborated afterwards foresees a set of actions to be carried out by 2020; these are oriented towards energy saving, improving energy efficiency and the use of renewable energy sources. Therefore, fifty-one different actions are planned in the housing and tertiary sectors, industry, transport, and local production of electricity, district heating, urban planning and green procurement.

Thus a 'TAPE Local team' – composed of both public managers and experts – was established for the actual definition of the plan and the overall review of the planned actions. In turn, each sub-group was then in charge of organising meetings with different stakeholders in order to illustrate, amend or integrate the proposed actions and seek for new collaborations in view of the implementation phase.

The TAPE was officially presented in November 2010. Monitoring and follow-up and evaluation of the actions aimed at CO_2 emissions reduction are foreseen to assure the possible adaptation of the process to changing conditions and to attain, nonetheless the overall final objectives. Officers directly involved in the elaboration of the SEAP in this case, point out how major difficulties were encountered during the process of data retrieval about the inner area of Turin as well as due to the absence of specific financial streams for the cities adhering to the CoM.

Conclusions: insights into the Europeanisation of energy saving in Turin

The Covenant of Mayors has the character of a 'voluntary activity' for cities. As goes for Turin, each of the decisions taken concerning the programme is in fact, the resultant of a council resolution (such as it was the case for the TAPE approval). Each of the planned actions, as afterwards featured in the SEAPs, depends on the 'city' and is addressed to the transformation of the city, as an overall demonstration of the voluntary action of the mayor. As such, the involvement of stakeholders – though encouraged by the Commission – is also at discretion of the municipal administration.

Interviews reveal how the city of Turin decided to take part in the CoM to pursue an already locally established path oriented towards the attainment of significant environmental objectives, specifically those aimed at boosting energy efficiency and energy saving in the urban territory. Additionally, participation in the CoM programme was perceived as a further occasion to foster the experience gained in the field of local development and environmental sustainability, thereby enhancing established practices of consultation and partnership already in place within the territory and part of the working method employed by the city administration.

Turin was the first 'big size' Italian city to adhere to the CoM and to present a sustainable energy action plan. In this connection, several meetings were organised with the CoM office in Brussels to coordinate the initial phases of the programme. Contextually, a national focus point – at the Ministry for Environment – was created to coordinate the interplay between the Italian local administrations that signed for the programme and the European Commission.

Nonetheless, the city administration of Turin and the European Commission – CoM Office – maintain a rather direct relationship in this sense. Contextually, the provincial services acting as supportive structure for the municipalities of the territorial area of Turin (and of the province) that take part in the programme entertain regular relations with other supporting structures – in Italy and abroad – as well as acting in the coordination group for the Italian local authorities taking part in 'Agenda 21'.

Turning our attention to the range of transformations occurred within the policy structures in the territorial system of Turin during the timeframe considered for the analysis of *ideation* as a mode of Europeanisation, it is possible to formulate some considerations on the perspective character of the process of Europeanisation.

As confirmed by officers in charge of the overall coordination of the programme in the city of Turin – particularly those involved in the elaboration and management of the sustainable action plan – taking part in the CoM programme has not translated in remarkable changes as to the number and type of actors involved within the policy domains here concerned. The involvement of stakeholders in the case of the CoM in Turin is, in fact, the resultant of a series of processes that have long been in place within the urban territory. This is further proven by the TAPE structure, presented and afterwards approved by the city of Turin. Amongst the proposed actions leading to CO_2 emissions reduction by 2020, a considerable bulk was partially already in place before the actual involvement in the community programme. In this connection though, the increased legitimacy of local actors – and more generally of the 'model' proposed by the city of Turin as a whole – *vis-à-vis* other Italian cities, other 'urban partners' in Europe and thus the EU institutions (e.g. the European Commission) – will largely depend on the overall deployment and eventual success of the actions as proposed in the TAPE. A more tangible upgrade in the degree of innovation will be finally reached with the possible participation of Turin in the EU 'Smart Cities' programme[34] for which the elaboration and implementation of a SEAP is perceived as a necessary condition.

---

34. http://www.smart-cities.eu/index2.html.

As to the instruments promoted over the last decade to reduce CO_2 emissions and to favour energy saving – also through renewable energy use – a number of initiatives can be attributed to the municipality of Turin, especially to the mayor and the different services within the Department for Environment and the Housing Sector. Hence, the only relevant EU-induced innovation in this sense corresponds to the financial instruments at support and incentive of the actions foreseen by the TAPE that will be deployed following the final approval of the Turin Action Plan by the Commission.

Concerning the procedures accompanying the CoM programme, key actors involved in the TAPE elaboration revealed that several of the practices employed thus far are similar to those already in place in the city before the involvement in the communitarian programme. Nonetheless, participating in the CoM – especially during the 'Energy Plan' organisation and drafting phases – favoured synergies and a continuous dialogue between actors within the city. Extended expert group consultations were organised for the construction of the emissions inventory and the elaboration of the action plan afterwards.

In this connection, the action plan is considered as an instrument to favour an overall dynamic of consultation and information sharing between public and private subjects, as well as social and economic actors. These can be actors external to the municipal administration, who are willing to, or have already promoted actions for energy saving and production within the urban territory. Moreover, the implementation of the action plan is considered necessary to boost partnership arrangements between different operators (public and private) in the urban territory.

The TAPE as such is the resultant of a certain convergence between initiatives of various type that found coherence in the plan redacted on occasion of the city's participation in the CoM. Veritably, the coordination between various departments within the municipal administration as well as between the city administration and other institutional and 'semi-private' subjects involved in the overall programmes showed rather problematic. This is also due to practical drawbacks in collecting, organising and interpreting information as to energy consumptions and use. Thus, the elaboration of the TAPE represents a first, but significant attempt for establishing 'dialogue channels' between subjects and administrative bodies otherwise detached one from the other within the same administrative compound. This will prospectively contribute to foster the technical training of staff within the communal administration, via processes of reflexivity and extended communication, and to elaborate specific methodologies for collecting information and for its use and diffusion.

A partial gap can be noticed between the guidelines and requirements proposed by the European Commission in this case and the factual reality characterising local administrations, where the integrated approach to policy development as well as the integration of administrative practices are often not fully in place. To this end, the process leading to the systematic elaboration of strategic plans – such as a SEAP in the context of the CoM – in various sectors and within different, but integrated, policy domains, is perceived as the real added value brought about by communitarian programmes of this kind. This is also a necessary capacity that the city needs to acquire to attain the sustainable and efficient development of the territory.

To conclude, the analysis of the CoM programme reveals two main insights, as far as it developed in the EU-wide arena and has been dealt with in the city of Turin. On one hand the role of the European Commission, which acts as the *catalyser* and therefore the *sender* of a certain set of ideas for energy planning and development for urban territories. On the other hand it shows how cities – Turin in this case – mainly act as *receivers* and *developers* of these ideas and instruments on the basis of a common EU-platform for communication, dissemination of information and benchmark of best-practices.

6.5 Energy efficiency at the forefront of the EU policy action

The promotion of a 'resilient Energy Union with a forward looking climate change policy' was one of the ten policy priorities set out by the then incoming President of the Europe Commission, Jean Claude Junker, in July 2014. Building on the 2030 policy framework for climate and energy[35] and on the European Commission's energy security strategy[36], a target of at least a 40 per cent cut in greenhouse gas emission by 2030 compared to 1990 will apply in the EU; this complements the intention to reach a target of at least 27 per cent market share for renewable energy and 27 per cent for improving energy efficiency. The EU Energy Union package[37] was adopted by the European Commission in February 2015. The issue of energy efficiency features prominently as part of the framework strategy underpinning the legislative package, where the promotion of the 'energy efficiency first' principle implies a fundamental rethinking of energy efficiency and to consider 'efficiency' as an energy source in its own right. Additionally, the 2030 energy framework indicates that the cost-effective delivery of the greenhouse gas emission reduction target for 2030 would require an increase of energy saving of the order of 25 per cent (by 2030)[38]. A more efficient use of energy would lead to a reduction in energy demand, thus triggering savings for consumers, lower emissions of greenhouse gases and eventually to an increased energy security through a reduction of imports.

35. A full array of information of the EU 2030 energy strategy can be found at: http://ec.europa.eu/energy/en/topics/energy-strategy/2030-energy-strategy.

36. The strategy aims to ensure a stable and abundant supply of energy for European citizens and the economy. Its organisation and implementing instruments can be retrieved at http://ec.europa.eu/energy/en/topics/energy-strategy/energy-security-strategy.

37. The package consists of a communication accompanied by a roadmap detailing fifteen different initiatives to be adopted; an interconnection communication describing the measures needed to reach the target of 10 per cent per cent electricity interconnection by 2020, and a communication 'on the road to Paris', setting out the EU's vision of achieving a binding climate agreement in 2015.

38. Communication from the Commission to the European Parliament and the council, *Energy Efficiency and its contribution to energy security and the 2030 Framework for climate and energy policy*, COM(2014) 520 final, July 2014.

Despite the regulatory environment already in place – comprising the set of energy efficiency target – the overall implementation of energy efficiency policies faces several challenges, which include high upfront investment costs, access to finance, lack of information, split incentives and rebound effects (Erbach, 2015). As part of the Energy Union strategy, the European Commission is proposing to revise the relevant energy efficiency legislation – including the revision of the existing directives on energy efficiency (2012/27/EU) and the directive on the energy performance of buildings (2010/31/EU) – where special attention will be paid to the issue of finance for energy efficiency.

The Energy Efficiency Directive in force sets for a framework aimed at promoting energy efficiency in the EU via the removal of existing barriers and tackling market failures that hamper the efficient supply and use of energy. In this case, targets are set at member state level in the magnitude of an annual final energy saving for final consumers of 1.5 per cent between 2014 and 2020; this is to be achieved through obligation schemes or alternative policy measures[39]. Amongst the different policy components of the 'energy efficiency' pillar, it is particularly relevant the issue of energy efficiency improvement in building; according to available data, EU households spend on average 6.4 per cent of their disposable income on home-related energy use and in 2012 almost 11 per cent of the population of the EU were unable to keep their homes properly warm[40]. The existing Directive on the Energy Performance of Buildings establishes a common framework for the calculation and certification of buildings' energy performance and requires member states to set minimum energy performance standards for new buildings, major renovations and the replacement of building elements. Ahead of the revision of the existing legislation on energy efficiency, the current objective of the Commission's work is the full implementation of the existing legislative framework, and in particular to implement measures aimed at increasing investments in energy efficiency. This includes boosting investments as part of the European Structural and Investment Funds for regional policy, directing investment for energy efficiency through the European Fund for Strategic Investments and strengthening the use of financial instruments via targeted initiatives[41].

---

39. Alternative policy measures to reduce final energy consumption may include: energy or CO_2 taxes, financial incentives that lead to an increased use of energy efficient technology, regulations or voluntary agreements that lead to the increased use of energy efficient technology, energy labelling schemes beyond those that are already mandatory under EU law, yet training and education, including energy advisory programmes. To date, twenty member states have notified the Commission that they will implement alternative measures.

40. Commission staff working document, *Energy prices and costs in Europe*, SWD(2014) 20 final, January 2014.

41. The EU already provides funding for energy efficiency measures through the European local energy assistance programme (ELENA) and the European Energy Efficiency Fund (EEEF). The EEEF is a public-private partnership focused on financing projects carried out by, or on behalf of, local and regional authorities. The European Investment bank's Private Finance for Energy Efficiency (PF4EE) instrument provides instead long-term financing for energy efficiency investments.

Building on this evolved background, and on the experience of the CoM, a new EU 'local initiative' – the Mayors Adapt initiative[42] – was launched in 2014. Its key objectives are to *inform* decision makers and other actors in local authorities on issues of climate adaptation, to *mobilise* cities to take action on climate adaptation and to *support* them in accessing existing expertise and implementing local plans for climate action. From October 2015, the initiative is part of the 'Covenant of Mayors'; the new integrated structure now involves more than 6000 cities committed to take action for securing sustainable and affordable energy, and sustaining climate mitigation/adaptation[43] with a shared long-term vision for 2050. In this connection, the signatories of the 'new' Covenant of Mayors commit to take actions to support implementation of the EU 40 per cent greenhouse gas reduction target by 2030; this is to be achieved through a series of concrete measures, including the submission of a 'baseline emission inventory' to track mitigation actions and climate risks and vulnerability assessment, and an adaptation strategy. Thus, participating local authorities also commit to reporting every two years on the implementation progress of their plans.

---

42. Details about the Mayors Adapt initiative can be found at: http://mayors-adapt.eu/.

43. Whilst 'mitigation' in the context of the Covenant of Mayors refers to the intention of accelerating the decarbonisation process within territories, the term 'adaptation' chimes with the intention of strengthening the capacity to adapt to unavoidable climate change impacts.

Chapter Seven

Europeanisation via Modes of Regulation: Waste Management and the Case of the EU Packaging Waste Directive

7.1 Introduction

The increasing waste production in Europe, and thereby the necessity for establishing a system of efficient waste management and disposal, emerged as a priority theme for the European Union and its territories. Not only do EU measures in this policy area detail a specific classification of the waste structure and streams, moreover, they define certain fundamental obligations for the management, recycling, treatment as well as the disposal of products. Thus, the EU's Sixth Environmental Programme identifies waste prevention and management as one of the four top priorities, where the main objective is to decouple waste generation from economic activity, so as to eventually reduce the production of rubbish.

The complexity of the EU waste legislation and the specificity of the multiple instruments through which EU action deploys in this issue area, have often led territorial administrations in member states to only partially comprehend the logic guiding EU provisions and to implementation problems. This implies considerable delays in the adoption of these measures within the domestic systems. In turn, this situation has at time fostered episodes of risk, both for the environment and for human health. The risks that recently hit some Italian cities and regions further testify the criticality of this policy area and the need for durable solutions both domestically and supranationally.

Thus, the management of waste in Europe has become a major challenge also for local authorities that are in charge of the collection, the recycling and the final disposal of waste. This takes place within a policy area where member states have defined regulations to implement the European legislation and where cities are confronted with a plethora of other administrative authorities and actors of different nature. The flourishing legislative production in this domain and the corresponding intensity of the EU policy action did not entirely translate into effective implementation domestically. In fact, the overly detailed nature of EU Environmental Action Plans, together with the specificity of the European directives and decisions, have sometimes hindered their full comprehension and implementation in several member states that consequently postponed the complete adoption of these measures (CITTALIA, 2010).

Different types of regulations were necessary to face the problematic implications of the growing production of waste and to reduce the types of waste produced, as well as to endure a design of new products that would facilitate waste recovery afterwards. Nonetheless, these regulations did not always take the form of command and control instruments; instead they can include economic and fiscal instruments as well as industrial codes of conduct (Chalmers, 1994).

Hitherto, only few 'command and control-like' measures have been adopted to address the excessive accrual of waste. In this connection, one of the most relevant attempts is represented by the enforcement of the Directive on Packaging and Packaging Waste[1], officially published on 20 December 1994. The directive required that, by 31 December 2001 – by weight – specific targets for packaging waste recovery have to be attained; additionally, within these general targets, there are other targets to be reached in terms of recycling of waste, with further specifications for each packaging material. The directive is accompanied by a series of supporting measures to help achieve these goals. Exceptions are moreover envisaged for some member states[2].

For the purpose of our investigation it is important to highlight how, a policy of this kind, and above its overall success, does not merely rely upon the deployment of regulatory instruments, but also on 'behavioural and attitudinal changes' (Chalmers, 1994: 277) that require the participation of a wide range of actors, including local authorities and private individuals. This implies the intensification of the relations between the community – and the EU policy making more generally – and these actors.

The remainder of this chapter is organised as follows. The next section shall give an introduction to the policy area of EU waste management by pointing out the structure of the EU waste legislation, its guiding principles as well as the main policy instruments promoted by the EU to attain its objectives in this sense. It also presents the archetypal game model we contend as exemplifying the main properties of interactions within this specific policy domain. Section 3 narrates the relevant historical background underpinning the promotion of the EU Packaging Waste Directive and its partial integration into the renewed Waste Framework Directive[3]. It also explains the elements that are likely to trigger change within the domestic systems considered. In the fourth section the theoretical and analytical frameworks presented in Part I of this book are extended to examine the case of Turin as regards the Packaging Waste Directive and the waste management policy more broadly. In particular, analytical attention is devoted to the nature of strategic interactions developing during the time frame considered and that may favour the deployment of specific mechanisms of Europeanisation and eventually transformation within specific domains of policy and politics in the urban system under analysis. Some preliminary considerations will be exposed in the conclusive section.

---

1. Council Directive 94/62 EC, OJ 1994 L 365/10.

2. Because of their specific situation, i.e. respectively the large number of small islands, the presence of rural and mountain areas and the current low level of packaging consumption, Greece, Ireland and Portugal, must aim to recover lower targets of packaging waste and meet the recycling targets by 31 December 2005.

3. Directive 2008/98/EC on waste and repealing certain directives.

7.2 Waste management policy in the EU

The waste management strategy of the European Union finds its roots in the adoption of the 1975[4] Waste Management Directive. It set – for the first time – important elements such as the waste hierarchy, the principles of proximity and self-sufficiency as well as indicates waste disposal modalities. Additionally, the directive included the requirement of establishing waste management plans. Despite these innovations, the EU action in this early stage limited to encourage member states to undertake appropriate steps towards the more effective prevention and recycling of waste[5], without instead advancing any sort of prescriptive measure (Chalmers, 1994).

Following the energy crisis that hit Europe in the 1970s, the question of raw material supply became of paramount relevance in the community, insomuch as economic reasons were brought forward for waste recovery. The duality of the waste issue, would then justify legislative intervention both for reasons of distortions in competition and for environmental purposes, thus opening up the question concerning the freedom of member states action in this domain (ACR+, 2009). Furthermore, the 1973 programme gave orientations aimed at establishing a waste inventory specific management plan and differentiated obligations according to the hazardous nature of waste[6]. Hence, the issues of resource conservation and waste management were more clearly addressed in the Second Environment Programme, where the European Commission introduced the watershed concept of tackling the waste issue according to a hierarchy of actions, namely *prevention, recover* and *hazard-free disposal*[7] as well as the idea of bridging the subject matters of 'waste policy' and 'clean products policy', thus potentially enlarging the interest to the whole chain of production.

In the light of this 'waste-hierarchy', where waste disposal in terms of discard and incineration are kept as last resort solutions, the role of local and regional authorities is decisive, not only operationally, but also for informational purposes towards the local populations.

Emphasis was also put on the necessity to prevent the production of waste by favouring the use of *clean technologies*. This would have been possible through the dissemination of knowledge and by concluding industry-wide agreements for the progressive replacement of certain polluting techniques. Yet, the programme further stressed the necessity to promote recycling by adopting different measures apt to support the secondary materials market. Waste management was *de facto*

---

4.   Council Directive 75/442/EEC OJ L 194, 25.7.1975.

5.   Provisions in this sense were not mentioned in the First Action Programme on the Environment, OJ 1973 C 112/1.

6.   Despite the adoption of a specific European regulation in 2002 (N. 2150/2002), the statistical system in this sense has not been fully harmonised and member states retain freedom in terms of the modes adopted.

7.   The concept legal basis is established by Directive 91/156/EEC that amends Directive 75/442/EEC and it has been further refined in the new Waste Framework Directives 2006/12/EC and 2008/98/EC.

placed on the same ground as pollution control with the Third Action Programme where greater emphasis is attributed to the issues of waste recovery and prevention. It was only with the sixth Environment Programme in 2001 that the question of *resources* was addressed in a fully integrated way. It pointed out the unsustainable nature of resource consumption and by suggesting measures aimed to promote research and development for better use of resources, better corporate practices and the diffusion of better performing economic instruments. These ideas have been reiterated in the thematic strategy on the sustainable use of natural resources published in 2005[8]. Benchmark objectives, including figures, were proposed with the fifth Environment Programme in 1992. These included a perspective reduction of dioxin emission by 90 per cent, the stabilisation of household waste production at 330 kg per habitant per year and an indicative target of 50 per cent recycling-reuse for paper, glass and plastic.

It was only in the late '80s that a debate developed around the possibility to establish binding objectives in terms of figures and precise targets. In particular, the need to review waste law in this sense clearly emerged with the fourth Action Programme in 1987 as part of the broader movement of the 'Better Regulation'[9], a concept that would have informed the subsequent Environment Programmes. Reviewing the legal definition of waste to guarantee a more effective regulation and a more general redefinition of the regulatory texts relating to waste was deemed necessary for the simplification, consolidation and clarification of the existing legislation already in 1994–95. During this period in fact, an independent group of experts was created by the European Commission to elaborate innovative proposals in this connection[10]. Nonetheless, only in 2005, the Commission announced that the promotion of innovative environmental policies – *thematic strategies*[11] – and in particular the thematic strategy on the prevention and recycling of waste[12] are

---

8. Communication from the Commission to the Council, the European Parliament, the European Economic and Social Committee and the Committee of the Regions – Thematic Strategy on the sustainable use of natural resources (SEC(2005) 1683).

9. The concept of better regulation is based on the conclusions of the Mandelkern group in November 2001 (http://ec.europa.eu/smart-regulation/better_regulation/documents/mandelkern_report. pdf (accessed 10 November 2016)) and was made official for the purpose of promoting greater transparency in the adoption of legal rules (White Paper –COM 2001/428).

10. Report of the Group of Independent Experts on legislative and administrative simplification. COM (95) 288 final/2, 21 June 1995.

11. Thematic Strategies have been elaborated for six different issue areas within the environmental policy domain, namely: air pollution, the marine environment, the sustainable use of resources, the waste prevention and recycling, the sustainable use of pesticides, soil protection, the urban environment.

12. Communication from the Commission to the Council, the European Parliament, the European Economic and Social Committee and the Committee of the Regions 'Taking sustainable use of resources forward: a thematic strategy on the prevention and recycling of waste', COM (2005) 666.

informed by principles aimed at regulatory improvements[13]. Apart from featuring a broad review agenda, the 2005 thematic strategy on waste prevention pointed out the guiding principle of considering waste not only as simple materials to be discarded, but more as a resource for energy recovery and to create new industrial opportunities and employability.

Since the adoption of the first EU directive in this policy area back in 1975, waste management and disposal have been subjects of intense normative action in the EU policy making. Today – due to the continuous technological development in this sector – they remain one of the priority fields in which the European Union promotes legislative measures. Nonetheless, more specialised legislative provisions had to be developed to turn the initial principles into operational targets.

Principles and structure of waste legislation

The main rationales underpinning the EU policy for waste management can be gathered from the two general waste strategies promoted by the European Commission, respectively in 1989, 1996[14] and the thematic strategies released in 2005 within the 6th Environmental Action Plan[15]. In turn, the strategies set out the guiding principles for the overall management of waste in the European Union.

Thus, in the 1989 strategy, a first distinction was made between *disposal* and *recovery* of waste and further specifications were delineated concerning the 'intra-Community movements' and 'other movements' of waste products. In relation to this latter point, two main principles emerged in terms of *self-sufficiency*, due to which the amount of waste produced in the Union must be disposed within its territory, and *proximity* foreseeing the disposal of waste at the closest installation to the place of generation. In this connection, this first communication pinpoints some major political orientations towards waste prevention, recovery through a series of voluntary measures, ensuring the security of waste transport, the optimisation of disposal as well as the endorsement of corrective actions for the recovery of contaminated sites (ACR +, 2009). The second strategy issued in 1996 contributed to slightly modify some of the earlier provisions. In particular, the waste hierarchy is therein made more flexible by further distinguishing between material recovery and energy recovery, and more emphasis is placed on the responsibility of waste producers. Yet, reference was clearly made for improving the free circulation of waste within the territory of the Union.

---

13. Commission Working Document 'Better Regulation and the Thematic Strategies for the Environment', COM (2005) 466 final.

14. The Community Strategy for Waste Management was adopted in 1989, see SEC (89) 934 final of 18 September 1989. The strategy was reviewed in 1996, see COM (96) 399 final of 30.7.1996.

15. Regarding waste in particular the European Commission published the following communications: Communication from the Commission to the Council, the European Parliament, the European Economic and Social Committee and the Committee of the Regions, 'Taking sustainable use of resources forward: a thematic strategy on the prevention and recycling of waste', COM (2005) 666 final.

The 2001 Green Paper on Integrated Product Policy[16] further reinforced the tendency to consider the integrated nature of waste production and management, by promoting three main objectives to improve participation at all action levels. This should be attained by better adapting price mechanisms through the extension of the 'polluter pays principle', by promoting more environment-friendly consumption based on environmental labelling and new communication techniques, and by promoting more environment-friendly production via the diffusion of information and the dissemination of guidelines on eco-design[17].

Relevant for the gist of this research are the Thematic Strategy on Prevention and the subsequent Thematic Strategy on Recycling. Already in 1998, the Commission addressed the subject matter of recycling and the competitiveness of related industries in a communication that took stock of the main initiatives to be developed towards improving the competitiveness of the recycling sector[18]. Questions relating more explicitly to recycling were addressed by the 2003 communication. In particular, the debate was therein centred on four main issues pertaining respectively to: the necessity to provision additional quantitative recycling objectives[19], the appropriate incentive to favour recycling actions, the further harmonisation of existing rules and the promotion of measures apt to promote forms of recycling that are both clean and 'easy' (ACR+, 2009). Building on these general intents, the provisions in thematic strategy formulated in 2005 aimed to increase the compliance with the existing legislations, thus redefining the current legislative provisions, developing joint benchmark standards for recycling and, more importantly, promoting recycling actions through material-based objectives and via the exchange of information.

Some general principles dominate the EU policy for waste management; these originated from both the treaties, the specific legislative acts adopted within this issue area, as well as from the case law of the Court of Justice. As such, their nature can be considered as both legal and political, and their scope can be somehow generalised to the overall environmental policy of the EU[20].

In this connection, five main environmental principles can be detached in the terms of *prevention, precaution, polluter-pays, protection* and *correction*. Thus, the former – despite the partial ambiguity as to its actual domain of application

---

16. Green Paper on Integrated Product Policy, Brussels, 07.02.2001, COM(2001) 68 final.

17. The Commission issued a further IPP Communication in 2003, which partially retracted the initial ambitions to 'only' three main objectives corresponding to: a life cycle analyses guide, public purchasing 'greening' measures, a discussion and negotiation process for certain priority products.

18. Communication from the Commission to the Council, the European Parliament, the European Economic and Social Committee and the Committee of the Regions 'The competitiveness of the recycling sector', COM (1998) 463 final. In particular, the communication envisaged initiatives to be undertaken in the field of standardisation, initiatives in favour of development and transparency of markets and in favour of innovation as well as the provision of new regulatory measures.

19. In this case reference was made to the 'Packaging' Directive 94/62, which already envisaged target objectives for waste collection and recycling.

(Scotford, 2007) – if applied to waste, envisages to targeting the disposal and reduction of waste at the very source of its production, by favouring the use of clean products and technologies; additionally, prevention is meant to apply both quantitatively (reduction of the total amount of waste produced) and qualitatively (reduction of danger)[20]. The precautionary principle – in a similar vein of the prevention one – emphasises the necessity to intervene, whenever possible, to prevent the accrual of environmental problems. Of particular relevance is the polluter-pays principle, which originated within sectors of the OECD. When applied to waste, it constitutes a sort of hindrance to certain types of state aid. The principle is actually embedded in numerous directives and can be subsumed as a charge of the disposal costs to the holder or the producer of the product that generated the waste. High levels of environmental protection in the case of waste, translate into formulating more ambitious policy measures than those already in place domestically. The latter principle, correcting environmental damages at source as a matter of priority, applies in particular to waste movements and notably to its disposal, which ought to be carried out as closely as possible to the place of production[21].

Besides these five main principles, additional principles concerning waste management more in particular, can be recognised. *Effective, hazard-free management* – provisioned by the first framework directive in 1975 – makes it mandatory to forward waste to a disposal or recovery service and calls for the 'ecologically rational' management of waste (ACR+, 2009). The principle of *waste hierarchy* represents a sort of watershed concept in the domain of waste management, since it links many of the other principles at stake, in particular waste prevention and sustainable development. Hence, in its latest form, the principle sets an 'order of priorities' in terms of prevention, preparation for reuse, recycling, energy recovery and finally disposal[22]. Finally, the principle of *producer responsibility* obliges those who place products that generate waste on the market to be concerned about their management after consumption.

The aforementioned principles find expression in the wide waste legislative package developed by the EU over the last thirty years. Considering the current structure of EU waste legislation, a three layers constitution stands out, where the already mentioned Thematic Strategy of Waste Prevention and Recycling[23] lays down the general orientation to be pursued by means of more detailed acts.

---

20. The prevention principle, as it is illustrated in the following sections finds expression in both the Packaging Waste Directive (94/60) – in terms of 'national programmes' for prevention – and the new Framework Directive (2008/98) – in terms of 'prevention programmes'.

21. This provision is also known as the 'proximity principle'. In particular, the principle only applies to movements intended for waste disposal and not for recovery. Proximity is backed by the principle of self-sufficiency both at the level of the EU and within each of its member states, meaning that the waste produced with the territory of the EU must be disposed within it, and ideally within each of the domestic territories.

22. The waste hierarchy has been presented in this form with the new 2008 framework directive (2008/98/CE).

23. COM (2005) 666 final.

Thus, two main legislative instruments are at the bases of the framework legislation. The revised Waste Framework Directive issued in 2008, that sets the basic concepts and definitions related to waste management and lays down waste management principles such as the 'polluter pays principle' or the 'waste hierarchy'. Besides the general framework directive, the Waste Shipment Regulation[24] aims to introduce control waste shipment procedures and to ensure an environmentally sound management of the waste and the Directive on Hazardous Waste[25], which provides record keeping, monitoring and control obligations from the waste producer to the final disposal or recovery. Two main instruments regulate waste treatment operations. The Incineration Directive[26], whose main aim is to prevent or to reduce as much as possible the negative effects on the environment caused by the incineration and co-incineration of waste. Directive 1999/31 disciplines landfill of waste. The main objective of the directive is to prevent or reduce negative effects on the environment from the land filling of waste as much as possible, by introducing stringent technical requirements for waste and landfills.

Different waste streams are instead dealt with by a series of specific directives whose provisions have been in some instances embedded in the architecture of the Framework Directives. Thus, the Sewage Sludge Directive 86/278/EEC seeks to encourage the use of sewage sludge in agriculture and to regulate its use in such a way as to prevent harmful effects on soil, vegetation, animals and man. The Batteries and Accumulator Directive 2006/66/EC aims at minimising the negative impacts of batteries and accumulators on the environment and also at harmonising requirements for the smooth functioning of the internal markets. Packaging of waste management is regulated by directive 94/62 EC, which introduced a comprehensive legislation on this issue[27]. Other waste streams include mining waste[28], end of life vehicles[29], electrical and electronic equipment[30], polychlorinated biphenyls and polychlorinated terphenyls[31] and restrictions on the use of hazardous substances in electrical and electronic equipment[32], each of which find expression in a specific directive[33].

---

24. 91/259/EEC.

25. 91/689/EEC, then amended by Directive 94/31/EC.

26. 2000/76/EC, It repealed former directives on the incineration of hazardous waste (Directive 94/67/EC) and household waste (Directives 89/369/EEC and 89/429/EEC) and replaced them with a single text.

27. The EU first introduced measures on the management of packaging waste in the early 1980s. Directive 85/339/EEC covered the packaging of liquid beverage containers intended for human consumption only.

28. Directive 2003/319/EC.

29. Directive 2000/53/EC.

30. Directive 2000/96/EC.

31. Directive 96/59/EC.

32. Directive 2002/95/EC.

33. For a more comprehensive overview on the EU waste policy structure, including a description of each of the legislative measures referred above, reference is made to the European Commission website at: http://ec.europa.eu/environment/waste/index.htm (accessed 10 November 2016).

Archetypal game model

The conditions that characterise this mode of Europeanisation and the set of interactions wherein potentially occurring, can be analytically represented by a *Battle of the Sexes* game, and more generally by the class of 'games of coordination with conflict over distribution' (Scharpf, 1997). According to the logic of the game, the parties involved in the interaction have a common interest in coordinating their choices in order to reach a welfare-superior outcomes (S.A-s.A and S.B-s.B) although the parties are initially orientated towards different options.

In particular, if the game is played as a non-cooperative one with simultaneous moves in the absence of prior communication there is no certainty of reaching the preferred outcomes. Nonetheless, communication and binding agreements do not solve these difficulties; in fact, disagreement over the coordinated outcomes with different distributive characteristics would still persist. Hence, agreement over outcomes is eventually reached since both sides still prefer to accept the less attractive outcome rather than fall in a situation of non-coordination.

$p2$ / $p1$	S. A	S. B
s. A	3 1	0 0
s. B	0 0	1 3

This is actually the case in European environmental policy – and notably the case for the negotiation over the contents of the Packaging Waste Directive – where the competition between those 'activist' member states willing to establish common European regulations at high levels leads to a 'race' for uploading solutions as aligned as possible to their national regulatory system to the EU level, thus lowering the costs of adjustment (Héritier, 1996). In our case though, interaction is more likely to be played conforming to a non-cooperative, but sequential game.

In this case, the party that has the first move selects its preferred outcome and it would be in the other party's best interest to coordinate on the same outcome. In this occurrence – as previously illustrated – communication and negotiations will not necessarily lead to outcomes that are socially superior to unilateral action. Thus, a first pattern of coordination is generated during the problem definition and agenda setting phases, when, following the strategic *first move* of a country, all the other countries 'adjust' to the position of the first mover, which succeeded in defining the scope and eventually the instruments to deal with the policy problem now part of the EU agenda (Héritier, 2002; Scharpf 2000)[34]. This

---

34. Adjustment in this sense presents the features of modes of 'mutual adjustment' as presented by Scharpf (1997), or instead dynamics of 'parametric adjustment' as presented by Lindblom (1965), where actors are likely to reach Nash equilibrium outcomes at which they will remain insofar as long as their available strategies, their associated outcomes and the preferences of actors over this outcome are stationary. Therefore, national governments would continue to adopt their policy nationally in response to, or in anticipation of, the policy choices of other governments.

also means – Scharpf argues – that in constellations resembling the Battle of the Sexes, 'the choice of the second mover will be adjusted so as to achieve perfect coordination, even if a different outcome would initially have been preferred' (Scharpf, 1997: 111).

Overall, the success of the first mover depends on the eventual adoption of its proposal by the Commission that acts as 'gate keeper' for the possible translation of the first mover strategy into a corresponding EU proposal[35]. Further patterns of coordination – Héritier contends – are likely to emerge during different phases of the policy process, depending on the specific nature of the instrument at stake. For the purpose of our analysis, the European Commission acts as first mover *vis-à-vis* cities, which in turn are also subject to further regulatory provisions by central governments, and eventually to plans established at the regional administrative level. Therefore, as already argued, in this case mechanisms of transmission of EU measures based on compliance patterns are expected to be prevailing within urban areas.

In this connection, the logic of action at the base of the regulatory measures considered in this research does not entirely conform to the logic of the Prisoners' Dilemma, but to the Battle of the Sexes-archetypal models (Krasner, 1991)[36]. If regulation consists of making efficient movements within the Pareto frontier on the bases of persuasion and reasoning, then the logic is of standard setting, which almost invariably conforms to Battle of the Sexes-game types, or to similar game models of coordination. The Prisoners' Dilemma is used instead to represent dynamics of tax competition and social dumping (Radaelli, 1998). Those are also regulatory problems, although they are different from those at the centre of this research.

In the case of coordination games of this type, the time factor plays a relevant role; in fact, the reiteration of the game makes players more sensitive to the distributional character of the outcomes arising from coordination (Snidal, 1985). As recalled by Radaelli (1998), in the Prisoner's Dilemma, the time factor provides incentives to cooperation, but in the Battle of the Sexes time may induce players 'to upset prevailing coordinated outcomes in an attempt to institute a movement to other conventions which are more favourable to them' (Snidal, 1985: 936). Leadership also matters in this case. It does so, by providing adaptability when circumstances change and by promoting change in otherwise static regimes (Snidal, 1985: 939). In this sense, the action of the European Commission features these characteristics.

---

35. The role of the Commission is further strengthened in this sense by an EU decision that obliges member states to inform the Commission about all relevant community drafts of national primary and secondary legislation on which the Commission is thereafter supposed to notify about possible EU legislative actions in the same area. This establishes a direct link between national and European policy initiatives, thus eventually favouring the diffusion of national measures via European legislation (Héritier, 2002).

36. Also see McAdams (2008) for a detailed differentiation between the Prisoners' Dilemma and other coordination games.

7.3 The Packaging and Packaging Waste Directive

After nearly three years of negotiation, on 20 December 1994, the Council of Ministers adopted Directive 94/62/EC on Packaging and Packaging Waste (thereinafter PWD). The directive is considered to be the key to understanding the entire municipal waste management systems in the European Union (Haverland, 2000; Fischer, *et al.*, 2002). As the first major EU environmental piece of legislation under the Treaty of Maastricht (Golub, 1996; 2002), the PWD represents a suitable means for investigating questions concerning the interplay between, and the role of actors in various territorial systems towards the implementation of its provisions. The directive sets the harmonisation of national measures concerning the management of packaging and packaging waste as its overall objective, in order to prevent impacts on the environment and to secure the proper functioning of the internal market within the community (Art. 1). The directive also establishes targets for the recovery and recycling of packaging waste within the member states[37].

As the previous section shows, the EU legislation for waste management and disposal is mainly regulated through specific directives whose provisions leave considerable room for manoeuvre to member states as to the choice of instruments for their implementation. In this connection, the diffusion of multiple domestic-territorial strategies may imply that problematic implications arise. This is mainly due to lack of compliance with the EU targets, difficulties in carrying out comparative analysis of the distinctive elements of the multiple strategies put in place domestically as well as the absence of legal requirements for member states to inform the European Commission as to the levels and composition of the recycling of municipal waste (CITTALIA, 2009).

A more comprehensive appreciation of the current discipline for the management of waste in Europe and within its territories may be acquired by drawing on the contents of the Waste Framework Directive – the most recent legislative document issued by the European Commission for the treatment and management of waste – and the requirements for waste management planning differently provisioned into the WFD and other directives[38]. A brief analysis of the content issues of the WFD, we assume, will facilitate the understanding of the Packaging and Packaging Waste Directive that constitutes the *proxy* instrument for the assessment of the *regulatory* mode of Europeanisation.

Instruments for waste management – WFD and waste management plans

The original waste management directive adopted in 1975 underwent a series of significant amendments, especially during the '90s to be afterwards replaced by

---

37. The term recovery denotes the collection of packaging waste for the purpose of recouping value, including composting, combustion with energy recovery, or recycling (OJ 1994, Art. 3).

38. The WFD 2006/12/EC on waste sets out general requirements for waste plans in Art. 7, while specific provisions are laid down with regard to hazardous waste in Art. 6 of Directive 92/698/EC and packaging and packaging waste in Art. 6 of Directive 94/62/EC.

a 'codification' framework directive in 2006[39]. In turn, this latter directive was partially repealed with the entry into force of the last framework directive 2008/16/EC that had to be transposed by December 2010. Both of these documents reaffirm general principles such as the obligation of environmental and health sound waste treatment. Additionally the new framework directives further specify the notions of waste collection, treatment, recycling and disposal of waste as well as including a more stringent definition of the obligations and responsibilities for a correct management of waste streams; the new provisions follow the waste hierarchy indicated by the European Strategy that privileges prevention, re-use and recycling over simple disposal of waste.

As such, the waste framework directive is the cornerstone of the EU waste policy architecture, whose overall objective is 'the protection of human health and the environment against the harmful effects caused by the collection, transport treatment, storage and tipping of waste'[40]. Despite the innovations brought about with the 2008 document, the directive features three main functions, common to both its latest versions.

As suggested by Scotford (2007), the directive acts as a *framework* for EC waste legislation by setting a comprehensive agenda for EC waste regulation. According to a *policy-directing* function, a waste hierarchy is indicated and member states are invited to adopt appropriate measures to respect its objectives. Thirdly, the establishment of a system for the supervision and control of waste within the EU fulfils a regulatory intent, whereby principles and rules discipline the regulation of waste and its treatment (Scotford, 2007).

In this connection, some main innovations introduced with the latest version of the framework directive can be worth mentioning before we outline the content issues of the directive 94/62/EC, since they consolidate or extend what initially provisioned in the directive on packaging. As to the *scope*, the new framework directive excludes from its provisions certain substances that remain nonetheless encompassed by the definition of waste[41], in which waste is defined as 'any substance or object which the holder discards or intends or is required to discard'. The directive also introduces assumptions concerning the distinction between waste and by-products as well as specifications relating to the end of waste quality after recovery operations. Most relevant is the provision for a five-level waste hierarchy in terms of prevention, preparation for re-use, recycling, other recovery (including energy recovery) and disposal. In particular, member states have to consider this newly framed hierarchy when endorsing domestic legislation and policies for waste prevention and management, although, in this case some major

---

39. The major amendments where included in the directive 91/56/EEC, whereas the directive 2006/12/EC represents, *de facto*, the first codified Waste Framework Directive.

40. Second recital of the 2006/12/EC WFD.

41. In particular article 2 of the directive establishes a distinction between substances falling outside of its scope unconditionally, those which fall outside its scope provided that they are covered by other European legislation, and lastly those that fall outside its scope subject to certain conditions relating mainly to the way they are managed (ACR+, 2009: 76).

exemptions are also provisioned for specific waste streams. Member states are asked to draw up waste prevention programmes no later than December 2013 (Art. 29) by taking appropriate measures to promote the re-use of products and activities. In this sense, the directive also sets quantitative objectives for certain specific streams as far as specific waste streams are concerned[42]. The new directive further specifies some conditions under which the operations carried out by incineration installation – mainly processing solid municipal waste – ought to be qualified as recovery operations, with specific regard to the production of energy. Some new requirements are also formulated for the management of specific streams such as hazardous waste, waste oil and bio-waste.

Relevant for this study, is the explicit formulation of the obligation to draw up waste prevention programmes and waste management plans. Prevention programmes must be drawn up – no later than five years after the directive comes into force – so as to breaking the link between economic growth and the environmental impact associated with the generation of waste[43]. These can be integrated into waste management plans that must be drawn up with the aim of covering the entire territory of the member states concerned; they contain the type, quantity and source of waste, existing collection systems and location criteria. In particular, the plans must contain an analysis of the current situation in terms of waste management of the geographical entity in question, determine the measures to be undertaken for waste preparation, and provide an assessment of how the plan will support the implementation of the provisions. Plans have also to include a specific chapter on the management of packaging and packaging waste, including the measures taken in terms of prevention and reuse. Such provisions, as formulated in the WFD, leave a substantial margin of manoeuvre to the competent authorities when it comes to implementing their details.

Implementing the EU Packaging Waste Directive

The disposal of tonnes of packaging waste produced each year and the already existing 'waste mountains' (Golub, 2002) has confronted EU member states with increasing environmental and economic problems. In this connection, voluntary and compulsory agreements with industry have been introduced in EU member states to try and reduce the production of packaging waste by at the same time favouring processes of reuse and recycling. Hence, particularly ambitious programmes were implemented during the 1980s and 1990s in Denmark, Germany and The

---

42. Art. 11 (2) imposes that '...by 2020 the preparing for re-use and recycling of waste materials... shall be increased by a minimum of 50 per cent by weight', without nonetheless specifying whether the imposed percentage objective applies only overall or instead also to the flows set.

43. Prevention programmes must set objectives in terms of waste prevention, describe the existing prevention measures, assess the usefulness of the measures provided as well as set qualitative and quantitative reference points (Art. 29).

Netherlands[44], although member states continued to highly differ as regards their packaging policies and regulatory styles (Bailey, 1999, 2003; Haverland, 2000).

However, before eventually reusing or recycling waste, methods for waste 'recover' must be put in place so as to collect and separate various materials from the general waste stream. These procedures are not exempt from problematic implications, especially when it comes to waste disposal. Thus, on one hand restrictions imposed on land-filling, incineration and recycling of domestic waste in some member states constituted a hindrance for those countries relying more heavily on exporting used packaging, on the other hand, the restriction imposed on waste imports opened up questions about the free movement of goods in the community. Against the background of this apparent contradiction, and to reduce the environmental risks implicated in the production of packaging waste in the EU, the Commission began to consider the introduction of preventing and harmonising measures (Golub, 1996; 2002). The Commission proposal on packaging and packaging waste – under Art. 100 of the Treaty – and the successive adoption of a directive in 1994, represented a formal step in this direction (Bailey, 1999; Fischer, et al., 2002).

Hence, in the aim of preventing green protectionism from hindering the free movement of packaging waste in the community, the proposal initially advanced by the European Commission contained far reaching targets[45], which substantially exceeded the plans already in place in many member states. Their full respect would have implied considerable pressures for adaptation on the majority of national systems. Although supported by the more 'green states' (Germany, The Netherlands and Denmark), the proposal was opposed by several member states and industrial groups that claimed for more flexible targets and a comparatively low level of environmental protection. The European Parliament second reading substantially mirrored most of what was conveyed in the council's position, thus endorsing a set of lower standards; exceptions were nonetheless granted for those 'greener' member states willing to maintain – rather introduce – more ambitious measures (Golub, 2002; Haverland, 1999).

Objectives and targets of the Packaging Waste Directive

The PWD lays down measures aimed at preventing the production of packaging waste as well as reusing and recycling packaging so as to reduce the final disposal of waste (Art. 1) and its provisions cover all packaging placed on the market in the community and all packaging waste, regardless of the material used (Art. 2).

---

44. For an extended overview of different national strategies for waste management and recycling policies, including examples from extra-European States as well as statistical overviews, reference is made to Chalmin, P. and Gaillochet, C. (2009) *From Waste to Resources: World Waste Survey 2009*, Paris: Economica.

45. The original proposal provided for three major elements: 150kg/yr of packaging waste to be achieved in ten years, a minimum 'recovery' rate of 60 per cent for all packaging within 5 years, rising to 90 per cent after ten years, the inclusion of a hierarchy of goals in terms of prevention, reuse, recycling, incineration with energy recovery, incineration without energy recovery, landfill.

Thus, the directive sets a series of targets for recovery[46] and recycling to attain in the whole of the EU territory. In particular (Art. 6):

- By 2001, member states must recover between 50 per cent as a minimum and 65 per cent as a maximum of the packaging waste produced within its markets or imported;
- Between 25 per cent and 45 per cent (by weight) of the totality of packaging materials must be recycled, with a minimum of 15 per cent by weight for each packaging material;

The directive also foresaw the progressive refinement of targets for recovery and recycling every five years from the date of its entry into force in national systems[47]. Therefore, the directive requires the recovery and recycling of packaging waste in accordance with these targets; additionally, the reduction and reuse of packaging are objectives of the directive, although without the specification of definitive targets. Another set of standard limits is instead fixed as to the concentration of heavy metals in packaging (Art. 11). In line with the original purposes that led the Commission towards proposing a directive containing measures to solve the apparent trade-off between environmental protectionism and free movement of goods, the directive also prohibits member states from impeding any packaging which satisfies the provisions of the directive being placed on their markets (Art. 18).

In confirmation of the conflict between member states during the negotiation phase (Golub, 1996), the directive contains a series of derogations to accommodate the specific situation of certain domestic systems. Thus, more relaxed measures and targets are provisioned for those member states with particular territorial morphology and low levels of packaging consumptions, whereas, nation-States willing to exceed the directive's targets are also permitted to do so. The directive also allows member states to introduce economic instruments in their packaging recovery systems, under the condition that this does not hinder the free trade within the Union (Art. 15). Finally, the directive – as successively reiterated in the new waste framework directive – calls for the establishment of national databases on packaging and packaging waste flows (Art.12), the diffusion of information to users of packaging (Art. 13) and the inclusion of a specific chapter on packaging and packaging waste in management plans.

7.4 Exploring the mode: waste management in the city of Turin

The legislative set presented – waste framework directive and packaging waste directive – does not directly address cities and municipal authorities; it does

---

46. The term recovery denotes the collection of packaging waste for the purpose of recouping value, including composting, combustion with energy recovery, or recycling (*OJ*1994, Art. 3).

47. In this connection, directive 2008/50 (waste framework directive) states that, by 2020 preparing for re-use and recycling waste materials (packaging) shall be increased to a minimum overall 50 per cent by weight and the preparation for re-use, recycling and other material recovery shall be increased to a minimum of 70 per cent by weight (Art. 11).

nonetheless deal with two aspects that bear a strong relevance for the territorial units. These are the prevision of economic instruments as well as a better participation of citizens. member states are in fact asked to foster the participation of the interested parts (waste producers), of local authorities and of the general public in the elaboration of management plans and prevention programmes (Art. 31).

Although local authorities, and cities in particular, have indeed little influence on the negotiation of waste legislation at the European level, the progressive elaboration at the EU level of measures for promoting and eventually improving the selective collection of waste represents the main – and commonly recognisable – feature of potential EU influence on cities within this policy area. In this connection, the Packaging and Packaging Waste Directive (94/62/CE) not only stands out as an early EU legislative instrument for the regulation of waste management, but it contains above all provisions whose attainment and correct implementation is of main concern for urban authorities in Europe. It can be considered as the key to understand the entire municipal waste management system in Europe (Buclet, 2002: 3) and, we argue, one of the EU instruments leading to the Europeanisation of cities within this specific policy domain.

The set of interactions developing upon the provisions of these directives – and around the set of instruments domestically elaborated for their transpositions and eventual implementation – as well as the concrete policy initiatives undertaken within the territories considered for the analysis, allow, we argue, to consider the social mechanisms structuring such interactions.

The following sections will respectively make sense of how EU instruments – PWD and more generally the WFD in this case – have been transposed and domestically addressed (within both national and local administrations) and of how they have been reacted to and 'used' in the city of Turin.

By taking into account the contents of previous sections of this chapter, as well as what was indicated in Part I – in particular the possible mechanisms for Europeanisation and the different components of the dependent variable (actors, instruments, procedures and paradigms/cognition) – in this section we deal more specifically with the series of actions undertaken in the city of Turin for the management of waste (waste collection and recycling in particular), thus tackling step 2 of our research strategy (as outlined in Chapter Four).

Legislative context and waste management in Italy

Together with other Mediterranean countries, Italy is often considered as a laggard in the process of policy promotion at the EU level, or labelled as a 'fence-sitter' with specific reference to environmental policies (Börzel, 2002), thus occupying an intermediate position in terms of domestic environmental regulation. The Italian Constitution includes – Art. 9 – environmental protection as one of its fundamental principles; nonetheless, the effective implementation of the environmental instruments and policy measures remains problematic.

Therefore, environmental legislation figured as an ensemble of fragmented and contingent measures, thus making Italy a 'net exporter of pollution'

(CITTALIA, 2009)[48]; however, this is a tendency that has been partly counterbalanced by the activism of certain regions and notably some local administrations. Part V of the constitutional chart, as partially amended in 2001[49], lies down a strict division of competences between state, regions, provinces and municipalities, thus leaving the central administration exclusive competence to legislate in environmental matters (amongst others). Furthermore, the definition of environmental norms and instruments in the Italian system (at least until recently) mainly originates from EU legislative initiative. The transposition of EU measures into the Italian law has generally followed the emergency procedure, or instead the delegation of authority to the Government (*decreto legislativo*), thus avoiding the ordinary validation procedure which involves the state and the regions (Chalmin and Gaillochet, 2009).

Relevant for our purposes are in particular the 'Ronchi' order (n. 22/97) that transposed the packaging and packaging waste directive and the measures introduced through order n. 36/03 on landfilling of waste. This fixed values for volume reduction applicable to landfilling of the organic fraction of waste, and introduced measures to encourage the selective collection of municipal waste under the responsibility of the municipalities, which are indicated as responsible for the management of municipal waste (with the exclusion of recovery and recycling). The enactment of order 203/03 was meant instead to improve the market conditions for recycled products by extending provisions to textiles, paper, wood and plastic waste streams. Part IV of the 2006 order n. 152 recognised the EU principles of precaution, prevention and producer responsibility as well as the 'polluters pay' principle. In particular, the decree specified the division of competences for waste management and acknowledged the waste hierarchy as defined in the EU framework directive[50]. However, the central administration keeps control over the definition of general criteria and of the initiatives apt to pursue the prefixed objectives.

In turn, regions, provinces and municipalities maintain competences in the definition and implementation of the necessary actions for the management and disposal of waste. In this connection, amongst the competences recognised to the regional authorities there are regulation of activities for waste management – notably for the definition of the optimal territorial areas (ATO) and the promotion of integrated management of waste – as well as the adoption of the regional plans for waste management. Provinces are instead in charge of the administrative functions for programming and organising the recovery and disposal of waste within the provincial territory. Municipalities can concur in disciplining the management of

---

48. Industrial clustering, the diffused utilisation of private vehicles, problems linked to waste management and the high density of the population in some areas are factors that contribute to accrue these phenomena.

49. Title V of the constitution was modified through constitutional law no. 3, 18 October 2001.

50. Competent authorities at different territorial level should therefore act in order to favour prevention and reductions of waste production, as well as favouring the reduction of final disposal through re-use, recycling and other forms.

municipal waste through the adoption of *ad hoc* measures (*regolamenti*)[51] and are expected to disseminate the necessary information concerning urban waste management to the provincial and regional authorities.

As defined in order n. 152, the system for waste management is organised on the bases of optimal territorial areas (Ambiti Territoriali Ottimali – ATO) (Art. 200) that need to satisfy some defining criteria[52]. Hence, territorial waste management is defined in the regional plans that need to assure the implementation of measures for the reduction of waste production within the territories concerned as well as paying due attention to the identification of the appropriate sites for the construction of the disposal plants. Moreover, regions are expected to promote a series of initiatives aimed at reducing waste production and favouring re-use and recycling through the involvement of the public opinion and citizens. Provisions as lied down in the order 2006/252 were only tangentially modified by order n. 4 enacted in January 2008. Besides regulatory instruments, some economic instruments have also been promoted. These include the Sustainable Development Fund created in 2001, a series of tax waivers for enterprises producing bio-diesel and bio-ethanol and a regional tax for open cast sites.

Furthermore, the extended responsibility of the producer and importer was introduced in Italy and applied to packaging waste to improve their treatment and recycling. In this connection, the 'Ronchi' order instituted the eco-organisation CONAI[53] (Official Waste Packaging Recycling Association) to coordinate the action of a series of recovery consortia. CONAI signed an agreement with the National Association of Italian Municipalities (ANCI) to improve urban waste collection according to which, virtuous municipalities receive financial assistance and support in the communication and awareness campaigns at the local level. The former tax on municipal waste (TARSU), has been instead replaced by a mixed payment system based on both operating/maintenance costs and quantity produced by household, thus any longer depending on the surface area of the household property[54] (Chalmin and Gaillochet, 2009).

---

51. Such measures are meant to assure hygienic safety during all phases of waste management, the modalities for the collection and transportation of urban waste, the appropriate management of the different waste streams and their recycling, including weighting and quality-assessment operation before the eventual disposal of waste.

52. Amongst the criteria to be followed there is the pursuing of an integrated system for waste management, attaining a dimensionally efficient managerial system, an appropriate evaluation of the territorial capacity for transportation and communication, the full valorisation of the need of the municipalities present on the ATO perimeter and the careful evaluation of the existing conditions.

53. As of today CONAI is one of the biggest consortia of its kind in Europe with more than 1,400,000 affiliate enterprises. Additional information can be retrieved at: www.conai.org (accessed 10 November 2016).

54. Other tax-type instruments include the rates introduced for the reduction of waste production, a tax on incineration without energy recovery and above all the promotion of a market for 'Green certificate' so as to favour the production of energy from renewable resources.

Nonetheless, some recent changes that occurred in the legislative framework for the integrated management of waste, both domestically and at the level of the EU, are likely to partially modify the working modalities adopted thus far. In particular, the enactment of order n. 135 in 2009[55] for the progressive adaptation to the communitarian provisions in the field of services of general interest at the local level, foresees limits for public share in service societies, and above all public competitive tenders, so as to favour private interventions. Relevant for our topic in this case, is also the provision for dismantling the so-called 'in house' authorities by the end of 2011. Furthermore, new dispositions were foreseen by the budget act for 2010 and law order n. 2/2010 in terms of dismantling the functional consortia between local authorities in 2011 and the ultimate suppression of the existing territorial optimal areas (ATO). Future attribution of competences is loosely defined; nonetheless, regional authorities in respect of the principles of subsidiarity, differentiation and adequacy should decide competences[56].

This brief overview shows how the application of environmental laws and regulation in the waste management domain in Italy, not only has proceeded almost invariably as a response to corresponding European legislation, but it has mainly followed the 'regulatory way', in the form of governmental orders and laws. In the next section we make sense of the way the city of Turin, and in turn the main actors therein operating, have 'encountered' the EU within this specific area, by addressing, implementing and eventually making use of the instruments initially promoted by the EU and thereafter transposed into the Italian system, thus revealing the main mechanisms for Europeanisation. The PWD remains the yardstick for analysis.

The situation in Turin: logic of action

The frame legislation for the territorial organisation of waste management in the city of Turin – aimed to promote an integrated system of activities – is rooted in regional law n. 24/2000[57], which makes provisions for the creation of a series of *territorial optimal areas (ATO)*, generally corresponding to the provincial territory. In turn, the province of Turin is in charge of issuing and implementing the provincial plan for waste management. In compliance with the regional framework legislation for waste management, the present plan sets as overall objective for separate refuse waste collection at a percentage value of 52.1 per cent, whereas the new plan foresees an increase up to 55 per cent, with a specific value for the city of Turin set at 52 per cent[58]. Following the 2006 document,

---

55. These provisions feature in Art. 15 of the Order n. 135 (Decreto Ronchi) under the heading: adaptation to the communitarian discipline in the field of local economic public services.

56. Order n. 2/2010 is normatively converted into law n. 42 of March 2010.

57. *Norme per la gestione dei rifiuti.*

58. The current national legislation fixes an overall objective of 65 per cent for selected waste collection. The objective seems rather unattainable, whereas the province acts towards attaining a percentage target of 57 per cent including 50 per cent of effective recycling.

the new provincial plan for waste management, under negotiation in 2010, sets objectives and interventions for the 2010–20 period. Thus, the activities for the realisation and management of the technologic plants for the recycling and disposal of waste are organised within ATO-R[59], which includes a total of eight *basins* for the management of the structures aimed at waste collection, transport and the disposal of waste (basin services). The governing of activities for each of the basins and ATO are, in turn, carried out by the so-called *Consorzi obbligatori di bacino* (compulsory basin consortia) and *Associazioni d'ambito* (area associations), whereas *management companies* are in charge of the operational management of the activities. In particular, basin consortium '18' corresponds both territorially and institutionally to the city of Turin and represents 40 per cent of the provincial population (909.538 as of Dec. 2009) and covers an overall area of 130,5 km[60].

The consortium for the city of Turin is in charge of the procedures for waste disposal and of the agreement for the supply of service with AMIAT, a company mainly owned by the municipality, which is in charge of the actual management of the services for waste management[61]. Thus, the region, the province and the city of Turin in synergy with AMIAT, regulate – although with different competences – waste management in the territory of Turin. Besides that, waste management is coordinated via ATO-R, the Optimal Territorial Association, which was a 'Consorzio dei Comuni' prior to 2002. Additional provisions for waste management within the city territory are outlined in the municipal regulation n. 280/2002[62]. In particular, with this regulation the municipal administration sets up the specific modalities for the collection of different urban waste streams and establishes the corresponding sanctions to be applied in case of infringement of the provisions. Thus, provisions are made for the prevention of waste production, waste recovery (re-use and recycling) and services for waste collection.

---

59. *Associazione dambito Torinese per il governo dei rifiuti* was constituted in October 2005. ATO-R is in charge of accomplishing the so called 'Piano d'ambito' (Area Plan), in particular as to the parts of: waste streams (undifferentiated components); partial treatment of organic waste; organisation of waste disposal and distribution of the waste streams (www.atorifiutitorinese.it (accessed 10 November 2016)).

60. Some of the guiding principles of the EU Environment policy have been presented in Chapter Five. A more extended presentation of the fundamental legal principles here briefly introduced, reference is made to ACR + (2009); Chalmers (1994) and Scotford (2007).

61. The Turin Multi-services Company for Ambient Hygiene was a 'special company' of the municipality of Turin till 1997, whereas in 2000 it was transformed into a joint stock company. Since 2010, the city of Turin has been the only partner of AMIAT Ltd. The relation between AMIAT at the city of Turin is regulated through the so called 'service contract' lasting about fifteen years (to be renewed in 2011). The main tasks AMIAT is in charge of are: waste collection, cleaning of containers, cleaning of the public soil, waste treatment and discharge (www.amiat.it (accessed 10 November 2016)).

62. Municipal regulation n. 280/2002 endorsed via Municipal Council decision 12136/21 and entered into force from 24 June 2002 and subsequently modified through decision 11826/112 in April 2005.

In this connection, the main referent for the city of Turin as regards the sector of waste management is the provincial administration, even though the regional administration is also part of the systems deputed to the management of this sector. On the other hand, the municipal administration manages the actual collection and disposal of waste via the operative managements of AMIAT, which is also member of ACR+, the pan-European association of cities and regions for recycling and sustainable resource management[63]. This allows for accessing important information in the sector, to follow up the legislative evolution and development in the domain as well as to benchmark practices for waste management. Beside AMIAT, the city of Turin is also the main shareholder of TRM Ltd.[64], the company in charge of realising the new waste to energy plant in the Gerbido area (Turin south) by 2013.

Within its residual competences, the city of Turin – through the action of the Department for Environment – has promoted a series of actions to enhance both public awareness and the actual capacity for separate refuse collection in the urban territory. Therefore, initiatives for improving waste disposal and recycling were launched in 2004 in the context of the community programme URBAN II (*see* Chapter Nine) and recycling was promoted for all waste fractions and disseminated among 50 per cent of the city population, starting from the peripheral areas to be then progressively extended to its inner boroughs. A 'stand to stand' service for waste collection during open markets was promoted in 2005/2006 and experimental programmes addressed to specific commercial activities in the city and for the promotion of ecologic underground 'collecting islands' are currently undertaken.

Conclusions: insights into the Europeanisation of waste management

The financial shortages characterising Italian local administrations – especially in a high fixed-costs sector like waste management – associated with some organisational drawbacks in the system of waste collection[65], partly due to the specific infrastructural situation of the estates in Turin – will hinder the attainment of the overall targets for separate waste collection (50 per cent by 2013) as set in the Provincial Plan[66]. The recent endorsement of directive 2008/98 into the Italian system through order n. 205, in particular as to the parts concerning the collection

---

63. ACR+ is an international network of members who share the common aim of promoting sustainable consumption of resources and management of waste through prevention at source, reuse and recycling (www.acrplus.org (accessed 10 November 2016)).

64. TRM Ltd. (Trattamento Rifiuti Metropolitani) received the – *in house* – concession for the planning, realisation and management of the 'Gerbido' waste to energy plant in 2005 by the Province of Turin (www.trm.to.it (accessed 10 November 2016)).

65. The pathway towards a more efficient – target oriented – collection of municipal waste is additionally thwarted by the quality of separated rubbish as well as the problems of private differentiation of the plastic fractions.

66. The figure for the year 2009 was at around 42 per cent for separate waste collection for the city of Turin according to the 2010 provincial report on the state of the system for waste management.

and recycling of waste, has not translated into a clear set of plausibly attainable objectives and above all in the net distinction between the phases of collection and re-use/recycling.

The territorial organisation of waste management is deemed, by some, to suffer from *loose coordination*, where the provincial administration tends to mainly interact with the service company in charge of the management of waste (thus mainly with AMIAT). Nonetheless, the city of Turin remains national 'leader' amongst urban areas as to the overall level of separate waste collection, with a percentage of 42 per cent attained in 2010, and a plethora of actions – both legislative and operational – have been put in place during the period of time considered in the analysis.

Turning our attention to the transformations within the policy structures of the territorial system of Turin during the timeframe considered for the analysis of *regulation* as mode of Europeanisation – where EU directive 1999/30 (2008/98) is the *proxy instrument* selected to exemplify this mode – it is possible to formulate some considerations on the prospective character of the Europeanisation process.

The partial absence of a regulatory framework for waste management in the territory of Turin up until 2000, associated with an overall national situation where the majority of actions undertaken in the field of waste management (including packaging and packaging waste) are the consequence of legislative measures adopted by the EU since the mid-1990s, determine that also within the territorial system of Turin a prevalent bulk of instruments adopted were legislative in character[67], and followed – both temporally and in terms of their provisions – what was previously adopted since 1994 at the EU level. In this connection, amongst the monetary instruments promoted there is the TARSU tax, which was nonetheless already introduced in 1993 following national decree n.507/1993 and thereafter integrated locally via a mixed collecting system. Additionally, more 'target oriented' policy instruments, in the form of pilot projects to boost the system of separate collection of waste or extended awareness campaigns have been promoted, often in synergy between the municipal administration, the competent departments of the province and AMIAT.

Although the city administration does not directly take part in pan-European networks for waste management, the territory is 'represented' within the EU policy making by the participation of AMIAT and the provincial administration in the ACR+ thematic association. Additionally, the analysis reveals that the number of local actors involved in the system of waste management within the territory of Turin has increased during the period of time considered. These are moreover institutional collective actors – competent departments of the municipal, provincial and regional administrations – other municipalities of the metropolitan area of Turin, but also private collective actors taking part in public-private partnerships

---

67. Regional Law n. 59 for Waste Management (1997), the first provincial programme for waste management adopted in 1998, the city regulation n. 280 for municipal waste management and regional law n. 24 for waste management (2002), are the main legislative measures adopted within the territory of Turin in the field of waste management.

for the management of the service (AMIAT), instead of for the realisation of infrastructural plants (TRM Ltd.). Furthermore, also in this policy domain, the competences of the Mayor – thus also those of the municipal administration more generally – widened following the wave of reforms in 1993 and more importantly the reform of the constitutional chart's fifth deed in 2001[68].

Concerning the procedures that preside over policy making during its different phases as well as the policy styles eventually developing during the phase of program formulation and implementation, it is relevant to highlight the shift towards an integrated system for waste management. The original 'sectorial character' of the operations for waste management has progressively been replaced by a system where integration is applied both in terms of the sectors affected by the policy measures adopted[69] and the administrative bodies involved at the stage of policy programme formulation and implementation within the territory, as testified by the negotiation of the provincial waste plan. Despite following recommendations included in the national transposition acts of the corresponding European legislation, the integrated character of the structure for waste management clearly follows a trend initiated at the EU level, which recommends relevance to be given above all to prevention, recycling and re-use of waste. Furthermore, the system for the collection of information, data and statistics on the separate collection of waste and on waste streams is now also jointly managed by regional, provincial and municipal services.

Interviews with key actors at both the municipal and provincial departments dealing with waste management reveal how the main factor of change actually perceived is the significant increase in the percentage of collected waste, especially during the 2003–10 period. Nonetheless, differentiated waste collection and recycling are now maintained as 'acquired topics' within the territorial area of Turin. This translated into a greater consciousness of the local administrations and therefore in the increasing number of policy provisions adopted to improve the overall situation in this policy sector, and also into a different attitude of consumers towards the 'waste problem', which is now perceived more pro-actively, as testified by the relative success of the various projects promoted to improve the 'door to door' system for waste collection. In this connection, the advent of the Olympic Games in 2006 is also considered to have been conducive to greater awareness and then relative success within this policy domain.

---

68. Whether the 1993 reform led to the direct election of the mayors and the provincial governors, the reform promoted in 2001 involved a more encompassing redistribution of the territorial competences and the partial redefinition of the relations between the central administration and local authorities.

69. One amongst other examples is the promotion of an experimental system for 'door to door' waste collection within the environmental *volet* of the URBAN II community initiative for urban regeneration during the 2000–06 period.

7.5 New perspectives on waste management in the EU

Although the economic production and consumption in the EU evolved to become less waste intensive, the overall production of waste remains important; 2.5 billion tonnes of waste (about 5 tonnes per capita) were generated in the European Union in 2012[70]. Worth mentioning for the discussion on this occasion are the improvements recorded in the treatment of *municipal waste* in the EU, which represents some 10 per cent; the per capita fraction has decreased from 523 kg in 2007, to 474 kg per capita in 2014. Improvements have been recorded also in the proportion of waste recycled; in particular, the share of recycled or composted municipal waste in the EU-28 has shifted from 35 per cent in 2007 to 43.5 per cent in 2014, although a certain variation persists between countries. Whilst recycling of municipal waste reached around 64 per cent in Germany, it remained as low as 10 per cent in Slovakia, whereas the per capita fraction ranged from 752 kg in Denmark to 254 kg in Romania in 2013. Similarly, the overall progress towards the targets to recycle 50 per cent of household waste by 2020 – as foreseen in the Waste Framework Directive – has been patchy. According to the European Environmental Agency[71], while a number of member states has already achieved the 50 per cent threshold, a majority of EU countries need to maintain a steady annual increase of their recycling rate or accelerate the annual rate of increase to meet the target by 2020. However, nine countries (Cyprus, Czech Republic, Estonia, Greece, Hungary, Iceland, Malta, Poland and Portugal) will need an annual increase rate between two and four percentage points to achieve 50 per cent recycling in 2020.

Despite the progress made in the overall management of waste in Europe, a number of challenges persist; the varying monitoring systems and methods makes the available statistics often uncertain, thus often making difficult any comprehensive attempt to compare figures across different relevant directives or to interpret variation between territories. The lack of harmonised legislative framework outside the EU – and the often weaker requirements – creates the conditions for economic operators to export waste for treatment. Yet, the production of energy from waste (energy recovery of waste) may in some cases disincentives recycling as a waste treatment method. Concerning waste prevention, the most part of member states in the EU lack effective measures to limit the overall quantity of produced waste, thus hampering further the process of waste management.

Recent developments in waste management point to the opportunities offered by the shift towards a more *circular economy*, where higher economic value is given to the products and the materials they contains, rather than to the 'linear chain' of purchase and final disposal of products. This shift also implies that

---

70. Eurostat (env_wasgen), 2015. As for the breakdown of waste generation in the EU-29 by sector, while the greater fraction came from the construction sector (33 per cent) and manufacturing (11 per cent), household waste still represented about 8 per cent of the total.

71. European Environmental Agency, managing municipal solid waste – a review of achievements in thirty-two European countries, EEA Report n.2/2013.

growing policy attention is given to further limiting landfilling, thus investing additional action in promoting recycling, reuse and manufacturing. Shifting policy action and consumers behaviours towards the 'circular economy' paradigm would be justified on both environmental and economic rationales[72] (Bourguignon, 2015); higher recycling rates can contribute to reduce air, soil and water pollution, reduce greenhouse gas emissions and enhancing the status of ecosystems and biodiversity. This would also imply overall benefits for human health. Economic advantages of a circular approach could translate in additional jobs – despite the initial increase in the costs for sorting, collecting and recycling of waste, and net material cost savings for EU companies, varying according to the magnitude of the shift. It is against this background that in July 2014, the European Commission launched a circular economy package, which was soon replaced by a new set of legislative proposals in December 2015. The new package contains an action plan for the circular economy, mapping out a series of actions planned for the coming years, as well as four legislative proposals on waste, containing targets for landfill, reuse and recycling, to be met by 2030. The new legislative package contains a number of policy measures on waste management; these include – *inter alia* – new waste management targets to be met by 2030, in particular increasing the share of municipal waste prepared for reuse and recycling to 65 per cent. Additional measures foresee the introduction of an 'early monitoring system' for monitoring compliance with targets and the setting of minimum requirements for 'extended producer responsibility' schemes whereby the contribution paid by producers depends on the costs necessary to treat their products at the end of their life[73]. For the full deployment of a circular economy model – at least for the part regarding the management of waste, a number of challenges need to be accounted for by both policy makers and consumer. Thus, the shift of consumer behaviour and business models would require the adoption of new forms of finance to compensate for unavoidable transition costs (i.e. research and development, asset investments and subsidy payments) as well as the progressive introduction of a pricing system triggering the efficient resource reuse, incentives for producers and recyclers for improving performances. Additionally, the workforce would need new technical skills (i.e. eco-design) which are currently lacking, especially within the small and medium enterprises.

---

72. Bourguignon, D. (2015) Closing the Loop: *New Circular Economy Package*, EPRS 'Briefing' note, January 2016.

73. Other areas for action are provisioned in the *action plan* accompanying the new circular economy package. These includes improving product design and resource efficiency in production processes; regarding consumption, new actions are foreseen to better inform consumers about the sustainability of products through labelling. The Commission also intends to favour the creation of a market for secondary raw materials by setting quality standards for materials recovered from waste and to facilitate the safe use of treated wastewaters.

Chapter Eight

Europeanisation via Modes of Coordination: Ambient Air Quality Control and the Case of EU Directive 1999/30

8.1 Introduction

The European Union has been particularly active in the air quality sector over the last three decades. Apart from acting to mitigate the adverse effects of climate change – mainly by adopting measures for the control of greenhouse gases (Jordan, *et al.*, 2010) – a key objective of EU environmental legislation has been to improve the quality of ambient air, above all to limit the dangerous effects of polluted air on humans' health as well as the progressive eutrophication of the environment. Thus, measures in this sense have been adopted to control the emission of harmful substances in the atmosphere, improving the quality of fuels and by progressively integrating the requirements of environmental protection into the transport and energy sectors.

Despite significant progress in this direction having been made, and the emissions of certain substances reduced considerably, air pollution remains a source of concern, as limit values for certain pollutants – in particular ground-level ozone and fine particulates – are regularly exceeded (EEA, 2002; Baldasano *et al.*, 2002). In this connection, the European Commission calls for more action to be undertaken at various levels of regulation, both internationally and locally, where the damaging effects of air pollution loom largest. The inclusion of air pollution within the target area of environment and health of the sixth Environment Action Programme of the EU (European Commission, 2001a) is a first step in this direction.

In the field of EU clean-air policy, patterns of coordination within different systems of territoriality and during various phases of the policy process reflect the patchwork character of the EU action in this field. This is a process that has mainly proceeded through successive steps of interest accommodation between the European legislator and the diverse regulatory traditions of member states, where at times the regulatory style of one member state features as the yardstick for modelling European measures afterwards (Héritier, 2002)[1].

---

1. Similarly to the dynamics occurred in other fields within environmental policy (*see* Chapters Five and Six), also in the case of EU policy for clean air some national traditions have been imposing over others. Hence, for instance, some directives clearly reflect the German tradition of technology-based emission control, whilst others are more aligned with the British model of ambient air regulation.

For the gist of our analysis, it is relevant to point out that EU regulation in the policy field of air quality has traditionally followed logics of standard setting based on persuasion, reasoning and evidence-based measures aiming at effectiveness in reaching the prescribed levels of environmental quality. Majone often referred to standard setting as a regulative problem in his early works (Majone, 1992; 1994)[2]. Thus, effluent (or emission) standards set the quantity of certain types of pollutants that are allowed from a particular source. In particular, Majone shows how the common notion of purely scientifically based standards presents in fact serious fallacies (Majone, 1975; 1984). He argues that 'the popularity of standards is not due to their 'scientific' character but, on the contrary, to an intrinsic vagueness, hiding behind a specious appearance of precision, which offers strategic advantages to the regulated, both at the level of standard setting and in the process of implementation' (Majone, 1975: 8).

In this connection, we argue, considering the deployment of Directive 1999/30 – and its successive incorporation into the new 'framework directive' for air quality – that set limit values for the concentration of certain substances and promotes common methods for monitoring and evaluation, well exemplifies those modes where mechanisms of coordination are thought to be prevalent and the perspective influence of the EU on domestic systems is likely to trigger processes of Europeanisation within various arenas of policy in cities.

The remainder of this chapter is organised as follows. The next section shall give an introduction to the EU air quality policy by pointing out the structure of the EU air legislation, its guiding principles as well as the main policy instruments deployed by the EU to attain its objectives in this domain. It also presents the archetypal game model we contend as exemplifying the main properties of the interactions producing within this specific policy domain. Section 3 narrates the relevant historical background underpinning the promotion of EU directive 1999/30 and its merge into the renewed 'framework directive' in 2008. In the fourth section, the theoretical and analytical frameworks presented in Part I are used to examine the case of air quality policy in the city of Turin.

8.2 Air quality policy in the EU

Particularly over the last two decades, developed countries have paid increasing attention to air quality and to the adverse effects of polluted air on human health. Thus, various clean air plans have been adopted to introduce measures for the regulation of emissions, regular air quality monitoring in urban areas, and the promotion of less noxious fuels (Baldasano, et al., 2002).

In this connection, the EU acts within various jurisdictions in the attempt to ease the adverse consequences of air pollution and promote different instruments to pursue this objective. In particular, the EU Commission has oriented its

---

2. Distinction is made between different types of standards in environmental policy in terms of ambient (or environmental quality) standards, affluent (or emission) standards and technical standards.

action towards the development of an overall strategy for air quality control and prevention, wherein member states are expected to transpose and implement a series of directives that set long-term objectives. Thus for instance, the launch of the CAFE[3] programme in 2001 opened a new phase in the EU policy for air quality, which led to issuing a thematic strategy on air pollution setting objectives for the reduction of certain pollutants and reinforcing the legislative framework in this sector through the mainstream of air quality issues into related policy areas.

Within this portrayal, not only are urban areas the places where the adverse effects of poor air quality conditions loom largest – mainly due to the use of road vehicles – but also the contexts where practical solutions are often put in place, monitoring and assessment of air quality are performed and where most information is collected to allow the overall evaluation of air quality trends, thus eventually facilitating the elaboration of most efficient solutions.

Principles and structure of air quality legislation

Standards and objectives are set through EU legislative measures for various pollutants. These are applied over diverse time spans, to account for different health impacts associated with the exposure to various pollutants.

Certain basic principles are at the foundation of EU air quality legislation; these are, in turn, recalled within the air quality directives, in particular in the parts dealing with implementation and management. Thus, the principle of *zoning* foresees the division of national territories in zones and agglomerations for the assessment of air pollution levels through measurements and other techniques. On the other hand, *assessment* implies the actual measurement of air quality and the evaluation of the compliance with the environmental standards fixed by the EU and domestically; *management* of air pollution is about the promotion of measures aimed at reducing the adverse effects of air pollution on human health. These can be undertaken at the EU level as well as integrated with national initiatives in air quality plans that outline their nature and methods for implementation. The principle of *information* – cornerstone in this field – requires providing a minimum amount of information to the public as to the assessment of concentrations, as well as the public availability of abatement plans and programs. Related to information, *reporting results* is thereafter required by the Commission to assess the compliance with the standards as set in the directives and to enable the public to have access to harmonised information on air quality.

In this connection, EU legislation on air quality has developed in an overall attempt to preserve levels of air quality sensitive to human health and the

---

3.   Clean Air for Europe Programme. Its aim was to establish a long-term, integrated strategy to tackle air pollution and to protect against its effects on human health and the environment, which substantiated in the Commission communication of 4 May 2001 'The Clean Air for Europe (CAFE) programme: towards a thematic strategy for air quality'.

environment. Thus, in line with the provisions of Art. 174 TEC[4], the relevant EU legislative action for the management and quality of ambient air applicable to all member states can be summarised in the first air quality framework directive 96/62/EC[5], in the so called 'daughter' directives[6] 1999/30, 2000/69, 2002/03 and 2004/107 on limit values for different pollutants, and the new air quality and cleaner air for Europe directive 2008/50/EC that proposes – within others – the progressive merging of the existing legislation.

The first 'ambient air quality' framework directive of 1996 established the basic principles of a common strategy to define and set objectives for ambient air quality based on common methods and criteria for the assessment and diffusion of information on air quality. In particular, methods to monitor air quality within the territories of member states were indicated in the directive, where assessment would have been compulsory in urban areas with more than 250,000 inhabitants or in areas with concentration values close to the threshold limits. Furthermore, the directive brought about requirements for member states to draw up a list of the areas and conurbations where pollution levels exceed the limit values and to provide information accordingly. Together with the 'daughter directives' fixing limit values and long term objectives for specific pollutants, a series of implementing measures[7] in the form of decision has been subsequently adopted to provide further guidance especially as to reporting and submission of information[8]. European legislation has been revised by Directive 2008/50/EC, which established

---

4. In particular, according to Art. 174 the Community policy on the environment shall contribute to pursuit of the following objectives: preserving, protecting and improving the quality of the environment; protecting human health; prudent and rational utilisation of natural resources; promoting measures at international level to deal with regional or worldwide environmental problems.

5. Council Directive 96/62/EC of 27 September 1996 on ambient air quality assessment and management.

6. Council Directive 1999/30/EC relating to limit values for sulphur dioxide, nitrogen dioxide and oxides of nitrogen, particulate matter and lead in ambient air; Directive 2000/69/EC of the European Parliament and of the Council relating to limit values for benzene and carbon monoxide in ambient air; Directive 2002/3/EC of the European Parliament and of the Council relating to ozone in ambient air; Directive 2004/107/EC of the European Parliament and of the Council relating to arsenic, cadmium, mercury, nickel and polycyclic aromatic hydrocarbons in ambient air.

7. Decision 2004/461/EC laying down a questionnaire to be used for annual reporting on ambient air quality assessment under Council Directives 96/62/EC and 1999/30/EC and under Directives 2000/69/EC and 2002/3/EC of the European Parliament and of the Council; Decision 2004/279/EC concerning guidance for implementation of Directive 2002/3/EC of the European Parliament and of the Council relating to ozone in ambient air; Decision 2004/224/EC laying down arrangements for the submission of information on plans or programmes required under Council Directive 96/62/EC in relation to limit values for certain pollutants in ambient air.

8. Council Decision 97/101/EC of 27 January 1997 establishing a reciprocal exchange of information and data from networks and individual stations measuring ambient air pollution within the member states. In particular, the decision introduces a reciprocal exchange of information and data from the networks and stations set up in member states and the air quality measurements taken by those stations.

a new comprehensive framework for air quality control in Europe by progressively merging previously adopted measures.

A concrete attempt to establish an integrated strategy to tackle air pollution is represented by the Clean Air for Europe programme (CAFE), launched in 2001. Amongst the main objectives of CAFE there were the establishment of a system for developing, collecting and validating scientific information on the effects of air pollution, the support to effective implementation of the existing legislation on air quality and the eventual development of new proposals to favour the appropriate observance of the requisite measures.

Furthermore, the programme aimed at developing new systems for the dissemination of information, meaning the information gathered during its development and also relating to air quality values that is collected in different EU countries. The main proposal issued in this context was, nonetheless, the development of an overall thematic strategy for air quality.

Therefore, the thematic strategy on air pollution[9] launched in 2005 (to be revised in 2010) set objectives and limit values for the concentration of certain pollutants so as to avoid excessive damages on human health, thus proposing measures to achieve these objectives by 2020[10]. A further simplification of the existing legislation was also proposed, as it was the modernisation of the monitoring and measurement systems for ambient air quality. Relevant in this sense is also the declared intention to improve the coherence with other environmental policies, in particular with those bearing a direct impact on the emission of pollutants in the atmosphere – namely policies for energy use, transport policies regulating the use of cars and heavy-duty vehicles, industrial policies and agricultural policies concerning the use of animal feedings and fertilisers.

Archetypal game model

Taking into account the actual limits of the Prisoners' Dilemma in exemplifying interactions where mechanisms of coordination are prevailing, modes of coordination in our typology can be generally represented – we maintain – by the well-known *Assurance Game*[11], where players have a clear common interest in coordinating on common efficient options, hence providing both of them with

---

9. Communication of 21 September 2005 from the Commission to the Council and the European Parliament – Thematic Strategy on Air Pollution, COM (2005) 446.

10. Main objectives were: 47 per cent reduction in loss of life expectancy as a result of exposure to particulate matter; 10 per cent reduction in acute mortalities from exposure to ozone; reduction in excess acid deposition of 74 per cent and 39 per cent in forest areas and surface freshwater areas respectively; 43 per cent reduction in areas or ecosystems exposed to eutrophication.

11. 'Assurance game' is a generic name for the game more commonly known as 'Stag Hunt'. The French philosopher, Jean-Jacques Rousseau, presented the following situation. Two hunters can either jointly hunt a stag (an adult deer and rather large meal) or individually hunt a rabbit (tasty, but substantially less filling). Hunting stags is quite challenging and requires mutual cooperation. If either hunts a stag alone, the chance of success is minimal. Hunting stags is most beneficial for society but requires a lot of trust among its members.

their best possible payoffs (s.A-S.A). As such, the game features the character of games of pure coordination; we need nonetheless to account for the risk factor involved. If, for instance, one of the two parties chooses to defect, then the other part that has decided to 'cooperate' will end up with the worst possible outcome (s.A/S.B). In this connection, if the player that has decided to cooperate is unable to trust others' understanding of the common situation, he would be logically led to defect in order to avoid the worst-case outcome of a cooperate/defect situation.

If also the other player in our example should be persuaded by the same initial uncertainty, then both would end up with an overall second-worst outcome solution (s.B/S.A). There are two pure strategy equilibriums[12]: s.A/S.A and s.B/S.B. Both players prefer one equilibrium to the other (A/A) – which is both Pareto optimal and Hicks optimal. However, the inefficient equilibrium is less risky than the payoff variance over the other player's strategies is

$p1$ \ $p2$	S. A		S. B	
s.A		4		3
	4		0	
s.B		0		3
	3		3	

lower. Specifically, one equilibrium is payoff-dominant while the other is risk-dominant[13]. The game owes its name – *assurance* – to the fact that, when played out in the normal form, each player needs to assure the others that he is going to play the most risky strategy, so the other can act accordingly. Additionally, we argue, in real interaction, this type of game is more likely to be played in situations of *incomplete information*. Agents, in this eventuality, do not know the payoffs of the other players and the game; nonetheless, the game can be transformed – formally at least – into complete but *imperfect information* by simply including a fictional player (nature) in the game that moves first[14], thus drawing the utility functions of the agents from a probability distribution (known by players), thus conditioning payoffs on nature's (unknown) moves.

Thus, for the purposes of our analysis, the game in its most simple form reminds us of the great importance of actors' perceptions and mutual predictability in social

---

12. A 'pure strategy' is one that selects (in a given circumstance) a certain 'move' or behaviour with certainty. This approach is contrasted with a 'mixed strategy,' which involves (in a given circumstance) selecting between at least two moves with some probabilities that sum to one. Accordingly, in a pure strategy equilibrium, 'each player adopts a particular strategy with certainty,' whereas in a mixed strategy equilibrium 'one or more of the players adopts a strategy that randomises among a number of pure strategies'. See McCarty and Meirowitz (2007) on this point.

13. Pareto optimality is a measure of efficiency. An outcome of a game is Pareto optimal if there is no other outcome that makes every player at least as well off and at least one player strictly better off. That is, a Pareto optimal outcome cannot be improved without hurting at least one player. Often, a Nash Equilibrium is not Pareto optimal implying that the players' payoffs can all be increased. Hicks' optimality is also a measure of efficiency. An outcome of a game is Hicks optimal if there is no other outcome that results in greater total payoffs for the players.

14. Harsany has first introduced this standard practice in 1968. For a formal definition of games of incomplete information and their modelling, see McCarty and Meirowitz (2007, ch.6).

interactions, as well as of the value of argumentation between the actors involved (Majone, 1994). It also points out the role that 'external actors', such as the EU – European Commission – can exercise towards enhancing reciprocal assurance between the agents and their role in limiting the preference set.

8.3 Implementing Directive 1999/30/EC (and 'framework directive' 2008/50)

As showed in the previous section, in the attempt to improve the quality of ambient air, the EU has acted mainly by setting standards for the concentration values of various pollutants, such as sulphur dioxide, nitrogen dioxide and oxide, particulate matters and leads, as well as establishing alert thresholds for the concentration of sulphur dioxide and nitrogen oxide in ambient air.

In this connection, the Council Directive 1999/30/EC represents the earliest EU – legislative – instrument to coordinate action towards the achievement of a better quality of ambient air. In particular, the 'first daughter directive' contained limit values for concentration of sulphur dioxide, nitrogen dioxide and oxide from nitrogen, particulate matter and lead[15]. For each of these substances, the directive lays down upper and lower assessment thresholds and asks member states to draw up a list of zones and agglomerations within which the margin of tolerance for the limit values is exceeded[16]. In turn, member states must take action to ensure that an action plan that makes the achievement of the limit value possible is drawn up and implemented within the fixed deadlines.

As to particulate matters $PM_{2.5}$ and PM_{10} the directive foresees the installation – by member atates – of appropriate measuring stations to collect data on concentrations. Within nine months from the end of each year, member states must inform the Commission on the assessed measurements. Furthermore, member states are asked to assure the collection of *up to date* information on the pollutants concentrations and to make it available to the public, to appropriate bodies as well as to the European Commission for all the other pollutants.

The new air quality 'framework directive' 2008/50/EC – that progressively repeals directive 96/62/EC and the four 'daughter directives' – confirms the mechanism for air quality management and more specifically addresses some polluting substances that are particularly dangerous for human health.

In particular, the new directive sets out for the definition of objectives for ambient air quality designed to reduce harmful effects on human health and the environment, evaluating air quality according to common methods and standards, collecting information on ambient air quality so as to make this information

---

15. The limit values for the concentration of the pollutants addressed by directive 1999/30/EC are indicated in table 8.1.

16. The alert threshold levels set for the pollutants addressed in directive 1999/30/EC correspond to 500 µg/m³ measured over three consecutive hours at locations representative of air quality over at least 100 km² for sulphur dioxide and 400 µg/m³ measured over three consecutive hours for nitrogen dioxide.

available to the public, and maintaining air quality conditions or eventually improving them, through appropriate actions to be undertaken domestically.

Directive 2008/50 defines the concepts of limit values, target values, information threshold, alert threshold and critical level, thus fixing targets and threshold of evaluation for the emission in the atmosphere of certain pollutant substances[17]. In this connection, member states shall designate the competent authorities for evaluating the quality of ambient air and ensuring the accurate measurement pollution levels. Additionally, national administrations must put in place systems to guarantee the coordination of initiatives promoted by the EU to protect air quality as well as establish zones and agglomerations for evaluation and reporting.

Therefore, specific methodologies and measurement criteria are set for each pollutant covered by the directive and measuring stations must be set up territorially. As regards the management of air quality, the appropriate authorities must guarantee the maintenance of the *status quo* and eventually improvements where the levels lie under the limit value; otherwise they must implement air quality plans in order to achieve the limit or target values where the limits are exceeded. In particular, management plans must be organised according to the planned zones and agglomerations where the limit values are surpassed. Short-term action plans are instead foreseen wherever the risk of exceeding one or more alert thresholds is envisaged. These plans define the action to be undertaken to avoid the risk, in particular through the temporary interruption of the activities co-responsible for the risk or via measures for traffic suspension and the regulation of domestic heating.

Exemptions from the application of limit values for PM_{10} are nonetheless granted to those member states characterised by zone or agglomeration, where the limit value cannot be achieved because of specific adverse climatic conditions or cross-border circumstances.

8.4 Taking stock of coordination: air quality control in Turin

In European cities, urban sustainable strategies are put in place to contrast air pollution. Integrated solutions are therefore necessary to prevent the excessive concentration of pollutant substances, in particular nitrogen dioxide and particulate matters ($PM_{2.5}$ and PM_{10}), which are amongst the major responsible for urban pollution caused by excessive traffic jams, bad fuels quality, obsolete vehicles and inappropriate heating and air conditioning systems.

---

17. In particular, the protection of human health is framed in the concept of *information threshold*: a level beyond which there is a risk to human health from brief exposure for particularly sensitive sections of the population and for which immediate and appropriate information is necessary; *alert threshold*: a level beyond which there is a risk to human health from brief exposure for the population as a whole and for which immediate steps are to be taken by the member states and *critical level*: a level fixed on the basis of scientific knowledge, above which direct adverse effects may occur on some receptors, such as trees, other plants or natural ecosystems but not on humans.

Thus, the variety of causes at the source of increasing levels of air pollution has induced European cities to undertake general action plans, not only to contrast contingent emergency factors, but above all to reach the gradual reduction of pollutant substances in the transport and public housing sectors, which are generally recognised as the principal sources of particulate matters production within urban areas.

As to the case of northern Italian cities, in particular those located in the Po-valley – including the city of Turin – the concentrations of pollutant substances remain well above the alert thresholds established by the EU, thus exposing inhabitants to a situation of risk. With a specific decision in 2009, the European Commission granted Italy an extension relative to PM_{10} for five zones, whereas a second decision emanated in 2010 declined the second Italian request for further extension, thus approving just a single respite for a zone in the region Campania.

Many local administrations in northern Italy yet embarked on infrastructural and organisational initiatives aimed at reducing the emissions and concentrations of pollutants, although this does not seem to be enough to attain the standards as fixed by the new directive 2008/50/EC. In this connection, recommendations point to the need of strengthening integrated urban strategies able to take into full account the geographical characteristics of the territory as well as the organisational assets of the cities (CITTALIA, 2010).

Legislative context and air quality control in Italy

The Italian system for air quality is originally based on statutory order n. 351/99[18] that transposed EU directive 96/62. In particular, according to the decree, regional administrations have the duty to define plans for improving air quality; regional plans must include indications as to air quality assessment, the specification of zones and agglomerations as well as the concrete actions to be implemented to improve air quality. Further to that, statutory order n. 60/2002 – transposing into the Italian system directive 1999/30/EC – confirmed what was previously established, although with specific reference to the pollutants addressed in the European legislative act. Finally, the new 2008/50 EU directive was acknowledged through order n. 155/2010[19] that substantially confirmed the system for air quality management previously established.

As regards the territorial division of competences within the policy area of air quality in Italy, the central administration – Ministry for Environment (thereinafter MATTM) – sets the limit values and air quality targets, whereas regions organise the operational roles of local administration through regional laws. In this connection, it is up to the regional administrations to fix the criteria for air quality assessment and the operational plans aimed at predisposing actions

18. 'Attuazione della direttiva 96/62/CE in materia di valutazione e di gestione della qualità dell'aria ambiente'.

19. 'Attuazione della direttiva 2008/50/CE relativa alla qualità dell'aria ambiente e per un'aria più pulita in Europa'.

for the prevention, preservation and eventually the amelioration of air quality, also by setting limit values for the concentration of pollutants. Provinces instead are in charge of identifying – on the bases of regional criteria and limit values – the territorial zones where it is necessary to intervene and action must be undertaken to contrast pick phenomena of atmospheric pollution. Municipalities are therefore in charge of approving provincial plans and of organising structural interventions for the amelioration of air quality conditions, and – relevant in this case – can decide on traffic control and limitations.

As for the concentration of pollutants within the Italian territory, data confirms that over 40 per cent of total PM_{10} and NO_2 emissions originate in the Po Valley (CITTALIA, 2010). Over concentration of these pollutants is therefore due to a concatenation of factors that relate to the morphology of this portion of territory and to atmospheric conditions of high stability, scarce ventilation and seasonal rainfalls that do not favour the dispersion of air pollutants. Additionally, the territory is characterised by high concentrations of road traffic, settlements and industrial activities. Therefore, the daily limit value for PM_{10} (50 μg/m3 not to be overcome more than thirty-five days in a year) has been regularly surpassed in almost all the urban measurement stations of the Po-Valley, where also the values recorded in the non-urban stations revealed excessive concentrations, thus confirming the persistence of highly unfavourable background conditions[20].

Within this rather deluding portrayal, the initiatives undertaken by some mayors led to positive results for the possible amelioration of air quality conditions. This occurred despite the absence of emergency provisions at the national level and the increasing levels of house settlements (and heating systems) and road traffic.

In particular, cities' administrations have sought to promote the use of methane plants through district heating systems; initiatives have also been deployed to facilitate alternative mobility, especially to promote the use of public transports, the realisation of more efficient cycle lanes and new limited traffic areas in the inner parts of the cities[21].

Logic of action in the city of Turin

The role of the city of Turin in the policy domain of air quality mainly follows the provisions of Regional Law n.43/2000[22], which gives application to the measures endorsed at the central level. It specifies the distribution of competences to provinces and municipalities and lies down the regional plan for air quality

---

20. In 2009, the limit value for PM_{10} was attained in fifty-seven out of eighty-eight provincial capital cities (equal to 65 per cent of the total).

21. ISTAT data for 2008 reports that the limited traffic areas in the provincial capital cities of the Po Valley grew from 2000 to 2007 by 22 per cent and the total length of cycle lane approximate now to 1200km.

22. Regional Law 7 April 2000, n. 43, laying down dispositions for environmental protection within matters of atmospheric pollution and including the first actuation of the regional plan for the recovery and preservation of air quality.

control. In particular, the plan details the criteria for air quality assessment, outlines the classification of the regional territory in zones and agglomerations and sets the range of emergency actions to be undertaken in case acute episodes of air pollution occur[23].

Overall, the regional government is responsible for matters of orientation and coordination, whereas, according to regional law 43/2000, the provinces are in charge of drawing up action plans to be implemented in coordination with the municipalities. The latter instead, undertake concrete and final actions.

In this connection, the actual role played by the city of Turin in the domain of air quality control can be summarised through the competences of the Environmental Department of the city in this sector. In particular, the municipality is in charge of collecting and managing different data sets on various streams of pollutants and diffusing information on air quality in collaboration with ARPA, as well as undertaking actions for the regulation of vehicular traffic in relationship with the Department for Mobility. The mayor, as 'responsible for the protection of citizens' health' is authorised by the *Testo Unico Enti Locali* (Single Law on Local Authorities)[24] to adopt extraordinary measures, such as the 'urban traffic limitations'. The city has acted prevalently within the 'negotiation table' of the province without renouncing nonetheless to adopt 'autonomous measures' in coordination with other urban areas (such as daily traffic limitations)[25]. In particular, a new limited traffic area accessible to only ecologic vehicles was established in 2004.

Additional actions and initiatives have been therefore promoted to favour the use of public transport and to boost the sustainability of individual displacement. This can be summarised, on one hand, in the introduction of green procurement plans in 2004 in collaboration with the competent provincial authority, the presentation and successive realisation of a new system of bicycle paths in 2004, the realisation of a new underground line in 2006[26] as well as the prolongation of the Porta Nuova rail station to the adjacent Lingotto rail station. On the other hand, new forms of individual mobility were promoted via the launch of a new system for car sharing and an efficient system of bike sharing in 2010[27], backed by a series of economic incentives to favour the purchase of low-impact/environmentally-friendly means of transport. Relevant in this sense, have also been the recent adoption of an Urban

---

23. Regional law 43/2000 was endorsed when the 'new' EU directives were not yet transposed into the national system.

24. Order n. 267/2000 'Testo unico delle leggi sull'ordinamento degli enti locali'.

25. There is indeed a growing concern for the state of air quality within the Po-Valley; in this respect it is worth mentioning the so-called 'Mayors Alliance' signed in 2010 to which more than 200 municipalities adhered. The participant signed a document containing target values for air quality and the coordinated traffic bans during specific days of the year.

26. This is the first automated underground line introduced in Italy. In particular, line 1 connects the peripheral city of Collegno with the inner part of Turin and carries 80.000 passengers on average every day.

27. The new bike sharing system 'To Bike' allows users to collect a bicycle in one of the 116 bike stations in the city and is endowed with a total of 1200 bicycles.

Plan for Sustainable Mobility (PUMS) in 2010 – first national experience of this kind – that lays down guidelines for the realisation of initiatives and infrastructural actions over the next 10–15 years, and the adhesion of the city of Turin to the EU 'Covenant of Mayors' programme for CO_2 emission reduction (*see* Chapter Six).

Conclusions: insights into the Europeanisation of air quality control

Despite the implementation of several action plans for air quality control, the territory of Turin remains mainly characterised by zones where the limit values for certain pollutants (in particular PM_{10} and NO_2) are constantly overcome. The particular morphological conformation of this area, together with adverse meteorological conditions – scarce ventilation and seasonal precipitations – plays an unfavourable role in this sense.

Nonetheless, interviews revealed how scarce coordination at various levels of administration – especially in the attempt to effectively comprehend the causes leading to the huge gap in achieving the standards for emissions – is the main hindrance for the actual respect of the limit values. In turn, this translates into delays in implementing the legislative provisions at the regional level as well as in the sub-optimal division of territorial competences at the national level. In this connection, in 2008 the whole country asked for a temporary dispensation on the limit values for $PM_{10,}$ to compensate for a situation characterised by the absence of a coherent national plan and where the transposition of the new EU 'air quality' directive 2008/50 is still somehow uncertain at the moment of writing.

Notwithstanding a rather deluding national situation, where the existing policy for air quality control is moreover the resultant of a series of contingent measures to face critical situations and where the provisions attached to the EU action in this field feature, at time as a indispensable lifebuoy, at time as untenable constraints, there has been room for innovation and progress within the localities. EU opportunities as well as constraints have been used for the amelioration of urban territories and their air quality.

In this connection, our analysis shows that even in the case of the policy for air quality control as related to the deployment of the EU directive 1999/30 – and directive 2008/50 later on – national measures have been adopted in order to respond to EU requirements, although the implementation of these requirements mainly bears on local authorities. It is within cities and local territories that concrete actions to contrast the adverse effects of air pollution are elaborated and eventually promoted.

Thus, in the specific case of Turin, where the air quality conditions have traditionally been critical and to some extent continue to remain above threshold, the action of specific sectors – and individuals – in the municipal, provincial and regional administration, not only has led to the efficient promotion of contrasting and proactive measures for air quality control, but eventually to the amelioration of air quality (at least for certain pollutants) within an objectively problematic context. Our narrative in this case reveals how the legitimacy of local actors underwent decisive changes during the period of examination, both in terms of actors' discretion to take initiative somehow independently of central authorities and *vis-à-vis* the European legislator, which recommends actions to be taken as close as possible to the source of the problem to be tackled. Therefore, although neither the city of Turin, nor the other local administrations acting in the territory, directly take part in the *fora* for discussion and group of experts at the EU level[28]– notably within the council – renewed synergies were put in place for the elaboration and implementation of the regional plans for air quality and provincial plans for action. This was especially for the part concerning assessment, measurement and diffusion of information on air quality in collaboration with research institutes such as ARPA and ISPRA.

As to the instruments eventually promoted over the last decade to contrast air pollution and to incentive alternative use of transport, a bulk of initiatives can be attributed to the municipality of Turin, especially to the mayor and the different services within the department for environment and the mobility sector. In this connection, although generalised urban toll for vehicles transiting in the inner part of the city (a solution employed in many other urban cities in Europe) were not introduced in Turin, the surface of limited traffic areas has been substantially increased during the period considered for the analysis and a renewed system for vehicle certification ('bollino blu') was instituted in 2003. Furthermore, the mayor (Mr Chiamparino during the 2001–11period) exercised his special competencies in this sector several times through the establishment of traffic closures in coordination with the mayors of the other main cities of the Po-Valley.

Concerning the procedures underpinning policy development in this domain – similarly to the case of waste management – different administrations acting in the territory of Turin have sought to tap the benefit of the integrated approach as promoted by the EU. Therefore, whether horizontal integration has translated into initiatives undertaken within different policy sectors but with high reach on matters of air quality, the vertical outlook revealed more problematic. As reported, action coordination was perceived (sub)-optimal at the local level, instead more difficult *vis-à-vis* the central administration, which is often deemed to be inconsistent as to the measures promoted, and somehow lacking in terms of coordinating actions with the localities. Besides embarking on a more integrated approach to tackle the issue of air pollution, new procedures for data collection and evaluation were put in place. In particular, through the monitoring system set up by the competent service of the provincial administration – where seven out of twenty-eight detection stations are located in the city of Turin – data are collected and elaborated by ARPA, which is in charge of the technical management of the regional system for monitoring air quality. Therefore, data on air quality are benchmarked between the municipal, provincial and regional level, and eventually comparatively analysed regionally in view to their submission to the national competent authority, which is in turn expected to report annually to the European Commission.

---

28. Amongst the *fora* where air quality issues are debated there are the 'expert' working groups within the council (part of the co-decision procedure), the consultation process in place for the impact assessment of matters linked to air quality as well as the groups of inter-services consultation.

Actors at the local level commonly recognise that since the introduction of the first EU directive on ambient air quality in 1999 – directive 96/62/EC – attention has been more decidedly focused on matters of sustainable development – in particular sustainable urban mobility – and more generally on the necessity to move towards policy integration also in the sector of air quality control. This tendency is further strengthened by the successive promotion of more detailed EU measures – directives 1999/30/EC and 2008/50 – which led to change in the perception of the specific problems linked to air quality and favoured the endorsement of initiatives in a sector not fully regulated by law. In this connection, many of the officers directly involved in air quality management witness a partial modification of policy makers' attitudes and perceptions after EU requirements became local policy yardsticks. At the same time though, the influence of the EU within this policy domain is often identified with the economic sanctions applied when air quality standards are not attained. Hence, not only the city of Turin – which is nonetheless at the forefront in contrasting air pollution – but also the other major Italian cities (through ANCI) are urging both the EU and national authorities for greater financial resources to be attributed directly to local administrations to grant interventions in this specific – and highly complex – sector. Public administrations – and notably the mayors – in urban territories are aware of the necessity to boost synergic agreements between municipal administrations in the same territory, where policy actions to ameliorate air quality can be more efficiently pursued.

8.5 A renewed EU policy for air quality?

Over the last decade, significant progress – both in terms of legislative quality on the subject and day by day practice – has been made to curb the levels of air pollution in the European Union, the negative impacts of pollutant emissions on the environment and human health still loom large. According to the figures released by the European Environment Agency, the emission of most pollutants (i.e. sulphure oxide, nickel, carbon monoxide, nitrogen oxide, non-methane volatile organic compounds) has been decreasing between 2003 and 2012 – also due to the downturn of the EU economy over the same period, so did the overall emission rate of different sectors (e.g. with the transport sector that achieved the highest reduction in carbon monoxide, 61 per cent and nitrogen oxide, 29 per cent)[29]. Concerning the possible adverse effects of air pollution on human health, high concentrations of $PM_{2.5}$ and ozone in the atmosphere; have been deemed as particularly impacting. Estimates showed that in 2011 concentrations of these two pollutants were responsible respectively for 43,0000 and 16,000 premature deaths in the EU28[30]. From an environmental point of view, the main effects of air pollution remain the excessive presence of nutrients in soil and water (eutrophication) that

---

29. European Environment Agency/Eurostat (env_air_emis (accessed 10 November 2016)), 2003–13.

30. According to the impacts assessment analysis of the European Commission accompanying the 'Clean Air Programme for Europe', the health-related costs of air pollution in the EU are estimated in the range of Euro 330 and 940 billion per year.

may lead to the exhaustion of oxygen and the progressive change of soil's pH level – acidification – mainly due to the concentration of sulphur and nitrogen compounds. Considering the legislative/regulatory environment, today's air policy in the EU is structured around the Clean Air Programme for Europe framework; this is made of a series of acts related to different sources of pollution on the one side[31], and three major legal acts on the other. Thus, the 'Ambient Air Quality' directive defines binding limits values for the concentration of the main air pollutants in the atmosphere and requires member states to define zones where to monitor, manage and assess ambient air quality; the directive on 'arsenic, cadmium, mercury, nickel and polycyclic aromatic hydrocarbons in ambient air' sets instead non-binding targets for the concentration of these substances; thirdly, the 'National Emission Ceiling' directive (NECD), which sets maximum amounts of four pollutants responsible for acidification, eutrophication and ground-level ozone that each member state is entitled to emit every year as of 2010. As to the requirements set in the 'Ambient Air Quality Directive', 2014 data shows that about two thirds of EU member states were non-compliant with the limit values of emission fixed for particulate matters (PM_{10}) and nitrogen oxide, whereas the target value for fine particulate matters ($PM_{2.5}$) were exceeded in six member states over the same year; thus, infringement procedures were launched by the European Commission against twenty-three of the twenty-eight member states. Amongst the factors undermining the attainment of the set target and limits there would be the over reliance on domestic heating and the lack of adapted filtering systems in industrial plants (this applies in particular for PM_{10}) and on heavy traffic in large urban areas, where diesel vehicles constitute the primary cause of persisting exceedances (in particular for the emission of NO_2). On this latter aspect, some impute the persistence of such a situation to the non-delivery of Euro standards for diesel passenger cars and light duty vehicles, whilst others maintain that a complete ban on diesel vehicles in inner cities areas would be necessary to achieve compliance[32]. In respect of the 'National Emission Ceiling' directive, a new proposal – which would repeal the current legislative act – has been tabled by the European Commission in December 2013; this sets binding reduction targets for 2020 and 2030 and introduces ceilings also for fine particulate matters and methane as well as introducing flexibility mechanisms. As reported in the impact assessment analysis accompanying the new proposal, the efficient implementation of the new requirement would entail benefits for Euro 40 billion per year, against a cost of compliance estimated in the range of Euro 3.3 and 2.2 billion. Contextually, potential adverse impact may occur for the competitiveness of sectors exposed to

---

31. The main legal acts attached to the Clean Air Programme for Europe relate to different sectors, such as 'road transport' (Euro 5 and Euro 6 Regulation, directive on clean and energy-efficient vehicles, directive on volatile organic compounds from petrol), 'non-road transport' (directive on the sulphur content of certain fuels), and 'industry' (pollution prevention and control directive, large combustion plant directive, industrial emissions directive).

32. A complete analysis of the implementation of the 'Ambient Air Quality' directive has been performed on behalf of the European Parliament Committee on Environment, Public Health and Food Safety.

international competition (i.e. petroleum refining and agriculture, chemicals, iron and steel). Thus, under the current regulatory arrangements, it is rather unlikely that the objectives set for 2020 in the clean air policy package will be achieved for particulate matters, fine particulates and nitrogen oxide; depending on the implementation of the existing emission reduction technologies, full compliance – at least for particulate matters – with limit values is deemed more likely to be achieved by 2030.

Chapter Nine

Europeanisation via Modes of Distribution: Regional Policy and the Case of the Community Initiative URBAN II

9.1 Introduction

Over the last two decades, the European Union – particularly on the initiative of the Commission – has played an increasing role seeking to favour and shape development within urban and city areas. The 'Urban Policy' of the EU has developed, so far, mostly within the competences of the EU for economic and social cohesion and its funding mechanisms. Even within this 'policy realm', the European Commission maintains the formal right of initiative to the council and the European Parliament. In reason of this right, the Commission promotes policy development and to include proposals from relevant stakeholders, such as *cities*. Moreover, thanks to the availability of certain budgetary rooms, the Commission could carry out some 'independent' programmes to support innovative actions according to former Art.10 of the structural funds provisions (European Commission, 1989).

Amongst the actors involved, cities could boost their mobilisation thanks to the growing significance of measures for urban development within the structural funds (Hooghe, 1995; Marks, 1992). Urban measures began as innovative actions under Art.10 of the ERDF and Art.6 of the ESF in 1988 – in the form of experimental projects – and continued in 1994 and 1999 through the URBAN/ URBAN II community initiatives and the enhanced urban targeting of Objective 2 programmes.

The community instruments addressed to urban areas have multiplied over the years, ranging from environmental programmes and transport, to research and development. Nonetheless, the urban action of the European Union, as of the mid-1990s, mainly translated into programmes for *urban regeneration*. The 'integrated approach' represented the innovative feature of the EU action in this domain.

In this connection, the EU *integrated approach* consists of both a horizontal and a vertical component. The former entails overcoming the sectorial approach and contextually tackling multiple domains (i.e. environment, employment, transport, financing, etc.). The latter, instead, builds on involving different institutional and administrative bodies (EU, central government, regions, municipalities) during the programming and control phases, and on the participation of private actors and the civil society living in the concerned area of action. Thus, the urban policy of the European Union has mainly focused on programmes for urban regeneration whose principal instruments have been the Urban Pilot Projects over the 1988–1999 period (second phase) and the programmes financed under the CI URBAN between 1994 and 2006.

Considering the development and the implementation of the CI URBAN II, with reference to a specific territorial context – we argue – shall allow unveiling the causal mechanisms structuring the interactions upon the specific policy issues at stake, thus eventually leading to transformations within different policy arenas in the territory taken into consideration. In this connection, the Europeanisation process would follow patterns of territorial rescaling, programming between different administrative layers acting in the localities as well as of compliance with the targets recommended by the EU provisions in this instance.

9.2 Regional policy in the EU: what space for cities?

The European Regional Development Fund (ERDF) was established in 1975, following the entrance in the EU of Denmark, Ireland and the UK. In this early stage, the Commission had, nonetheless, a limited role. The Commission retained a certain role in approving applications and responsibility for ensuring that the funds were additional to other planned domestic expenditure. The approval of the Single European Act (SEA) in 1987 – and the insertion of a new Title V into the Treaty of Rome (Art. 13a-e, now 158–62) – led to the quest for strengthening economic and social cohesion so as to reducing the disparities between levels of regional development.

Following the SEA, resources allocated to regional policy increased decisively and the budget of the structural fund for the 1988–1993 programming period reached ECU 14 billion, approximately 25 per cent of the EU budget. The initial allocation of ECU 257.6 million in 1975 represented solely 4.8 per cent of total EC spending (Bache, 1998: 70). Following negotiation in 1993, the TEU established the cohesion fund. Together with the approval of the *Delors-1 package*, providing for a doubling of the structural funds, the cohesion funds brought the total structural fund action to ECU 27.4 billion projected for 1999, thus representing 35 per cent of the total EU budget (Tofarides, 2003: 42). After the 1988 reform, the Commission played a more proactive role in regional policies.

In the strategic document *Agenda 2000: for a Stronger and Wider Union*, published in July 1997 (European Commission, 1997b), the Commission outlined the structural programme for the first period of the new millennium (2000–06). On this occasion – first time thus far – the total financial envelop attributed to regional policy was reduced; contextually, a series of supporting measures were elaborated and financed for the 'new member states' entered in 2004. Furthermore, the reform led a partially new role for the Commission, now mainly in charge of managing the initial programming phases, thus leaving rooms for manoeuvre and discretionarily to national and sub-national governments[1].

---

1.   For a complete overview of the development of EU regional policy see for instance: Bache (1998) and Brunazzo, M. (2005).

The EU principles of structural action

Four main principles stand behind the structural action of the European Union and guide the Commission throughout the different phases of the policy process, from the negotiation to the management and implementation of the programmes.

Thus, *concentration* is about focusing the funds on areas of greatest need. After the 1993 reform, national government reasserted control over the selection of areas eligible for European funding. With respect to concentration, it is rather evident that there has been a constant tension between the Commission's commitment towards more concentration and the concern of member states to obtain bigger share of the structural funds. *Programming* instead, involves switching from the project-based approach of pre-1988 regional policy to a multi-annual programme. After 1993, member state authorities were required to submit a single programming document, which would include a development plan, as well as applications for aid related to this (European Commission, 1989). The principle of *additionality* in EC regional policy dates back to the establishment of the ERDF in 1975, but only after the reform of the structural funds in 1988, the Commission stated that a monitoring system was necessary to assess the extent to which the community effort finds matching at the national level (European Commission, 1989). Alongside the enforcement of additionality, the Commission pushed forward the principle of *partnership* in order to strengthen the role of regions in relation to the EU, and partly beyond the control of the nation state.

Since the establishment of the ERDF in 1975, the European Commission stated that 'Community regional policy is by nature a partnership between the Community and its member states, with the former at the present stage the junior partner' (Tofarides, 2003: 51). Partnership was initially defined as a 'close consultation between the Commission, the member states concerned and the competent authorities designated by the latter at national, regional, local or other levels, which each partner in pursuit a common goal' (Commission, 1989: 15).

The scope of *partnership* widened with the inclusion of the principle of *subsidiarity* into the TEU signed in 1991. Through subsidiary, non-governmental partners started to take part in the implementation of European structural funds, thus reflecting the idea that 'community structural action depends for its implementation, not only on the national and regional authorities, but also on the various economic and social partners' (Commission, 1989: 15). By endorsing this additional principle, the Commission sought to bring new partners into the implementation process, in order to improve the delivery mechanisms and effectiveness of regional policy.

In addition to the major programmes – accounting for over 70 per cent of the entire structural fund budget – for the 1989–1993 programming period the Commission allocated almost ECU 4 billion to a series of community initiatives (CIs). These could contain a combination of funds (ERDF, ESF, EAGGF), depending on the problem tackled. Over the period 1989–1993, 4 ECU billion were spread between twelve different CIs, covering different policy themes. Although at an embryonic stage, CIs promoted dialogue and interaction between the European Commission and a broader range of actors. Over this programming period, there were not specific CIs devoted to cities and urban problems. In the wake of the second round of reforms (covering the 1994–99 period), the Commission or European Commission proposed to increase the percentage of funds for CIs up to 15 per cent of the structural funds general budget. In response, a new council committee on community initiatives was established in the aim of tightening the control of member governments, and the proposal of the Commission was limited to solely 9 per cent by the council.

Finally, the 1999 reform substantially simplified the organisation and number of CIs, by reducing them to only four, with a financial availability of 5 per cent of the total structural funds' budget for the 2000–06 period (European Commission, 1999). The regulation for the 2007–13 period does not explicitly foresee any community initiatives and the 'working methods' characterising three of the former CIs – Interreg III, Equal and Urban II – is incorporated within the three new regional objectives of the EU regional policy.

The launch of thirty-three Urban Pilot Projects over the 1989–1993 period and of a further twenty-six projects during the 1994–99 period can be directly related to developments following the 1988 structural funds reform and to the possibilities entrenched in Art.10 of the ERDF[2].

A second phase of the Urban Pilot Projects was approved in July 1997 with the aim of continuing to support innovation in urban regeneration and planning. Amongst the beneficiary cities in this period, there were both cities belonging to areas covered by objective 1 and 2 of the structural funds and cities 'out of objective'. The average dimension of each UPP was ECU 6.1 million (1 ECU= 1 EURO), 50 per cent of which was financed by the ERDF. The UPPs stressed the innovative nature of the action undertaken and a different approach in carrying out interventions in urban areas.

Since that time onwards, 'urban policy' has been part of the agenda of the regional policy of the Commission, even though the treaties did not recognise an official urban policy of the EU and this was outside the competences of the Commission. In the early 1990s, DGXVI (now DG for Regional and Urban Policy) within the Commission decisively oriented its action towards urban areas by underlining the need for increasing cooperation between cities, information exchange and diffusing expertise. The Commission or European Commission proposed an amendment to the regulation of structural funds, with the aim of including 'urban decline' in the definition of ERDF objectives. Nonetheless, the European Council rejected the Commission proposal for a more formal urban competence in the treaties in 1991 (Tofarides, 2003). Only after the first round of CIs, a process based on a more systematic consultation between DGXVI and representatives of cities took place. It was the favourable response of the European Parliament to the 'Green

---

2.   In this early stage, UPPs have been used by the Commission to promote innovative approaches in cities, amongst them the Antwerp project directed to the establishment of strong neighbourhood partnerships and the Dublin project, addressed to regeneration initiatives, mainly in the field of arts and culture (European Commission, 1997a).

Paper on the future of Community Initiatives' published by the Commission in 1993 (European Commission, 1993) that encouraged the Commission to include an explicit reference to 'Urban Initiatives' in its communication in March 1994 (European Commission, 1994).

URBAN, as an official community initiative was formally adopted on 15 June 1994. No additional treaty competences were required as URBAN was within the framework of CIs that had existed since the 1988 reform (Nanetti, 2002). In 1999, besides the community initiative URBAN II, which pursued the approach adopted by URBAN I the launch of URBACT[3] and the second phase of the urban audit confirm a trend within which a large part of the financial resources of Objective 1 and 2 of the structural funds is addressed towards urban-related measures.

For the programming period 2007–13, the Commission reinforced (at least formally) the place of urban issues by fully integrating actions in this field into the programmes. Additionally, the functioning mechanisms of the cohesion policy were simplified further. From the past nine objectives and six financial instruments, the cohesion policy 2007–13 was based on only three objectives (convergence; regional competitiveness and employment; European territorial cooperation) implemented through three financial instruments (ERDF; ESF; Cohesion Fund).

Within this new structure, there was not specific community initiative and the ex-URBAN II and EQUAL programmes will be part of the convergence objective, as well as of the regional competitiveness and employment objective. Thus, urban-related programmes are part of the mainstream regional programmes under new objectives 1 and 2; consequently regional authorities are responsible for the programming and management of perspective urban initiatives.

Table 9.1: EU programmes specifically directed at cities

Programming Period	Programme	Nr. of Projects/ Cities	Budget
1989–1993	UPP 1	33	ECU 102 M.
1994–99	UPP 2	26	ECU 63.6 M.
1994–99	URBAN I	118	EUR 900 million
1994–99	Urban audit I	58	EUR 2.2 million
2000–06	URBAN II	70	EUR 728 million
2000–06	Urban audit II	258	EUR 1.6 million
2000–06	Obj.2- Urban areas in difficulty	Data not available	Data not available
2007–13	NONE		
2014–20	Urban innovative actions	ongoing	EUR 372 million

---

3.   http://urbact.eu (accessed 10 November 2016).

Archetypal game model

Interaction, in this case, can be paired – at least initially – to game models of bargaining in non-cooperative situations; the original model proposed by Rubinstein (1982)[4] well exemplifies this set of games, where the players involved interact in reiterated ways (Roth and Malouf, 1979). In the negotiation of structural funds, local representatives are often involved in the phase of domestic consultation, and only in 'second facie' at the supranational level when dynamics of *grand bargaining* can be considered completed (Pollack, 1997; Sandholtz, 1992).

Another way to conceive interaction within distributive arenas is to think of a series of nested games (Tsebelis, 1990) taking place within different arenas of governance, where actors' suboptimal strategy in one game can be part of a strategy to maximise payoffs when all arenas are taken into account. This in turn may imply the shifting of arenas, thus moving to a different set of decisions and orders (Héritier and Lehmkuhl, 2008) or instead strategies for the creation of sub systemic arenas where partial positive-sum games may be reached within an overall situation of disagreement (Radaelli and Kraemer, 2008). Cities-EU interactions may also conform to mechanisms of 'two-level games' (Buchs, 2008; Putnam, 1988).

Thus, this type of interactive situations belongs to the family of *extensive form games*, where players choose their strategies sequentially and the time-factor holds an important role. More specifically in this case, since we are dealing with policies implying net distribution of funds from the EU to cities, it seems more likely that the model to employ is the one proposed by Romer and Rosenthal (Romer and Rosenthal, 1978; 1979) for resource allocation[5]. Two main aspects are relevant here: on the one side, the majority rule governing the decision process over collective expenditure determination. On the other, the presence of an agenda setter – the European Commission in this case, which 'has the power to make a proposal to the voters, and thereby set the agenda… and can confront the voters with a "take it or leave it" choice' (Romer and Rosenthal, 1978: 27).

9.3 CI URBAN II. A catalyst for urban Europeanisation

The URBAN Community Initiative represents – we argue – the most significant EU attempt to address urban areas in terms of policy promotion. It is one of the principal actions within EU policies favouring institutional transformation and policy change in cities and urban areas. This also permits to address the relations

---

4. Rubistein draws his model from the simple situation of two individuals with several possible agreements but with different interests as to how an agreement is made.

5. The example offered by Romer and Rosenthal in their original model formulation builds on a situation common in many local jurisdictions, where some collective expenditure is determined through the interaction between citizen-voters and a committee or a bureau charged with the provision of public services that typically formulates a proposal for the coming period's expenditures. In turn, the proposal is subject to approval or defeat in a referendum of the jurisdictions residents.

between the subjects affected by the set of instruments considered. Due to their involvement in EU-led urban programmes, and particularly in the URBAN Community Initiative – during the 1994–99 and 2000–06 programming period – European cities reacted to both the new opportunities offered, and the constraints sometimes accompanying the EU-grants (Atkinson, 2001; Halpern, 2005; Marshall, 2005).

Between 1994 and 1999, URBAN I Initiative financed programmes in 118 urban areas with a total of EUR 953 million of community assistance, 3.2 million people lived in the supported areas and projects focused on rehabilitation of infrastructures, job creation, combating social exclusion and upgrading of the environment. With a total budget of EUR 730 million, projects for sustainable economic development and social regeneration were co-financed under URBAN II in seventy urban areas throughout Europe (European Commission, 2003b).

Differently from the first edition, over the second round the financial equipment decreased substantially and URBAN became a mono-fund programme, financed exclusively by the ERDF. Building on the positive experience of the first edition, URBAN II is based on a series of Commission guidelines to finance projects aimed at improving living conditions, job creation, integrating the socially excluded, developing environmental friendly public transport and facilitating the use of information technologies in cities (European Commission, 2000a).

With the aim of pursuing these objectives, URBAN II focused on three main actions: physical and environmental regeneration, social inclusion, entrepreneurship and employment. Therefore, some of the main features of URBAN II programmes, constituting what can be termed the *acquis URBAN* (or URBAN model) were: targeting small areas, focus on social inclusion and integration of minorities, formation of local partnership and the exchange of experience and best practices, respect of local specificities and local capacity building.

By elaborating the contents of the Council Regulation 1260/1999 on general provisions for Structural Funds 2000–06[6], the Commission pointed out how the programmes funded under the URBAN CI since 1994 'are delivering visible improvements in the quality of life in their target areas' (European Commission, 2000a: 2).

In this connection, the two main objectives to possibly attain through URBAN were 'to promote the formulation and implementation of particularly innovative strategies for sustainable economic and social regeneration and to enhance exchange of knowledge and experience in relation to sustainable urban regeneration and development in the community' (European Commission, 2000a: 3–4).

As regards the 'way of doing' within URBAN CI, each city, town, or urban area to be supported has to present a single problem to be tackled, and a situation of effective need must be demonstrated on the base of relevant indicators proposed by member states, and thereafter discussed with the Commission. In this sense,

---

6.   Council of the European Communities (CE) (1999). 'Council Regulation (EC) No 1260/1999, laying down general provision on the Structural Funds', June 21 1999.

URBAN II programmes differ from 'pilot action' for their strategic nature, although territorially limited. The trend towards territorial development programmes and integrated strategic plans had been undertaken by many European cities over the same period, such as in the case of Bilbao, Birmingham, Lille and Turin.

Strategies elaborated in the community initiative programmes (CIPs) need to have a commitment to 'organisational change, participatory governance, empowerment and capacity-building transferable into mainstream practice at local and wider levels' (European Commission, 2000a: 6). Furthermore, each CIP must contain a description of the social and economic situation in terms of strengths, weaknesses, opportunities and threats, and a series of indicators regarding the labour market, the environmental situation and the sense of security perceived by citizens (European Commission 2000b: 7). Member states would have identified potentially eligible areas and to break down funding once they are granted; afterwards, the preparation of the CIP is up to the local authority responsible for the eligible areas, which should act in 'partnership with the regional and national authorities depending on the structure of each member state' (European Commission, 2000b: 7).

Operationally, a series of authorities and structures are in charge of programmes management and implementation. These usually are a *managing authority* – designed by the member state – a *paying authority*, with financial responsibility, and a *monitoring committee*. In this connection, the Commission invited to strengthen partnership relations and to promote wider consultation between the committed urban authority and other levels of governments, as well as with social and economic partners from non-governmental organisations.

As underlined in the presentation guide of URBAN II published by DG Regio in 2003 (European Commission, 2003b), key features of URBAN CI are the integrated approach to issues which elsewhere are often tackled in isolation, the high profile for EU priorities and the fact that programmes are run at the local level, close to people and to their problems. In fact, 'an important part of the rational for URBAN is to *contribute to the effectiveness of other urban actions. This would be achieved by acting as a testing ground, or a model, and by generating the raw material for the exchange of experience.* Much of the added value of URBAN therefore steams from the method of implementation' (European Commission, 2003b: 16, *italics added*). In comparison to its predecessor, URBAN II was characterised by a higher degree of management decentralisation to local authorities. In fact, one third of the seventy programmes initially selected, had a city council as managing authority (all the Italian, Dutch, Austrian, Finnish and Irish programmes, and most of the French programmes), for another third of the programmes the local authority was the key player in partnership with central government (i.e. England, Spain and Greece). In the remaining programmes, the city council was a full member of the monitoring committee (i.e. Germany and Portugal).

To conclude on this part, some considerations on the current architecture of the EU Cohesion Policy are worth mentioning. Besides a minor importance of URBAN CI in its second round – at least from a budgetary point of view – concern has been raised as to the interruption of community initiatives for the 2007–13 period and their 'inclusion' in the new objectives of the structural funds under the sole responsibility of regional authorities. Already in the course of the programming period 2000–06, the involvement of cities in the planning and implementation of regional programmes under former objectives 'one' and 'two' has turned out contrasting results.

The regulation of structural funds for the period 2007–13 stressed the importance of the urban dimension. It affirms that (13th whereas) 'in the view of the importance of sustainable urban development and the contribution of towns and cities, particularly medium-sized ones, to regional development, greater account should be taken of them by developing their role in programming to promote urban regeneration' (European Commission, 2006: 2). However, the regional authorities are in control of the entire process, thus implying that the development of urban actions is planned through regional programmes and municipal authorities are eventually in charge of the implementation of actions. Within this picture, outcomes depend – we argue – on national differences in the tradition of organising policies addressed to urban areas, and still more on the regional capacity to set up dialogue and effective partnerships with cities, especially with regional capitals.

9.4 Exploring modes of distribution: URBAN II in Turin

An explicit urban policy was not in place in Italy, at least until the mid-nineties. The concept of metropolitan cities was introduced for the first time only with the endorsement of law 142/90; although some attempts have been made by the government to start a discussion, especially as regards administrative reforms at the urban level, an explicit urban policy was missing in terms of contents.

Urban policy in fact, has not been a priority for the central government, which since 1942, on the contrary, favoured de-urbanisation based on Art.1 of urban law n. 1159, rather than managing the (then) ongoing process of urbanisation. This hampered any attempt of programming and defining the phenomena of urbanisation and its links to economic and social aspects. Only in the 1990s, terms such as urban planning and programming became familiar to Italian legislators, which, despite setting up instruments for an integrated urban policy, have not succeeded in drawing the clear contents of such a policy. Thus, it is of little surprise that still now, formal metropolitan cities have not been constituted in the country.

Therefore, if urban policies exist, they assume the feature of 'self-made individual solutions', partly due to the lack of coordination and cooperation between the several departments and institutions at the national, regional and local level in charge of competences in connection to urban matters. Up until recently, scarce coordination represented the main hindrance to the development of a clear national urban policy. This implied, in turn, worsening the performances of larger cities and maintaining the dichotomy between the conditions of northern and southern cities, where problems in urban areas are getting more complex.

Compared to other European countries, in Italy, the elaboration of viable solutions to manage transformations occurred within the urban system seems to remain outside the political debate. The transfer of the legislative production (on urban matters) and control of local plans from the state to regional authorities, limited further the possible development of a general perspective on urban development in the country. At present, competences on policies and interventions in cities and urban areas are divided and shared between all levels of government (state, regions, local authorities), and between numerous departments within each of the aforementioned levels. Moreover, at the central level of government, the main competences are in turn distributed amongst different departments; this has hampered the overall coordination of action and the effective organisation of a coherent urban policy for Italian cities[7].

In Italy, differently from other contexts, the evolution of urban themes has been characterised by a certain delay and above all by the territorial dualism typical of the Italian peninsula and by the social-economic situation at the national level. The 'crisis' of the city became manifest only in the mid-1980s, but without assuming a homogeneous territorial characterisation. In fact, the population – especially in municipalities with more than 100,000 inhabitants – underwent a decisive decline (a trend alike in both northern and southern Italy) – and the emergence of a range of problems of 'urban degradation' which, instead, assumed different connotations in different territorial areas (Centre-North/*Mezzogiorno*)[8].

It is within this picture, that a 'patchwork attempt' to organise a coherent urban policy took place; as already stated, it has been an effort made of repeated emanations of regulations, but missing a real strategy and a proper programmatic definition.

The only systematic analysis of the national urban policies in Italy dates back to 1968, when throughout the so-called *Progetto '80*, the then Ministry of Budget commissioned a compound study about the ongoing urban development characterising Italy in an attempt to gauge problems and potentialities of the Italian urban system. The image offered by this report was already a picture made of great dichotomies, not only between northern and southern areas, but also between big conurbations and medium-sized cities, between urban areas and countryside, between strongly hierarchal systems and polycentric ones (Dematteis and Bonavero, 1997: 89).

---

7. A similar fragmentation and overlapping of competences is mirrored at the regional and local level, where urban planning is organised around four main domains of intervention, namely *Territorial Plans of Regional Coordination, Territorial Plans*, Territorial Plans of Provincial Coordination and General Regulatory Plan. Especially in the case of the elaboration of the latter, problems related to the attribution of competences, problems of coordination, and then management of specific tasks are frequently at stake.

8. While in the case of northern cities problems of urban disease and degradation are located in well-defined areas and are typical of specific situations, in cities belonging to Regions Objective 1 of the Structural Funds, these problems have a dramatic connotation. They are in fact characteristic of the entire urban area and typical of solely a certain portion of the European territory, thus being hardly comparable to dynamics in other areas of the EU.

Multiple initiatives have been undertaken from then onwards, especially at the proposal of the DICOTER, the General Direction for the Territorial Coordination within the Ministry of Infrastructure and Transportation. Two general (and detached) categories of intervention marked this trend of action. On one side, initiatives oriented towards restructuring institutional assets and political-administrative structures with the aim of solving the problems of competence attribution; on the other side, programmes aimed at intervening on specific 'material' problems afflicting urban areas. Therefore, priority was given to infrastructural interventions, mainly linked to definite sectorial policies (i.e. services) or area-based policies (i.e. *Mezzogiorno*) and to actions related to peculiar events, thus confirming the objective difficulty to set up a coherent strategy of intervention.

Furthermore, also the accomplishment of these programmes has partially been hindered by technical-financial problems and by huge political-administrative inefficiencies. As regards interventions aimed at reasserting the institutional and administrative system, the establishment of the department for urban areas in 1987 and the already cited law 142/90 are worth mentioning, envisaging metropolitan areas and reforming the institutional assets of local governments; most of the articles here contained (especially those about metropolitan areas) have not found implementation thus far.

Therefore, the picture emerging in the Italian case is made of multiple strategies aimed more at containing the worst setbacks deriving from contingent situations, than at setting up a coherent development strategy. This should envisage the promotion of a more modern and efficient political and administrative asset within an urban system that needs to renovate in order to align with the new governmental and administrative exigencies of urban areas in Europe. The implementation and organisation of an integrated urban strategy at the national level has been missing, and only few cities, such as Genoa, Turin and Bologna have been endorsing strategic plans and integrated strategies of urban development, often by drawing on the model of guidelines and programmes promoted by the European Union.

Developing URBAN CI in Italy

The implementation of the first edition of CI URBAN is rooted in an experimental phase, where some Italian cities started to manage 'complex programmes' of urban regeneration aimed at re-qualifying the urban context, by seeking to reorganise urban services, quality of life and urban functionality.

These programmes maintained a quasi-exclusive sectorial character and were mainly oriented towards infrastructural regeneration. Despite the prevailing physical character of the initiatives carried out, URBAN represented an element of strong innovation, being one amongst few real occasions for Italian cities to handle the integrated approach to urban regeneration. In this connection, URBAN's 'added value' matches with the broader range of interventions pursued and with the search for the efficient involvement of the population and socio-economic actors at the local level. This was especially true for cities in the southern part of the country.

Between 1994 and 1999, URBAN I involved sixteen Italian cities, three of which were part of objective 2 areas of the structural funds (Trieste, Genoa and Venice), one being out of objective (Rome) and the remaining twelve were cities of southern Italy, part of objective 1 areas (Naples, Salerno, Foggia, Bari, Lecce, Cosenza, Catanzaro, Reggio Calabria, Palermo, Catania, Syracuse and Cagliari). The urban settings where the programme took place were highly diversified as regards both the problems at stake – declining working class quarters, de-urbanised areas, popular quarters in the historic city centre – and the extension of the area of action (ranging from 2000 inhabitants of the URBAN site of Trieste to 81,000 inhabitants in Rome).

Thus, at least in this first phase (1994–99) the CI URBAN I in Italy took the form of a unique general programme made of 16 sub-programmes corresponding to the cities selected by the central government. Municipal administrations were in turn responsible for the implementation of the sub-programmes managed by the central ministry, while the former Department for the Coordination of Communitarian Policies (now Department for European Politics) was the national authority responsible for the coordination of the operative programme in charge of managing the financial flux, evaluation and monitoring, and of the programme's general control.

Some relevant innovations characterised the second CI URBAN edition in Italy. In fact, unlike the first edition, the areas of intervention were not only cities with a population of over 100,000 inhabitants, but also medium and small cities located in metropolitan provinces[9]. Furthermore, the surveillance committee was no longer centralised, but rather localised. During the second edition (URBAN II) each municipal administration of the ten cities taking part in the programme assumed the role of the *managing authority*, thus in turn holding the presidency of the local surveillance committees. This arrangement was adopted with the main aim of favouring participation 'during the implementation of the programme on behalf of all local forces active in the area, which, within URBAN I, did not have the relevance and the visibility that they expected' (DICOTER, 2003: 3).

Additionally, during the second phase, intermediate evaluation of the projects became an established practice. This was carried out by the central administration in the attempt to unify the system for programme evaluation at the national level, thus offering participant cities a greater possibility of exchanging information. As regards this latter point, despite the activism of some Italian cities in URBACT (those cities directly involved in URBAN and other UPPs) and in EUROCITIES, the occasion for sharing knowledge and experiences with other Italian cities taking part in URBAN II has been rather limited, if not absent. *URBAN-Italia* network – embracing the cities participating in the CI URBAN and in other urban programmes

---

9.   If it is actually the case with Misterbianco and Mola di Bari where the programme has been applied to the entire municipal territory. The number of eligible cities, also due to inferior financial equipment, has been decreased from sixteen to ten (Carrara, Caserta, Crotone, Genoa, Milan, Misterbianco, Mola di Bari, Pescara, Taranto and Turin).

financed at different levels (national and regional) – did not develop effectively and its action was limited solely to the publication of on-line documents.

According to the available data, the overall expenditures of Italian cities involved in the second phase of CI URBAN were organised around different axes of intervention. Thus, about 56 per cent was attributed to physical and environmental regeneration, 7 per cent to entrepreneurship and employment, about 10 per cent to inclusion, 15 per cent to transport, 6 per cent to information technologies, and the remaining 6 per cent to technical assistance. This confirms the fact that in the Italian case, particular attention was devoted to infrastructural interventions.

Logic of action in the city of Turin

With the endorsement of decision n. C/2001/3531, the community initiative URBAN II 'Mirafiori Nord' was formally adopted in November 2001. The programme had an overall financial budget of 43 euro millions[10] and represented one of the biggest initiatives for urban redevelopment ever carried out in the city[11].

The period of implementation of the CI URBAN II corresponded almost entirely to the running up to the winter Olympics, held in 2006. Even in this case, the programme aimed at promoting projects of social, physical and economic transformation to favour development opportunities for the local populations.

From the moment of initial endowment of the programme, onwards, the city directly dealt with the responsible for the programme at the European Commission. In this connection, the regional administration remained rather tangential to the overall dynamic, and the central administration – besides its role as paying authority – was responsible for the selection of the cities that would have taken part in the EU programme.

Additionally, during the period of implementation of the programme, the city of Turin took part – and it is still involved – in several pan-European networks. While some are explicitly addressing matters of urban regeneration and recovery – *Urban Italia* and *Quartiers en Crise* – others are networks dealing with a broader range of themes concerning cities and local authorities, such as *Eurocities* and *Urbact*.

The implementation of the programme as such, fits in within a wider context of peripheral redevelopment that the city initiated back in 1997, when a new department of the municipality – *settore periferie* – was set up[12]. Before the city applied for the second edition of the CI URBAN in 2000, the periphery departments were already pursuing fifteen different complex programmes for

---

10. The overall funding was secured for ~45 per cent by the EU, ~40 per cent by the Central State and the remaining ~15 per cent by local financing, including private actors.

11. Apart from the relevant financial allocation, the CI URBAN II 'Mirafiori Nord' covered an area inhabited by ~ 250,000 people and a total surface of approximately 2 million square metres.

12. In 1997 in particular, a municipal decree institutionalised the 'Special Periphery Project' for the requalification of peripheries in Turin. This was the resultant of a particularly favourable political juncture, which saw the first direct election of the city mayor in 1993.

urban regeneration, territorial development and the overall requalification of the peripheries was established.

The renewal of the administrative class – following reforms in 1993 – has certainly boosted a new attitude towards matters of urban regeneration and territorial development. Following this trend, Turin embarked on an (EU) Urban Pilot Project in the 1995–96 period (The Gate), which constituted a sort of preamble to the latter participation in URBAN II. Hence, in 1998, the city carried out an additional programme for integrated urban regeneration – *contratto di quartiere* – which allowed for experimenting new financial and programmatic instruments.

Therefore, the fact of 'missing out' the first edition of URBAN created a rather convenient climate to feature the projects initially proposed for the CI into the new Urban Recovery Plans (PRU) promoted at the regional level. Already on this occasion, the integrated approach as promoted by the EU was perceived as a necessity to face the complexity of the urban peripheries and above all to respond to local populations' increasing demand for participation. This translated into the elaboration of appropriate methodologies for informing the population, thus favouring its efficient participation in synergy with the public administration.

The area affected by PIC Urban were southern outskirts of Turin, near the industrial complex of Fiat Mirafiori, and it is characterised by high concentration of public housing[13] where problematic dynamics of social, economic and cultural nature traditionally loomed large. Mirafiori Nord needed intensive actions in terms of urban requalification; this did not only concern public housing estates and the quality of public and green areas, but also the revitalisation of the socio-economic conditions of an area at risk of stagnation in this sense.

The overall project was therefore organised around three main axis of intervention. Under the *green axis* of rehabilitation and environmental sustainability, a set of actions were promoted with the aim of re-qualifying the physical environment, the existing green areas and creating new public spaces. Along a second axis of intervention – *red axis* – concerning social integration, reduction of social exclusion and creating opportunities for cultural and artistic expression, several actions were promoted to strengthen the existing social relations and the sense of belonging to the local community. Finally, initiatives were promoted to support existing businesses and create new job opportunities within the *blue axis* – creating infrastructures and knowledge for economic growth. In this case, projects were carried out to support small and micro enterprises, services for the new economy and training activities for job induction.

The structure put in place for the overall management of the programme, from the programming phase, through to the actual realisation of the planned projects, saw the involvement of several socio-economic partners and institutions acting

13. The commune, the Territorial Housing Agency (ATC) and the government own 1904 housing units, accounting for circa 20 per cent of the homes available in the area, compared to a city-wide percentage of 6 per cent (http://www.comune.torino.it/rigenerazioneurbana/ (accessed 10 November 2016)).

in the territory. In particular – as confirmed by the witness of key actors in Turin – the promotion of a synergic network of partnership from the early stages was perceived as an indispensable condition for the overall success of the programme.

Thus, the city of Turin acted as managing authority responsible for the overall supervision of the programme, whereas, the concrete implementation of the planned actions was entrusted to an *ad hoc* steering committee – 'Urban 2 Committee' – that remained formally in office until the end of 2008[14]. In turn, the committee was organised through a board (with twelve members), a director, an URBAN II office –staffed by municipal personnel and external collaborators responsible for the day-to-day management of the programme – and a *forum for local development* including social and economic partners with a consultative role. The structure and working method of the URBAN II committee were maintained afterwards in order to manage the regional funds (ERDF) addressed to urban areas during the current programming 2007–13 period. Besides that, a surveillance committee – including amongst others the Piedmont region and the Compagnia di San Paolo – was established in 2002 with purposes of control and monitoring of the actions carried out[15]. Additionally, a paying authority and an evaluation committee were respectively responsible for managing the initial cash flow and the ex-post assessment of the programme. The figure below exemplifies the organisational scheme for the management of the CI URBAN II as set up in Turin.

Conclusions: insights into the Europeanisation of urban regeneration in Turin

The actual implementation of the programme translated into actions carried out within nine different domains and around sixty people actively working for the appropriate realisation of the planned interventions. *De facto*, the integrated approach to policy development was already in place in the proposal and programming phase, above all due to the bulk of experience previously gathered over the same policy area. This was further confirmed by the successful 'integration' of the URBAN II-actions with the other initiatives in place over the same lapse of time (i.e. 2003–04 'Contratti di Quartiere').

Thus, together with an enhanced coordination achieved with the competent regional departments during the whole development of the programme, URBAN II has certainly favoured the participation of a broader range of actors. Therefore, enhanced participation was registered in the phases of negotiation and application for EU financial support, but above all during the programming stage, both

---

14. The managing authority relies on the committee to perform all planning and implementation, management and control activities for the broad and complex set of mutually interrelated and coordinated actions involved in the program, for the attainment of the established goals. In other words, the committee is the supplier and organiser of all the technical, administrative, economic and managerial intelligence needed to put the programme into effect.

15. As part of its tasks, this committee approves the Complement Programme and evaluates the need to perform appropriate actions, defined jointly with the city of Turin (i.e. the programmes management authority) in order to ensure a full and effective use of the resources available.

pre-candidature and post-implementation. In particular, citizens' participation was a real benefit during the programming phase since 2002, when a comprehensive process of *participatory planning* was initiated in the aim of finalising objectives, methodologies and the political choices for intervention[16].

Interviews at various levels – public officers and representatives of the economic sector – revealed how the truly innovative and transformative element brought about by the promotion of EU programmes consists of the integrated approach to policy development (urban regeneration in this case). The integrated approach was moreover perceived due to the multiple measures endorsed within the same programme as well as the governance architecture backing its overall management. In particular, the establishment of an 'Urban Committee' certainly represented a value-added to the way the city managed the preparation and successive implementation of the URBAN II community initiative. The committee was in fact interdependent with the other various components of the city but managed to hold a sufficient degree of independence so as to take operative decisions, especially concerning spending.

Officers in charge of the various components of the programme stressed how the EU rules governing the URBAN initiative were fully internalised during the period of implementation, and the actual matching between the programmed interventions and those actually carried out is evidence of this renovated attitude. Thus, the working methods as well as the organisational aspects as streamlined by the European Commission, represented a thorough yardstick for the actual implementation of the projects, which – owing to a strengthened decisional and spending capacity – could be performed with success in due time.

Working methods accompanying URBAN II then became standard modalities for the realisation of other initiatives for urban recovery initiated by the city of Turin without the financial support of the EU; it is the case of the new programme 'Urban Barriera'[17], whose steering committee was officially set up in April 2011. In this connection, despite the actual success of the integrated approach as translated in the case of Turin, there continue to be – practitioners argue – some difficulties in constructively involving the private sector.

Amongst the instruments that the promotion of URBAN contributed to settle in the policy making within the domain of urban redevelopment, there is the enhanced capacity to define an overall strategy of intervention as well as a series of indicators for the up-to-date evaluation of the interventions. Furthermore, URBAN allowed for the use of flexible financial instruments that made sense of

---

16. Worth mentioning in this sense is the method experimented for the ideation and successive implementation of the project that led to the realisation of the 'Roccafranca farmstead', oriented towards a research-action approach. Following the endorsement of the overall project presented by the city of Turin, a 'feasibility study' (October 2002-June 2004) was adopted to sort out an operative plan that viewed the participation of public and private actors present on the Mirafiori Nord territory.

17. Following the URBAN II model, the programme for integrated urban requalification 'urban Barriera' will commence with a 4.5 € million financial provision and more than thirty actions will be carried out for the overall recovery of an area of 2 square km.

the efficient application of the subsidiarity principle, thus making it possible for the local administration to deploy, in turn, various instruments of proximity (i.e. participatory planning), leading to the increasing involvement of the population living in the areas of intervention.

The increasing involvement of the city in programmes and initiatives promoted by the EU, together with the renewal of the administrative class – following reforms in 1993 – have boosted a new attitude towards matters of urban regeneration and territorial development. Thus, during the legislature of mayor Castellani (1993–2001), the city of Turin embarked on a flourishing development process, which culminated in the allocation of the winter Olympic games then hosted in 2006.

9.5 Streamlining urban actions in the new EU Regional policy

The European Structural and Investment Funds Regulation 2014–20[18] (common provisions regulation) – including the provisions for the European Regional Development Fund – stresses the importance of elements such as integrated urban development, sustainable growth, the protection of the environment and the promotion of resource efficiency. It also points out the need to further strengthen community-led local development and to better rely on simplified rules, more efficient financial instruments and a more systematic use of monitoring and evaluation techniques for the assessment of actions undertaken in the territories and the appraisal of the impact eventually attained. Over the last twenty years, support to deprived neighbourhoods has been one core rationale for the European approach to urban matters. It is still prominent in the new programming period of regional policy but with a main difference from the past regulations that clearly stand out: the need for an integrated approach. In the provisions for the European Regional Development Fund, Article 7 requires member states to allocate a minimum of 5 per cent of their resources for integrated sustainable urban development strategies. Thus, holistic strategies and integrated actions are now considered necessary – and not any longer as a preferred option – to deliver urban development; this shall be pursued also through a better integration between funds, in particular the European Social Fund, which is now explicitly referred to as functional to the integrated strategy. Contextually, the need of enhancing the role of urban authorities in Europe and the necessity to further strengthen the conditions for a better involvement and empowerment of cities is reflected by the same dedicated article which establish a minimum requirement of delegation to urban authorities for the implementation of sustainable urban development strategies. Furthermore, integrated territorial investments as a replacement for separate priority axes for

---

18. Regulation (EU) No 1303/2013 of the European Parliament and of the Council of 17 December 2013, laying down common provisions on the European Regional Development Fund, the European Social Fund, the Cohesion Fund, the European Agricultural Fund for Rural Development and the European Maritime and Fisheries Fund and laying down general provisions on the European Regional Development Fund, the European Social Fund, the Cohesion Fund and the European Maritime and Fisheries Fund and repealing Council Regulation (EC) No 1083/2006.

urban development should favour better and more efficient policy integration; the possibility of endorsing multi-funds operational programmes may support strategic actions instead.

At a strategic level, member states are required to provide a territorial and urban analysis in their programming documents – Partnership Agreements and Operational Programmes – and clear arrangements to ensure an integrated approach to the use of European structural investment funds in urban areas. The provision of new tools to deliver integrated territorial and urban actions is another key aspect. Integrated territorial investments, as provisioned in Article 36 of the common provisions regulation, is an instrument facilitating the implementation of integrated territorial strategies at sub-national level by allowing the bundling of funds from several priority axes of one or more operational programmes (combining different thematic objectives) in order to finance interlinked cross-sectorial investments focused at a certain territorial level. Community-led local development as in Article 32–35 – an extension of the LEADER approach – seeks to promote bottom-up approaches and community ownership supporting local development strategies prepared and implemented by involving representatives of all sectors of local interest. Furthermore, the new provisions seek to promote innovation in urban areas through a dedicated budget represented by the Urban Innovative Actions (Article 8 of the ERDF Regulation), with a total financial commitment of EUR 317 million over the period 2015–20 and operationalised through a system of calls for proposals whose topic will be defined annually by the European Commission[19]. The URBACT programme – Article 9 of the ERDF Regulation – focusing on capacity building and policy transfer between cities will be continued over the new programming period. Additionally, the creation of a new Sustainable Urban Development will contribute to strengthen networking among cities, to review how European funds are implemented on the ground in Europe's cities and to support information exchange between cities involved in integrated Sustainable Urban Development (Art.7) and in Urban Innovative Actions (Art.8)

---

19. The ERDF contribution will not exceed EUR 5 million per project and the co-financing rate is set to a unique maximum of 80 per cent. The criteria fixed for the selection of projects chimes with criteria of innovativeness, quality, the establishment of partnerships, measurability and transferability.

Chapter Ten

Implications for Theory and Perspectives

in collaboration with Nicolas Gharbi[*]

During the 2007–13 programming period the place for cities and urban areas in Europe was subject to an ambivalent attitude by the EU. On one hand, initiatives specifically addressed to cities were dismissed. Programmes for urban renewal and growth were part of mainstream regional agendas under objectives 1 and 2 of the EU structural policy. On the other hand, the EU intended to strengthen the place of urban issues by integrating actions, concentrating resources and by formulating recommendations on a broad set of fields, ranging from transport services, environment and energy, sustainable territorial development, and the elaboration of new financial instruments to boost local economies.

The progressive marginalisation of cities in the EU policy making to the advantage of regional administrations and central bureaucracies is one possible implication of the former aspect. However, the integration of the urban dimension across issues and policies may position cities at the forefront of the EU policy making, especially in the domains of environment and sustainable development.

This project arose out of this potential dichotomy in an attempt to make sense of the ways European cities encounter the EU. The paucity of studies specifically addressing the relation between cities and the European Union led to favour a theoretically oriented type of research. The motivation for this project was to disclose the character of, and scope conditions for the Europeanisation of urban governance. In this chapter, we will address the research questions initially set out and systematise the empirical findings of our analysis. Specific attention will be devoted to the issue of mechanisms and the logic of interactions, to the theoretical expectations on the modes of Europeanisation and to locating the research findings in the broader literature on Europeanisation and European studies. Finally, we will present suggestions on how the result of the research can be used by the actors mentioned in the analysis to tackle some of the current and future policy issues concerning cities in the policy making of the European Union.

---

[*]   Nicolas Gharbi is a policy officer at the Directorate General for Regional and Urban policy of the European Commission, where he works in the 'Urban and Territorial Development' unit. Amongst his research interests, there is the architecture and planning of cities, urban sociology and cohesion policy.

10.1 Are cities in the EU really Europeanised?

The main question guiding the research – *how does the European Union influence urban policy?* – led us to a conceptual exploration of how cities encounter the EU.

Overall, we built on the argument that to identify how the EU affects different domains of urban governance it is necessary to look beyond those policies and programmes with 'cities on their tin', meaning the policies formally targeting cities. In this connection, EU policies – and policy instruments – initially promoted at the national level, may have a deferred or indirect influence on other territorial systems, thus contributing to re-structure relations and the policy making in the localities. Our analysis enables us to establish whether specific modes of interaction conform to theoretically justified patterns (mechanisms), thus determining the character of Europeanisation of urban systems. Simplified game-theoretical models – we found – are particularly useful to exemplify and highlight the defining properties at the foundations of modes of Europeanisation. They complement our process tracing of the selected cases.

Our findings also underline the role of actors, thus providing a link between substantive policy analysis and interaction-oriented policy research. In a nutshell, the overall attempt was to revitalise the research agenda initially proposed by Theodore Lowi, which calls for a science of politics that treats *policy* as an independent variable influencing the type of politics. In short, the empirical part of the volume has highlighted a whole set of policy programmes and policy instruments with potential impact on urban systems, beyond the range of activities that explicitly address cities in a formal-legalistic way.

Following the initial investigation of the possible channels of EU influence on cities, a second research question dealt with the *set of mechanisms that structure the interaction between actors and shape the process of Europeanisation*, thus eventually triggering change. Mechanisms have been sorted out according to different *arenas* – ideation, regulation, coordination and distribution – and to their *procedural nature* in terms of mechanisms of change and transmission.

We found that the analysis of policy instruments reveals the causal mechanisms structuring the encounter of actors within different institutional orders. Thus, policy instruments shed empirical light on the *modes of Europeanisation*. We argued that it is important to see instruments in relation to mechanisms. The analysis of four instruments (i.e. the covenant of mayors, the packaging and packaging waste directive, directive 1999/30 on air quality control and URBAN II community initiative), has shown that some of the mechanisms initially (and deductively) associated with the modes of Europeanisation (i.e. ideation, regulation, coordination and distribution) actually shape interactions within the specific domain considered, whereas others, despite prevailing in one mode, are also present in modes other than the one originally theorised. This is shown in Table 10.1 and 10.2, where we distinguish between change and transmission. Recall that change is about the mechanisms of interactions between actors around a specific policy issue, whereas transmission refers to the mechanisms for the promotion of EU instruments and how cities respond to, and manage EU instruments.

Coordination is the main mechanism within domains where preferences are prevalently exogenous and where EU action mainly consists of setting standards and aims to reach effectiveness through evidence-based measures (e.g. domains of air quality control). However, coordination dynamics also structure relations within the other domains considered, and its shortfall is often deemed as the most problematic aspect for the efficient pursuit of the objectives attached to the policy programmes undertaken.

Mechanisms of coordination – we found – become more relevant inasmuch as programmes implemented locally follow the integrated approach as recommended by the EU. *Proceduralisation* was initially ascribed to the set of mechanisms featuring ideational modes. However, actors' agreement on procedures, and processes for the choice of instruments to be used, is typical of multiple policy domains. Thus, ideational components are present also within modes of regulation in the form of persuasion dynamics, rational reasoning and dynamics for the selection of the procedures to employ in the management of instruments and policy programmes.

Some mechanisms for the transmission of EU instruments are generally present independently from the policy mode considered. To exemplify, *communication* features in modes of ideation as the principal mechanism for the transmission of EU instruments, but it also characterises the development of instruments within other modes, especially during the early phases of the policy process.

This is also the case for *learning* and *networking* mechanisms. The capacity of cities to enter networks where they can flag their preferred options and draw on others' successful experiences influences the diffusion and the outcomes of EU programmes. Learning is considered a necessary condition; on the one side for urban actors to put in place actions that revealed successful elsewhere, and on the other for the EU to guarantee the sustainability and improvement of its action domestically.

Table 10.1: Common mechanisms of Europeanisation

MECHANISMS of CHANGE	MECHANISMS of TRANSMISSION
- coordination	- communication
- proceduralisation	- policy learning/transfer
	- networking

A third research question – *does the nature of strategic interaction determine the character of Europeanisation?* – led us to further analysis of the four cases. The ideal-typical distinction between modes of Europeanisation through a typological exercise based on two dimensions – *logic of preference* and *payoffs from Europeanisation* – gave the analytical springboard for the empirical appraisal of EU policy instruments in the city of Turin.

Our initial hypotheses were:

Hp. 1: if preferences are ENDOGENOUS and the nature of strategic interaction is ZERO-SUM, then the prevalent mode of Europeanisation is via IDEATION;

Hp. 2: if preferences are ENDOGENOUS and the nature of strategic interaction is PARETO OPTIMAL, the prevalent mode of Europeanisation is via REGULATION;

Hp. 3: if preferences are EXOGENOUS and the nature of strategic interaction is PARETO OPTIMAL, the prevalent mode of Europeanisation is via COORDINATION;

Hp. 4: if preferences are EXOGENOUS and the nature of strategic interaction leads to ZERO-SUM games, the prevalent mode of Europeanisation is via DISTRIBUTION;

The analysis revealed that some conjectures/expectations were confirmed, whereas others revealed only partially true. In particular, when the city of Turin was involved from the early phases of the policy-process and maintained a role during the implementation phase – i.e. in the domain of air quality control and energy saving – our initial conjectures were not rejected by the evidence. In fact, the involvement in the initiatives promoted by the EU, a direct role in the implementation of instruments, and sustained management of policy action by cities' authorities, are conditions favouring Europeanisation. When the involvement of local actors is limited to specific phases instead – predominantly the execution of task in the case of waste management and the overall management of the programme in the case of URBAN CI – the process of Europeanisation is less robust. We will explore this point further in sections 3 and 4.

Linked to this substantive question, we addressed a further question – *do policy instruments and programmes perform according to specific modes of interaction, or do they trigger unforeseen contingencies instead?* – so as to eventually produce some generalisations and suggest avenues for future research.

As for the performance of instruments against the properties attributed to each of the modes of Europeanisation, the four case studies show how policy instrumentation does not entirely conform to the whole set of mechanisms and logics of action initially conjectured.

Instruments 'move' from one cell to another of the typology in Table 4.2, thus eventually showing properties that are initially credited to alternative modes. In particular, instruments within modes of ideation have the potential to evolve into their regulatory components and to develop distribution-like characteristics. This is actually the case for the Covenant of Mayors programme, which, despite mainly representing the character of ideational modes – based on extensive dynamics of reflexivity and communication – has developed into a series of instruments of a more pronounced financial type. In a similar vein, regulatory instruments – the waste framework directive in this case – present ideational components as initially suggested.

Ideational components within regulatory modes are typical of the process leading to the elaboration of regulatory procedures and feature in different phases of the policy process. Therefore, during the implementation of the waste framework directive in the city of Turin, actions aiming to efficiency by respecting the targets fixed by the EU are paralleled by information and communication campaigns to raise citizens' awareness. This is even more so within domains where distribution is the prevailing mode. In particular, URBAN II CI revealed how a financial instrument evolved into a complex programme made of a plethora of different components.

In a sense, the contrast among the four instruments is less stark than originally theorised, especially if we consider that they can move from one cell to another.

10.2 Dissecting mechanisms

Some mechanisms characterise interactions and the transmission of instruments within all the four modes of Europeanisation (Table 4.2). However, others appear more specific to one or the other policy instruments.

Table 10.2: Mechanisms and modes of Europeanisation

	MECHANISMS of EUROPEANISATION	
	IDEATION	*REGULATION*
MECHANISMS of CHANGE	*Socialisation* *Legitimising discourses* *Deliberation and framing*	*Pareto efficiency* *Regulation* *Collibration*
	DISTRIBUTION	*COORDINATION*
	Strategic bargaining *Negotiation*	*Coordination* *Cooperation*
	IDEATION	*REGULATION*
MECHANISMS of TRANSMISSION	Benchmarking Promotion of new paradigms and tools of governance	Regulatory competition Regulatory compliance
	DISTRIBUTION	*COORDINATION*
	Institutional framing Programming Targets compliance Territorial rescaling	Self-regulation Cooperative learning Targets compliance

We must recall that policy instruments exemplify our modes of Europeanisation. Looking at modes, *ideation* was examined via the Covenant of Mayors programme. The CoM is promoted within a domain – sustainable development – where preference has recently been accorded to incentive-based measures. Such measures are founded on a mix of soft regulatory provisions and financial mechanisms that aim to favour the efficient action of local authorities, without nonetheless imposing excessive bureaucratic and administrative burdens on the action of actors and administrations involved.

Here the EU channels a legitimising *discourse* where cities are depicted as loci for experimenting innovative governance tools and where management and implementation of existing policies can be pursued more efficiently. Since the promotion of the CoM in 2008, until the phases of initial implementation in the city of Turin, the action of the Commission – through the CoM Office – mainly confined to favour the socialisation of actors within different arenas and to the initial approval of the sustainable action plans.

Extended dynamics of *socialisation* and *deliberation* were at play during the promotional phase of the programme, especially on occasion of the informative meetings organised by the Commission. These lead signatories to eventually change their initial preferences, thus committing to a common set of overall goals, to be nonetheless locally pursued via autonomous actions. In particular, during the stages following the initial adoption of the programme and preceding the final endorsement of the SEAPs by the competent office at the EU level, the main mechanisms were *framing* and *proceduralisation*.

The former mainly structures relations between signatories – the city administration in this case – and the CoM Office during the elaboration of the sustainable action plan. Actions to implement locally are selected and organised according to evaluative and analytical criteria responding to templates and guidelines set at the EU level. The latter – proceduralisation – features instead in the process of actors' interrelation within urban systems during the preparation of the action plan and eventually throughout its management and implementation.

Thus, in the case of Turin, whilst the actual preparation of the action plan for energy – including the part relative to the emission inventory – showed the main role of the competent services of the city administration in partnership with the 'Politecnico' University, the overall discussion and planning of the actions recorded a broader participation of stakeholders[1].

The experimentation of *new tools of governance* in this sector, as well as the EU attempt to promote *new policy paradigms* in urban areas to stimulate the production of renewable energies and adopt sustainable strategies for urban development through the integrated approach, found an early translation in the launch of thirty pilot projects, which gave indications for the successive elaboration of the CoM programme. Therefore, mechanisms of innovation underpin dynamics of enlarged participation and the application of new financial instruments. In this case, EU financing depends more on the ability of local actors and administrations to attract complementary funds from domestic financial backers and institutions – and on the efficient pursuing of targets – than on their actual spending capacity, which is no longer considered a sufficient condition for efficiency.

Communication constitutes the principal mechanism for the transmission of the instruments embedded in the CoM programme. Not only does this apply to the CoM Office's action vis-à-vis the signatory cities, but also locally from the city administration towards stakeholders and the local population, with the aim to raise awareness about sustainable development and energy saving

---

1.   Fig. 6.3 (The Covenant of Mayors in Turin), in Chapter Six, graphically represents the subjects involved in the process in the case of Turin.

matters. Mechanisms of *benchmarking* apply in different instances. Overall, the CoM is interpreted as benchmark for future initiative of a similar nature, such as for instance the SmartCities project, therefore as a necessary toolkit for local administrations to venture into more long-term programmes. Benchmarking and *policy learning/transfer* characterise the entirety of the programme development. Local initiatives that appear to be particularly innovative are in fact endorsed as useful actions for other local authorities to replicate, within a context where the European Commission is seeking to elaborate a system for the continuous learning and transfer of best practices among participants.

In this connection, mechanisms of transmission are to various extents associated with dynamics for the promotion of ideational tools and their possible inclusion into future initiatives to be carried out in the context of more extended policy programmes within urban areas. At the level of urban domestic systems, ideational-discursive policies translate into EU-led – locally managed programmes – for boosting 'active citizenship' in the form of partnership arrangements for discussion and deliberation. In this case, representatives of different segments of the society are involved in debating problematic situations concerning specific policy issues or instead cross-sectoral initiatives to be carried out in limited areas or neighbourhoods of the city.

Modes of *regulation* have been exemplified by considering the development of the packaging and packaging waste directive 94/62/EC, embedded afterwards within the provisions of the waste framework directive in 2006–08. On one side, the choice to consider this particular instrument within a highly regulated sector was motivated by the early promotion of the directive, and on the other side by its character of 'command and control', setting specific targets for waste collection and recovery.

In this connection, *regulation* as a mechanism of mediation between actors – public administrations in particular – characterised most processes surrounding the development of directive 94/62/EC and the implementation of EU instruments for waste management in the case of the urban territory of Turin.

Despite the numerous legislative measures adopted since the late 1980s, the action of the national central administration is mainly confined to the transposition of EU provisions – it does not provide a coherent regulatory system for waste management. Cities are generally subject to a double regulatory scheme. The action of the Commission mainly consists of technical measures for the regulation of different waste streams, whereas domestic measures (mainly set at the regional level in the case of Turin) are moreover addressed to set the plans for waste management and to grant authorisations for waste treatment.

Contextually, the action of the European legislator within this particular policy domain aims at gaining increasing *efficiency* through the *harmonisation* of procedures for waste management. In this connection, we considered *collibration* as a mechanism for the virtuous exploitation of 'existing social energy'. The EU does not intervene on the operative methods for waste collection and the logistic organisation of the territories to be regulated. Mechanisms of *regulatory competition* apply only indirectly within local territories, where the regulatory action of the EU proceeds through the mediation of policy channels within other arenas (i.e. national and regional).

Compliance with the tenets and targets accompanying EU provisions for waste management is the main pattern structuring the relations between urban actors and regulators within other systems, namely the EU and the regional administration. Compliance with EU provisions in the case of the packaging waste directive – particularly as regards the obligation to attend quantitative objectives for waste collection and recycling – favoured transformations concerning the organisational aspects of waste management, technical operations of treatment and actions for waste prevention.

EU-related regulatory actions in urban areas are therefore associated with dynamics for the *monitoring of performance* and for *assessing outputs* at various stages of the policy process. Monitoring and assessment are performed at various levels by the municipal services, AMIAT, the area consortium and the provincial departments. Also within this domain, loose coordination is considered the main hindrance towards reaching greater efficiency in the territorial management of waste.

At the same time, *regulatory mechanisms* tied up with the action of variable partnership arrangements for the provision of services, where the management of policy programmes increasingly relies on shared competences. In this connection, the waste management system in Turin is mainly made of public and semi-public actors, which act on the bases of regulated partnership arrangements. The realisation of the 'Gerbido' waste to energy plant brought into scene a plethora of new private subjects acting as investors and partially as future management of the plant.

Coordination as a mode of Europeanisation was exemplified by considering directive 1999/30/EC and framework directive 2008/50/EC. Processes of interaction within the domain of air quality control – since its early phases back in the 1990s – advanced through successive steps of interests' accommodation between the European legislator and the different regulatory traditions of member states. In turn, the 'regulatory' measures agreed upon at the EU level were mostly following a logic of standard setting grounded on evidence based reasoning, evaluation techniques and information gathering.

Patterns of coordination apply in this case between different territorial systems as well as between actors within each of them. In one case coordination mainly structures the relations between member states and the EU. In the other, mechanisms of *coordination* and *cooperation* feature in the implementation process of concrete actions for local air quality control. Here, different administrations and multiple subjects involved in the urban policy making act in the attempt to respect the standards accompanying EU provisions for air quality control.

In this connection, member states coordinate their reciprocal actions around the standards agreed upon at community-level, in a policy domain where the EU does not regulate through 'command and control measures', but it promotes common methods for the evaluation and collection of information for statistical purposes. In particular, air quality control reveals how coordination is the main mechanism shaping the relations between the city (Department for Environment), the province of Turin, and the competent sectors within the regional administration. Similarly, coordination characterises the relation between Turin and the other urban conurbations of the Po-valley.

Compliance with targets is a characteristic mechanism within this domain, where actions implemented locally aim to create the conditions to attain performance-values. Regional plans for air quality control – comprising the elaboration of criteria for air quality assessment and zoning – and actions promoted and implemented by the city rest on mechanisms of *self-regulation*. In this connection, urban authorities have a certain room of manoeuvre to elaborate solutions that are as efficient and coherent as possible in addressing the specific drawbacks affecting their territories.

In turn, the success of locally implemented actions relies on the capacity to advance mechanisms of *cooperative learning* and *information benchmarking*, both between the subjects involved in the process locally, between the city administration and other administrative bodies having a competence to intervene in this policy realm (i.e. region and province). The overall success of urban action in this sense, as well as the long-term attainment of the EU objectives of the air quality control policy, largely depends on the efficient use of techniques for assessing air quality standards and on collecting reliable information for computing statistical databases useful for future policy elaboration[2].

Reporting and continuous *assessment* are necessary principles to coordinate the action of different systems towards the attainment of common goals. Coordination of actions, especially as to the overall collection and reporting of data, must be guaranteed by member states, which are asked to annually report to the European Commission on the national performances and values relative to emissions and air quality.

Poor coordination amongst the public administrations involved in the process is the main hindrance towards gaining full efficiency in the actions to contrast excessive pollutant emissions and therefore to respect the limit values imposed by legislation. Notwithstanding this partial drawback, Turin has achieved results, especially in limiting the overall emission of pollutant substances.

Community initiative URBAN II is the instrument we looked at for the mode of *distribution*. Unlike the other instruments considered, URBAN was an initiative (dismissed for the 2007–13 programming period) that the EU explicitly addressed to urban areas, thus representing a veritable incubator for the early experimentation of the integrated approach to policy elaboration in the localities.

According to structural funds regulations, national central administrations are the subjects that negotiate with the Commission the overall distribution of funds to member states and regions. In turn, different financial streams are nationally allocated, where, depending on the domestic organisation of territorial powers, local authorities (including cities) put forward their proposals to carry out programmes

---

2. The range of actions put in place for the control of emissions and to limit the emission of pollutants in the case of Turin are outlined in Chapter Eight (Europeanisation via modes of coordination).

and initiatives under the EU financial assistance. *Negotiation* and *bargaining* are the mechanisms shaping relations between member state representatives and the Commission during the early stage of the policy cycle.

The analysis of URBAN II has exposed different mechanisms of transmission: *programming, institutional framing, territorial rescaling* and *targets compliance*. The absence of a coherent pre-existing national policy for urban development, associated with a tendency to favour infrastructural regeneration in order to face contingent situations, did not favour the diffusion of integrated strategies for policy elaboration in Italian cities. Turin, together with other cities – Genoa and Bologna – had long embarked on the path of long-term strategic territorial development through the endorsement of a strategic plan back in 2000.

In particular, institutional framing applies to the relations between the municipal departments involved in the management of the CI, which had to partially re-adjust their usual working methods to better respond to the requirements attached to EU financial assistance. Similarly, relations with the regional administration underwent progressive transformations insofar as the integrated approach to urban development featured in the programmes carried out in the city[3].

Mechanisms of territorial re-scaling, as initially hypothesised, can be detected to the extent that direct relations between the city and the EU became more institutionalised during the deployment of the programme, thus strengthening the 'relative positioning' of Turin *vis-à-vis* the regional and central administrations. Mechanisms of compliance loom large also in the case of URBAN II. Compliance with targets translates here into the abidance to specific procedures for accomplishing the planned actions – integration of interventions and recourse to partnership arrangements in particular – as well as in the attempt to respect tenets concerning spending, timing and reporting towards attaining the overall efficiency of the actions pursued.

Dynamics leading to the 'institutionalisation of weak ties' (Granovetter, 1973), follow the application of new arrangements for the management of policies. In particular, partnership agreements initially set up to manage the actions planned to satisfy the programme requirements, have the potential to become long-lasting arrangements for implementing similar initiatives planned by the city without the aegis of the EU.

Additionally, programmes within modes of distribution envisage a series of processes leading to the horizontal integration of policies through cross-sectoral initiatives, whose management often requires the partial restructuring of relations between urban, regional, rural and central state authorities.

10.3 The logic of interaction

We already concluded that policy instrumentation does not entirely conform to the whole set of mechanisms initially hypothesised. The contrast among the

3. The regional administration co-involved in the dynamics of urban regeneration, and participated in the management and implementation of EU-financed projects for territorial development.

four instruments is less stark than originally theorised. We now go back to the association between EU instruments (in turn, proxies of the 'modes') and simple game-theoretical models, and explore a key element of any game, that is, the logic of interaction.

Recall that we associated the Covenant of Mayors with *signalling* games; the packaging and packaging waste directive with the *battle of the sexes* game; Directive 1999/30 (and 2008/50) on air quality control with the *assurance game*, and URBAN II with *games of bargaining*. The main properties of each game paired with our modes of Europeanisation were confirmed during the analysis of EU policy instruments in Turin. This gave us leverage to assess the type of change occurred – if any – and the possible character of Europeanisation.

The analysis of the Covenant of Mayors shows a situation where the European Commission acts as *sender vis-à-vis* participant cities, which are generally less informed 'agents' willing, nonetheless, to embark on the path of innovation. Reiterated processes of communication and learning, and more generally the coordination role played by the Commission behind the two-fold veil of exclusion/ suspension and financial support, transform a potentially zero-sum game into a situation that is beneficiary for both parts.

The voluntary character of the overall programme, associated with the great freedom of action granted to the participant cities, makes Europeanisation in the case of the CoM a highly variable process. Its nature and scope mainly depend on the specificities of the urban system encountered, thus on its permeability to innovation and the working methods accompanying this EU instrument.

Our analysis shows how EU action through the CoM is *de facto* auxiliary to an overall process of domestic (local) reforms, where policy actions for energy saving and renewal were already in place. Embarking on the CoM contributed to enhance the overall coherence of the city activity in this sector. The preparation of the Action Plan for Energy fostered new synergies between local actors, thus favouring an overall dynamic of consultation and information sharing between public and private subjects differently interested in this sector.

Although the number of actors involved in the process has not consistently increased during the period of analysis, actors' legitimacy has strengthened following EU 'inducement'. More relevant here is the potential embedded in this EU instrument to persuade cities – and thus their actors – to systematically adopt the yardstick of the integrated approach for the elaboration of action plans and the strategic development of urban territories. In this connection, *signalling* is a distinctive feature of the European Commission's role during the development of the Covenant of Mayors in Turin.

The role of certain member states as 'first-mover' characterised the early phases of discussion and negotiation of the packaging and packaging waste directive, the instrument chosen to exemplify *regulation* as a mode of Europeanisation. Hence, those member states with a stronger tradition – and a more comprehensive regulatory framework – in the realm of waste management succeeded in channelling their preferred options, and to influence the contents of the policy measures adopted by the EU. In this policy domain, the European Commission acts as first mover *vis-à-vis* cities, which are generally subject to the regulatory provisions of the EU and the nationally endorsed laws for waste management (or by the regional administration, as in the case of Turin).

Regulation mainly consists of successive movements to reach efficiency following dynamics of reasoning and compliance grounded on specific targets and on the prevision of sanctions. The European Commission exercises partial leadership by providing adaptability to changing circumstances and by promoting change, also through the revision of existing measures, as it was for the endorsement of the 'waste framework directive'.

EU action within this policy domain assumed a particularly strong relevance in Turin. This was due to the lack of a comprehensive regulatory framework for waste management in the territory of Turin until recently, associated with the partial stalemate of the national administration, which limited its action to the transposition of EU legislative measures. In Turin, the promotion of regulatory instruments for waste management and prevention – including directive 94/62 – encountered a particularly 'fertile' context for channelling EU tenets of waste management and fixing targets for the collection and re-use of municipal waste. New actors got involved in the process, and the level of participation increased, following the involvement in pan-European networks for waste management (i.e. ACR+) and the merging of private investors in the project for the realisation of the new waste to energy plant (TRM Ltd.).

In the analysis of Directive 1999/30 on air quality control, *assurance*[4] – the defining property of the game we held as exemplifying interactions within modes of coordination – characterises the relation between actors involved in the process of air quality control within the urban territory, and the dynamic of coordination between Turin and other 'neighbourhood' cities on occasion of joint actions to face situations of emergency. The role of the European Commission consists of enhancing reciprocal assurance between the agents – also by limiting the set of preferences at disposal of actors – through the diffusion of information and empirical evidence on air quality.

Europeanisation of air quality control translates in greater legitimacy for local actors to undertake policy initiatives and to 'autonomously regulate' within the legislative framework of the regional law. Increased dynamisms of urban actors triggered stronger collaborations between the public administration and other research institutes (i.e. ARPA and ISPRA) and the promotion of new instruments for emission reduction, especially on the initiative of the city mayor within his special competencies. The diffusion of an EU narrative that portrays urban areas as the ideal dimension where to undertake actions to combat air pollution favoured the overall process.

Game-models of bargaining were considered to exemplify the main properties of interactions within modes of *distribution*, which we assessed through the analysis of URBAN II. The extensive nature of interactions over policy issues

---

4. See Chapter Eight for an illustration of the 'Assurance Game'.

characterises this mode, where actors' interplay usually takes place in different arenas of governance over time[5].

In particular, the Romer-Rosenthal model for resource allocation was thought as best fitting the action of the EU in the process of negotiation and successive management of structural funds and thus the financial endorsement of URBAN II CI. Therefore, the European Commission acts like an 'agenda setter' *vis-à-vis* member states in the initial phase of negotiation and allotment of funds.

In URBAN II, after the initial decision of the Commission concerning the national allocation of funds to carry out the initiative, the principle interactions take place between the competent services at the EC (i.e. DG Regio) and the cities willing to put forward their candidature for the programme.

In the case of Turin, following the approval of the programming document, city's authorities were interacting directly with the offices of the European Commission, which acted as surveillance and technical support during the programme development.

The main element of innovation linked to URBAN II CI is the diffusion of the *integrated approach* to policy development. Veritably, some of its constitutive principles were already part of the working methods employed in carrying out programmes for urban regeneration in the city prior to EU assistance. On this occasion though, the principle of 'participatory planning' found thorough translation in the involvement of citizens during the project selection phase, while enhanced actors participation characterised the overall development of the programme.

Thus, the necessity to put in place cross-cutting actions within multiple domains led to the creation of new – although temporary – managerial committees as well as to partially readjust relations between different sectors of the municipality. The long lasting involvement of Turin in programmes for urban regeneration and territorial development sponsored by the EU, contributed on this occasion to fully interiorise working methods and organisational practices foreseen by URBAN CI. However, we cannot affirm that EU principles for urban regeneration through the integrated approach will continue to be part of the city 'policy-making DNA' for the elaboration and implementation of similar initiatives in the future. *Agenda setting* by part of the European Commission is the defining property governing the overall logic of interaction within modes of distribution. However, the analysis of URBAN II in Turin showed that interaction assumes more nuanced fashions during the actual management and implementation of the instrument within the urban territory.

10.4 Using evidence to formulate propositions on Europeanisation

The main purpose of the investigation was to assess the nature of the Europeanisation process of the policy making of European cities. However, we can now use the

---

5. As already exposed in Chapter Three, interaction within arenas of distribution can be thought as a series of 'nested games' (Tsebelis, 1990), where actors suboptimal strategy in one game can be part of a strategy to maximise payoffs when all arenas are taken into account.

evidence to formulate propositions about Europeanisation that new projects may wish to test. Our expectations about the scope of Europeanisation are the following:

EXP 1: when the prevailing mode is 'ideation', stakes are big and Europeanisation is expected to be robust in the long term;

EXP 2: when the prevailing mode is 'regulation', the stakes are rather irrelevant and Europeanisation is expected to be contingent on compliance patterns;

EXP 3: when the prevailing mode is 'coordination', stakes are small and Europeanisation is expected to be robust;

EXP 4: when the prevailing mode is 'distribution', stakes are big and Europeanisation is expected to be contingent;

Let us see how we get to these expectations. Exp.1 is drawn from the argument that, despite the non-binding character of the policy measures promoted within ideational domains, there are latent potentials for their sedimentation into the logic of domestic action due to extended processes of confrontation and socialisation between city actors in the EU-wide policy arenas, thus eventually leading to the Europeanisation of policy areas other than solely the one initially concerned. Exp.2 arises out of the reasoning that, being stakes rather irrelevant, the eventual Europeanisation of domestic policy arenas is dependent upon the compliance with the EU provisions, which can be constraining to different degrees and in the case of cities, 'filtered' through additional provisions elaborated within central national administrations. In the case of coordination – Exp.3 – the relatively 'soft' role of the EU, and the coordination of reciprocal actions and exchange of ideas over policy alternatives – generally taking place within groups of experts – trigger the possibility for EU instruments to become substantial yardsticks for policy elaboration domestically. Expectations on the character of Europeanisation in the case of modes of distribution – Exp. 4 – are motivated by the nature of EU action within these domains and by the generally limited duration of EU programmes, therefore on the likely 'dispersion' of EU working methods after programmes terminate.

Table 10.3: Expectations on the scope of Europeanisation

| | POLICY MODES | | |
	IDEATION	REGULATION	COORDINATION	DISTRIBUTION
SCOPE OF EUROPEANISATION	Potentially robust	Contingent on compliance patterns	Robust, but based on small stakes	Contingent on stakes

Building on the now extended scholarships on *modes of governance* in the European Union (Eberlein and Kerwer, 2002; Héritier and Rhodes, 2011 Joerges, Mény and Weiler, 2001 Knill and Lenschow, 2003; Treib, *et al.*, 2005), we submit that the four modes can reveal differences based on the *policy making features* that we expect to exemplify the encounter between cities and the EU.

Thus, the *approach to implementation* can rely on rigid modalities (e.g. in regulatory modes), which define precise standards, rather than on more flexible criterion for the application of norms (e.g. modes of ideation). Yet, the implementation of instruments can be based on different sets of targets to pursue, or on provisions of mixed nature, like in the case of URBAN II.

The *nature of conflict* over resources can be material, thus involving political or societal confrontation over sensitive policy issues (e.g. ideation and distribution), or more centred on the specific procedures to carry out EU level policies and programmes. In this latter case, confrontation on procedures to be employed is about deciding the type of standards or the level of targets on which the instrument is based (modes of coordination).

The *character of proceduralisation* of policies also varies between areas or policy sectors wherein there are binding (mandatory) steps to follow – no matter what the substance of the decision (or policy) is – and less stringent requirements that allow the parts involved to manage the issue at stake through more bendy modalities. Examples of procedures are reason-giving requirements, compulsory inter-service procedures, all the bits of the treaties on the involvement of the EP and council for example in the community method, obligations to publish the list of participants in meetings, prohibition to convene informal meetings prior to a formal meeting, obligation to give a hearing to an interested party, obligation to perform an economic analysis of proposed regulations, yet obligation to publish proposed regulation for notice and comment or the requirement attached to procedures for the judicial review of certain rules.

In addition, a distinction can be made as to the level of *transparency* of the interaction within a specific area, and the *nature of deliberation* over policy issues, which can be encouraged and diffused (modes of ideation), or limited to a strict range of actors. Hence, deliberation can be of a more technocratic nature – as in the case of modes of regulation – instead the process can be essentially 'political'. This is prevalently the case within modes of distribution, where local authorities and actors eventually deal with the EU only when dynamics of 'grand bargaining and negotiation' over the distribution of EU funds are concluded.

Furthermore, the modes are likely to feature different *structures of actors*. Distinction in this sense can be made as to the institutional and territorial level of their 'affiliation' – EU, national or local – the fact that those are public rather than private actors, yet as to the source of their legitimisation, that can be technocratic or political. Besides that, differences are likely to be detected in relation to the *structure of networks* eventually operating, as well as regarding the type of *access to network structures*. Networks in which actors might interact can be open to access, or constrained in terms of actors' participation. In turn, their structure can be prevalently hierarchical, where participation is subject to defined sets of rules or characterised by a variable geometry with the prevalence of technical expert or political representatives. Finally, other distinguishing features relate to the prevailing *locus of authority* that can be centralised or dispersed, rather than diffused within groups of experts or following patterns with variable geometry.

10.5 Contribution to the literature and future research

By approaching Europeanisation as a process (rather than as an outcome), we were able to appraise the evolution and transformations of different arenas, thus generating findings that are more nuanced than propositions like 'Turin is highly Europeanised / is not Europeanised'. This also exposes an important way in which our work contributes to the literature: in our analysis of Europeanisation, the unit of analysis was not the city, but policy arenas where actors, instruments and modes of interaction have shaped a given type of political relationships – a distinctive way to produce policy and politics. This approach – we submit – has more leverage for generalisations than approaches based on units of analysis (like the city or the country) that have little to offer to genuine theoretical public policy analysis (Radaelli, et al., 2012).

This approach also speaks to those who are trying to promote a conversation between rational choice and constructivist approaches, rather than isolating them so they no longer communicate. On many occasions, we have seen that actors in our policy arenas have a sense of strategy, and pursue power rather than learning. Yet there are fundamental elements of their strategy that defy calculability: our actors can gamble rather than formulate probability estimates. More interestingly still, there is no uniform behaviour across arenas. Thus we observed that the rational choice game theoretical intuitions go a bit further in some cases than in others. Finally, the volume has confirmed a major tenet of a large collective work programme under way, based on the systematic study of policy instruments to expose the politics of policy making. Although this was present in earlier work by Lowi and Salamon, it was in the last twenty years that the theoretical implications of thinking in terms of instruments have been clarified. Hopefully our work contributes to this systematisation of the theoretical usages of policy instruments in comparative public policy.

At an even more abstract level, there is debate on the agenda for the 'normalisation' and 'sociologisation' of European Studies – the basic idea being that we should have the same concepts to study different political systems, so the EU empirical pieces should fall in the theoretical places that can be used also outside the EU (Hassenteufel and Surel, 2000).

This agenda ties in with the motivation to 'revitalise' the logic of social action. This understanding of Europeanisation, however, also connects with strategic interaction, the importance of considering 'micro-sociological' aspects, as well as the importance of referring to social mechanisms and the modes of interaction guiding actors within different systems of territoriality. Actors *use* the opportunities offered by the European Union, but at the same time they are transformed by these relations (Jacqout and Woll, 2008). Our approach, however, accounts both for the goals of rational actors as well as for the social and institutional environments in which they are embedded. This brings us to lessen the theoretical dividing between the approaches of rational choice and social-constructivism.

This approach to Europeanisation – which is not necessarily devoid of rationality and strategy – emphasises the value of micro-sociological analysis and the importance of considering the role of, and the interaction between actors (Carter and Pasquier, 2010; Pasquier and Weisbain, 2004; Guiraudon, 2000; Smith, 1999). It also considers the importance of conducting analysis *par le bas* in the attempt to assess the role of local actors and the ways through which they re-appropriate of EU and national institutional rules (Baisnée and Pasquier, 2007; Pasquier, 2005). We have to consider how actors within the localities *perceive* and *use* EU norms and policies, although they may have not directly taken part in the process of their initial elaboration and promotion (Smith, 2001). Hence, the Europeanisation of a certain phenomenon (or policy sector) 'resides in the constant interaction between the communitarian dimension and the national and international dimensions' (Pasquier and Weisbain, 2004: 9).

To make progress along these lines, we found it useful to take typologies of mechanisms seriously – yet another way in which our findings can speak to a wider literature in political sociology. Typological exercises create order and simplification out of otherwise overly complex situations. A typology, in this sense does not constitute an explanation; it does not provide accounts as to why a certain event happens or for the time–space co-variation of occurrences. Typologies are 'classificatory devices that allow to attach labels to different phenomena in an orderly fashion, but they not tell us why we observe the phenomena we observe' (Hedström, 2005: 13). In turn, the classificatory purpose helps to establish to which type a case can be associated with. Eventually – as it was actually the case here – the typology is used for the selection of cases, their mapping and their comparison on the basis of different values of the attributes of the property space (Elman, 2005).

We can now sum-up and describe the main innovations we have hopefully brought into this field. In contrast to the classic view of the cathedral based on EU instruments that have 'city on the tin', we have set out to explore an alternative, more encompassing view. In particular, this study has drawn on the 'sharp public policy analysis tools' advocated by Carter and Smith. We have been able to generate the initial catalogue of mechanisms and arenas to consider four ideal-typical modes. These modes – NOT the policies legally defined as EU initiatives for the cities – are the theoretical places wherein the Europeanisation effects can be traced, by examining public policies and their instruments across time. In this connection, our research endeavour contributes – we argue – to revitalise the literature on modes (or arenas) of policy, thus those scholarships assuming that the structuring of politics depends on the type of confrontation and strategic interaction producing around specific policy issues.

Hence, one advantage of our proposal is to extend the range of instruments that are (potentially at least) vehicles of Europeanisation way beyond the limited 'city-level initiatives' considered by the traditional view of the cathedral. Another is to enable us to reflect theoretically about governance, interaction, and logics of political behaviour, thus setting the ground for theory-based expectations of how urban governance is affected by the action of the European Union.

Further, the typological exercises at the base of our analysis contributes to the literature on modes of governance, policy instruments and Europeanisation by showing how the urban dimension can be integrated in the analysis. By doing so, our approach makes the urban dimension fully comparable with other territorial domains in which Europeanisation effects have been studied. Further research could integrate our typological exercise with the vibrant literature on EU modes of governance and EU policy instruments (Kassim and Le Galès, 2010). Finally, the analysis has considered policy instruments not merely in terms of their intended outcomes, as usually suggested by functional explanations, but rather as complex devices ensuing from conflict and specific modes of interaction (Lascoumes and Le Galès, 2007).

Some words of caution are in order, however – to begin with, our conjectures and expectations were tested on a single geographical context (i.e., the city of Turin). This is a good choice in terms of research design, because it allows us to examine the variation of theoretically-generated variables (like our modes) within a single institutional and territorial context. However, it limits the possibility to draw general lessons. At the theoretical level, we suggested one possible way to study Europeanisation. However, this is not the only possible way. Our approach has high costs in terms of abstractions about logics, preferences and other concepts. Because of this, our approach is useful to sort out categories and concepts, less to generate causal IF-THEN propositions that can be tested empirically, although in the previous section we have made an effort in this direction.

We also have to acknowledge that we have moved away from multi-level governance: this may be seen as both an asset and a liability. The main justification to develop the project outside the field of multi-level governance is the need to pay attention to actors' relations over specific policy issues and to give sense of their specific role during the policy process. This allows overcoming an approach – MLG – that has usually treated sub-national actors and institutions as constituting a unique and static layer of governance. Future research will have to re-connect research on urban processes of Europeanisation to the general propositions of multi-level governance – if anything, to prove them wrong.

On research design, more extensive research strategies may be employed to carry out future research on the same topic. Thus, for instance, the same policy instrument can be considered in its development over different programming periods with reference to different territorial contexts[6]. Not only would this improve the understanding of how different urban systems react to EU promoted. It would also make more sense of whether the logic governing the EU action over different spans of time actually impacts on urban systems and on the ways local actors use EU policy instrumentation. Alternatively, the same policy mode may be assessed through the analysis of multiple instruments. This could contribute to appreciate internal differentiation within each of the modes as well as improve our understanding for alternative case selection.

---

6.   This would be the case, in particularly for the analysis of those instruments within policy domains where the action of the European Union is organised through different programming periods, such as for instance the EU structural policy.

Further, the analysis can gain additional analytical leverage by simply extending the number of observations. This would have implied to consider, for instance, four different cities, contrasting cases of success and failure. This type of research strategy would nonetheless require a considerable amount of resources, both in terms of time and availability of a sufficiently reliable date-set for the initial selection of the cities and the eventual evaluation of the actual results afterwards achieved.

10.6 Between new regulatory provisions and a possible EU urban agenda

We wish to conclude by connecting findings to recent policy developments. Over the past two decades, cities have played at the forefront in the context of the structural and cohesion policy of the EU, by making use of the available instruments over the different programming periods. Such a dynamic takes place within a territorial structure which reflects an often conflictive dynamic of space production, where cities are poles assuming the two-faceted function of *attraction* and *distribution* of people and resources. With the increasing *metapolisation* of the European territory, which some already defined as the resultant of a dual process of 'metropolisation' on the one hand, and formation of distended and discontinuous 'metacities' on the other (Ascher, 1995), cities continue to reflect, and to determine the relationship between society and its territories. Despite their structuring function, the role of cities has been subject to alternate fortune in the debate around – and practice of – cohesion policy. This has paralleled the debate on the territorial dimension of cohesion policy, and the often ambiguous narrative produced on the relationship between 'the territorial' and 'the urban' dimension of Europe. Conceptual uncertainty has mirrored a certain difficulty to reach a shared understanding by part of national administrations and decision makers of the defining characteristics of a city, or the urbanised territories, which are subject of dedicated investment and policy action. Other distinctive feature of the urban dimension of cohesion policy over time consists in the partial mismatch between the continuity of EU investments in urban areas over time, and the rather discontinuous progress in terms of policy development. Against this background, the adoption of the Structural and Investment Funds (ESIF) Regulation 2014–20 – including the provisions for the European Regional Development Fund – stresses the importance of elements such as integrated urban development, whilst the debate around the need for a European Union urban agenda has taken a new drive, thus confirming the will to adopt of a new programmatic chart for cities in Europe. The communication released by the European Commission in 2014[7] sets the bases for a renewed EU urban agenda, by stressing the necessity to strengthen the conditions for a better involvement of cities and to place urban governance at the forefront of EU policy making. Despite underlining elements that were

---

7. 'The Urban Dimension of EU Policies – Key features of an EU Urban Agenda', Communication from the Commission to the European Parliament, the Council, the European Economic and Social Committee and the Committee of the Regions, COM (2014) 490final.

already part of the EU-wide narrative on cities, the communication bears some elements of novelty, including a certain critical stand on the overall 'urban Europe' question. It recognises that a future EU urban agenda should focus on a limited number of relevant policy areas – i.e. CO_2 reduction and climate adaptation, inclusion and demographic change, economic development and innovation – in the spirit of ensuring sectoral coherence and a better coordination between available instruments. Against the current climate of economic crisis and a general situation of shrinking tax revenues at the local level, many European cities suffer from an insufficient capacity to engage in, and achieve structural change, and a growing mismatch between administrative and urban structures, which in turn may reduce cohesion and impair competitiveness[8]. The public consultation[9] organised on the subject of a new EU urban agenda, highlights three main avenues to move forward: (i) result orientation through concerted action on a limited number of priority areas, (ii) development and better use of the knowledge base approach and the use of better regulation tools, (iii) improved policy coherence and coordination of instruments addressed to cities and urban areas, and (iv) improving the use of benchmarking and monitoring of activities. Concerning the priority areas for intervention, stakeholders showed support for upgrading actions in the context of the Smart Cities and Communities Agenda[10], in particular by better integrating interventions in the energy, transport, water and waste sectors with the environmental challenges of urban development and the necessity to support urban regeneration to tackle poverty and inequality. In connection with the elements emerged during the process of consultations, the informal declaration adopted by the EU ministers responsible for territorial cohesion and urban matters gives political support to the entire process; it underlines the necessity to take action by respecting the principle of subsidiarity and avoiding new regulatory requirements, as well as recognising the heterogeneity of EU cities, an aspect that requires a flexible framework.

Although it is somehow premature to formulate evidence-based judgement about the actual effects of the new regulatory provisions or to assess their potential, some preliminary observations can be made by considering the programming documents adopted thus far. Member states have allocated approximately a total of EUR 16 billion (8.6 per cent of the total ERDF financial envelope) to implement sustainable urban development under Article 7 ERDF, half of them well exceeding the 5 per cent obligation; moreover there is a relatively limited use of funds other than the ERDF. From a thematic perspective – and in contrast to the thematic concentration requirements, member states predominantly address urban challenges linked to sustainable and inclusive growth type of investments. Regarding the empowerment of urban authorities, member states opted massively for the minimum required level of delegation, which is the selection of operations

---

8. *Ibid.*, p. 5.

9. Commission Staff Working Document, result of the public consultation on the key features of an EU Urban Agenda, SWD(2015) 109 final/2.

10. https://eu-smartcities.eu/ (accessed 10 November 2016).

and only in exceptional cases, they did delegate additional tasks. Finally, the absence of an appropriate set of indicators measuring the added value of an integrated approach seems to be transversal to most part of the programming documents. The picture emerging from the few elements mentioned is a rather heterogeneous one, which reflects the variety of the EU urban and territorial structure and the high level of differentiation as to the level of political and administrative decentralisation among member states. The absence of legal basis for a EU urban policy in the treaties, the tripartite process of negotiation of the legislative packages together with the shared management of EU funds, create the conditions for a high level of compromise enabling (and echoing) the expression of heterogeneity among member states, which does not necessarily reflect the one among the urban territories.

Over recent decades the EU played a relevant role in the development of cities, notably through structural action; economic, social and territorial cohesion are all domains with a strong urban dimension, although within a policy that still lies in a sort of 'legal vacuum', where no real legal basis can be found in the founding treaties of the European Union. In connection with this, the current debate on the role of cities in the EU seems to evolve around two main alternatives. On the one hand, a basic approach that would focus on better understanding how EU policies affect urban areas and on increasing synergies. On the other a more ambitious approach that would transpose Europe 2020 objectives into urban equivalents, with actions adapted to the diverse realities of Europe cities, involving the national level to agree with their cities on targets and suitable indicators.

Two years into the new EU programming period, the role of cities within the EU-wide policy making and the effectiveness of policies in urban areas is at the crossroad of the efficient engagement of stakeholders in the conception of policies and the attribution of formal regulatory and budgetary power between different administrations. In the absence of binding legal basis and of the possibility to adopt a single approach, the urban agenda could instead establish a shared method to identify the best course of action following the different contexts. Contemporary urban policy needs to struggle in detecting problems and find solutions case by case, accumulating knowledge but without forcefully reproducing solutions. Therefore, the key aim should be the construction of a common logical framework and common rules enabling the conditions to stimulate synergies between actors. In this connection, we argue, to fully deploy the potentials of the integrated approach to urban development, cities' administrations and actors should better develop instruments for the collection of information and the diffusion of knowledge, in order to assess both their current situation and the prospective development of their territories. Thus, a thorough system of indicators is needed to gauge progress towards objectives and to evaluate both the effectiveness of the strategies put in place and of the actions to be planned. New and more results-oriented indicators would need to be combined with an improved capacity for cities to communicate and share information, both between departments within the public administration and stakeholders, and between urban areas within the same territory, where policy objectives and the axes of strategic development are allegedly more similar.

Bibliography

Abbott, A. (1992) 'From causes to events: notes on narrative positivism', *Sociological Methods and Research* 20: 428–55.

—— (2007) 'Mechanisms and relations', *Sociologica* 2: 1–22.

ACR+ (2009) *Municipal Waste in Europe*, Collection Environment, Paris: Victoires Editions.

Adler, E. (1997) 'Seizing the middle ground: constructivism in world politics', *European Journal of International Relations* 3(3): 319–63.

—— (2002) 'Constructivism and international relations', in Carlsnaes, W., Risse, T. and Simmons, B. (eds.) *Handbook of International Relations*, London: Sage Publications, pp. 95–119.

Allen, D. (2000) 'Cohesion and the structural funds: transfers and trade-offs', in Wallace, H. and Wallace, W. (eds.) *Policy Making in the European Union*, Oxford: Oxford University Press.

Amatucci, F. and Vestito, D. (2009) *Lo sviluppo di fonti energetiche innovative per la realizzazione di ambienti urbani sostenibili*, CITTALIA working paper 5/2009.

Anderson, J. L. (1997) 'Governmental suasion: refocusing the Lowi policy typology', *Policy Studies Journal* 25(2): 266–282.

—— (2003) 'Europeanization in context: concept and theory', in Dyson, K. and Goetz, E. G. (eds.), *Germany, Europe and the politics of Constraint*, NY: Oxford University Press.

Atkinson, R. (2001) 'The emerging urban agenda and the European spatial development perspective: towards and EU urban policy', *European Planning Studies* 9(3): 385–406.

Bache, I. (1998) *The Politics of European Union Regional Policy: Multi-level governance and flexible gate-keeping?*, Sheffield: Sheffield Academic Press.

Bache, I. and Flinders, M. (2004) (eds.) *Multi-Level Governance*, Oxford-NY: Oxford University Press.

Bache, I. and Marshall, A. (2004) 'Europeanization and domestic change: a governance approach to institutional adaptation in Britain', *Queen's Paper on Europeanization*, No. 5.

Bagnasco, A. and Le Galés, P. (2000) (eds.) *Cities in Contemporary Europe*, Oxford: Oxford University Press.

Bailey, I. (1999) 'Flexibility, harmonization and the single market in EU environmental policy: the Packaging Waste Directive', *Journal of Common Market Studies* 37(4): 549–71.

—— (2003) *New Environmental Policy Instruments in the European Union: Politics, economics, and the implementation of the Packaging Waste Directive*, Aldershot: Ashgate.

Baisnée, O. and Pasquier, R. (2007) (eds.) *L'Europe telle qu'elle se fait: Européanisation et societés politiques nationales*, Paris: CNRS Editions.

Baldasano, J. M. Valera, E. and Jiménez, P. (2002) 'Air quality data from large cities', *The Science of the Total Environment*.

Bates, R. H., Greif, A., Levi, M., Rosenthal, J. L. and Weingast, B. R. (1998) *Analytic Narratives*, Princeton, NJ: Princeton University Press.

Benington, J. (1994) *Local Democracy and the European Union*, London: Commission for Local Democracy.

Benz, A. and Eberlein, B. (1999) 'The Europeanization of regional policies: patterns of multi-level governance', *Journal of European Public Policy* 6(2): 329–48.

Bomberg, E. and Peterson, J. (2000) 'Policy transfer and Europeanization: passing the Heineken test?', *Queen's Papers on Europeanization* No.2.

Bonoli, G. (2007) 'Time matter: Postindustrialization, new social risks, and welfare state adaptation in advanced industrial democracies', *Comparative Political Studies* 40(5): 495–520.

Borras, S. and Jacobsson, K. (2004) 'The open method of coordination and new governance patterns in the EU', *Journal of European Public Policy* 11(2): 185–208.

Borraz, O. and John, P. (2004) 'The transformation of urban political leadership in Western Europe', *International Journal of Urban and Regional Research* 28(1): 107–20.

Börzel, T. (1999) 'Towards convergence in Europe? Institutional adaptation to Europeanization in Germany and Spain', *Journal of Common Market Studies* 39(4): 573–596.

—— (2000a) 'Member states responses to Europeanization', *Journal of Common Market Studies* 40(2): 193–214.

—— (2000b) 'Why there is no 'Southern problem'. On environmental leaders and laggards in the European Union', *Journal of European Public Policy* 7(1): 141–62.

—— (2002) 'Pace-setting, foot-dragging, and fence-sitting: member state responses to Europeanization', *Journal of Common Market Studies* 40(2): 193–214.

—— (2003) 'Shaping and taking EU policies: member states' responses to Europeanization', *Queen's Paper on Europeanization*, No. 2.

—— (2005) 'Mind the gap! European integration between level and scope', *Journal of European Public Policy* 12(2): 217–36.

Börzel, T. and Risse, T. (2000) 'When Europe hits home: Europeanization and domestic change', *European Integration on-line papers* 5(15).

—— (2003) 'Conceptualising the domestic impact of Europe', in Featherstone, K. and Radaelli, C. M. (eds.) *The Politics of Europeanization*, Oxford: Oxford University Press, pp. 57–83.

Brenner, N. (1999) 'Globalisation as re-territorialisation: the re-scaling of urban governance in the European union', *Urban Studies* 36(3): 431–51.

—— (2004) 'Urban governance and the production of new state spaces in western Europe, 1960–2000', *Review of International Political Economy* 11(3): 447–88.

Brunazzo, M. (2005) *Le regioni Italiane e l'Unione Europea. Accessi Istituzionali e di Politica Pubblica*, Roma: Carrocci Editore.

Buchs, M. (2008) 'The open method of coordination as a "two-level game"', *Policy and Politics* 36(1): 21–37.

Buclet, N. (2002) (ed.) *Municipal Waste Management in Europe: European policy between harmonisation and subsidiarity*, Dordrecht: Kluwer Academic Publishers.

Bulmer, S. and Burch, M. (1998) 'Organizing for Europe: Whitehall, the British state and European Union', *Public Administration* 76(4): 601–28.

Bulmer, S. and Radaelli, C. (2005) 'The Europeanization of national policy', in Bulmer, S. and Lequesne, C. (eds.), *The Member States of the European Union*, Oxford: Oxford University Press, pp. 338–55.

Bunge, M. (1967) *Scientific Research*, Volume 3 in Studies of the foundations, methodology, and philosophy of science, Berlin: Springer-Verlag.

—— (2004) 'How does it work? The search for explanatory mechanisms', *Philosophy of the Social Sciences* 34: 182–210.

Caporaso, J.A. (2007) 'The three worlds of regional integration theory', in Graziano, P. and Vink, M.P. (eds.) *Europeanization: New research agendas*, Basingstoke: Palgrave/Macmillan, pp. 23–35.

Carley, M. (1980) *Rational Techniques in Policy Analysis*, London: Heinemann Educational Books.

Carter, C. and Smith, A. (2008) 'Revitalising public policy approaches to the EU: "territorial institutionalism", fisheries and wine', *Journal of European Public Policy* 15(2): 263–81.

Carter, C. and Pasquier, R. (2010) 'The Europeanization of regions as 'spaces for politics': a research agenda', Regional & Federal Studies 20(3): 295–314.

Cento Bull, A. and Jones, B. (2006) 'Governance and social capital in urban regeneration: a comparison between Bristol and Naples', *Urban Studies* 43(4): 767–786.

Chalmers, D. (1994) 'Community policy on waste management: managing environmental decline gently', *Yearbook of European Law* 14: 257–312.

Chalmin, P. and Gaillochet, C. (2009) *From Waste to Resources: World waste survey 2009*, Paris: Economica.

Checkel, J. T. (1998) 'The constructivist turn in international relations theory', *World Politics* 50(2): 324–348.

—— (1999) 'Social Construction and Integration', *Journal of European Public Policy* (special issue) 6(4): 545–60.

Checkel, J. T. (2005) 'International institutions and socialization in Europe: introduction and framework', *International Organization* 59(4): 801–26.

Christiansen, T. and Piattoni, S. (eds.) (2004) *Informal Governance in the European Union*, UK-Northampton-USA: Edward Elgar.

Christiansen, T., Jorgensen, K. E. and Wiener, A. (eds.) (1999) *The Social Construction of Europe*, London: Routledge.

CITTALIA (2008) *L'ambiente e le Amministrazioni locali: analisi, politiche e strumenti di sostenibilità*, document drafted for the project 'La diffusione delle innovazioni nel sistema delle Amministrazioni locali', on behalf of the Department for Public Function.

—— (2010) *I Sindaci della Valle Padana contro le polveri sottili*, Fondazione Anci Ricerche, Rome: Cittalia.

—— (2010) *La questione dei rifiuti in Europa ed in Italia. Un'analisi della direttiva RAEE*. Paper series, February 2010.

Collier, U. (1997) *Energy and Environment in the European Union*, Aldershot: Ashgate.

Council of the European Union (2002) 1600/2002 Decision of the European Parliament and of the Council laying down the Sixth Community Environment Action Programme, Brussels: Official Journal of the European Communities.

—— (2006) 'Council Regulation (EC) No. 1083/2006, laying down general provision on the European regional Development Fund, the European Social Fund and the Cohesion Fund and repealing Regulation (EC) No 1260/1999', June 2006.

—— (2006a) 10917/06 Review of the EU Sustainable Development Strategy (EU SDS), Brussels: Official Journal of the European Communities.

Daviter, F. (2007) 'Policy framing in the European Union', *Journal of European Public Policy* 14(4): 654–66.

Dematteis, G. and Bonavero, P. (1997) (eds.) *Il sistema urbano italiano nello spazio unificato europeo*, Bologna: Il Mulino.

Dente, B. (2010) 'The transformation of regional and local governments: implications for environmental policy integration', in Goria, A., Sgobbi, A., and von Homeyer, I. (eds.) *Governance for the Environment: A comparative analysis of environmental policy integration*, Cheltenam-Northampton: Edward Elgar, pp. 77–87.

Dolowitz, D. and Marsh, D. (2000) 'Who learns what from whom: a review of the policy transfer literature', *Political Studies* 44(2): 343–57.

Dunsire, A. (1993) 'Manipulating social tensions: collibration as an alternative mode of government intervention', MPIFG Discussion Paper 93(7).

Eberlein, B. and Kerwer, D. (2002) 'Theorising the new modes of European union governance', *European Integration online Papers* 6(5) http://eiop.or.at/eiop/texte/2002-005.htm (accessed 10 November 2016).

—— (2004) 'New governance in the European union: a theoretical perspective', *Journal of Common Market Studies* 42(1): 121–42.

Eberlein, B. and Radaelli, C. M. (2010) 'Mechanisms of conflict management in EU regulatory policy', *Public Administration* 88(3): 782–99.

Egenhofer, C. (2010) *Greening EU strategy: The emerging EU strategy to address climate change*, CEPS task force report, www.ceps.eu/ceps/download/3915 (accessed 10 November 2016).

Ellingsen, T. and Östling, R. (2010) 'When does communication improve coordination', *American Economic Review* 100: 1695–1712.

Elman, C. (2005) 'Explanatory typologies in qualitative studies of international politics', *International organization* 59: 293–326.

Elster, J. (1998) 'A plea for mechanisms', in Hedstrom, P. and Swedberg, R. (eds.) *Social Mechanisms: An analytical approach to social theory*, Cambridge: Cambridge University Press.

Erbach, G. (2015) 'Understanding energy efficiency', briefing note, European Parliament Research Service, October 2015.

EURICUR, (2004) *National Urban Policies in the European Union*, Erasmus University Rotterdam.

European Commission (1989) *Guide to the Reform of the Community's Structural Funds*. Luxembourg: Office for Official Publications of the European Communities.

—— (1990) *Green Paper on the Urban Environment*, Communication from the Commission to the Council and the Parliament, Brussels: Commission of the European Communities.

—— (1993) 'The future of community initiatives under the structural funds', *Green Paper*, July 1993, Brussels/Luxembourg.

—— (1994) *The Future of Community Initiatives under the Structural Funds*, follow-up to the Green Paper. Brussels: Commission of the European Communities.

—— (1997a) *Towards an Urban Agenda in the European Union*, Brussels: Commission of the European Communities.

—— (1997b) *Agenda 2000: For a stronger and wider Union*, Brussels: Commission of the European Communities.

—— (1998) *Sustainable Urban Development in the European Union: A framework for action*, Communication from the Commission to the Council and the Parliament, the Economic and Social Committee and the Committee of the Regions, Brussels: Commission of the European Communities.

—— (1999) *The Community Initiatives in 2000–2006: Indicative allocation of funds among member states*, Brussels: Commission of the European Communities.

—— (2000a) 'Communication from the Commission to the member states, laying down guidelines for a community initiative concerning economic and social regeneration of cities and neighbourhoods in crisis in order to promote sustainable urban development, URBAN II', Luxemburg: Office for Official Publication of the European Communities.

—— (2000b) DG XVI, *Vademecum for URBAN II Community Initiative Programmes*, Office for Official Publication of the European Communities, Luxembourg.

—— (2001a) *A Sustainable Europe for a Better World: A European Union strategy for sustainable development*, Communication from the Commission to the Council and the European Parliament, COM (2001) 264 final, Brussels: Commission of the European Communities.

—— (2001b) *European Governance – a white paper*, Luxembourg: Office for Official Publications of the European Communities.

—— (2005) *Cohesion and the Lisbon Strategy: A clear signal to the cities and regions*, Luxemburg: Office for Official Publications of the European Communities.

—— (2006a) *LIFE in the City: Innovative solutions for Europe's urban environment*, Environment-Directorate General, Luxembourg: Office for Official Publications of the European Communities.

—— (2006b) *On Thematic Strategy on the Urban Environment*, Communication from the Commission to the Council and the European Parliament, COM (2005) 718 final, Brussels: Commission of the European Communities.

—— (2006c) *Cohesion Policy in Support of Growth and Jobs: Community Strategic Guidelines, 2007–2013*, Luxembourg: Office for Official Publications of the European Communities.

—— (2006d) *The Urban Dimension in Community Policies for the Period 2007–2013*, Brussels: European Commission-Interservice for urban affairs.

—— (2007a) *Integrated Environmental Management: Guidance in relation to the thematic strategy on the urban environment*, Luxembourg: Office for Official Publications of the European Communities.

—— (2007b) *Cohesion Policy 2007–2013: Commentaries and Official Texts*, Luxemburg: Office for Official Publications of the European Communities.

—— (2008) *Fostering the Urban Dimension: Analysis of the operational programmes co-financed by the European regional development fund (2007–2013)*, Working Document of the Directorate General for Regional Policy, Brussels: 25 November 2008, http://ec.europa.eu/regional_policy/sources/docoffic/2007/working/urban_dimension_en.pdf.

—— (2009a) *Promoting Sustainable Urban Development in Europe: Achievements and opportunities*, Brussels: Commission of the European Communities.

—— (2009b) *Guide to the Urban Dimension in European Union Policies*, Brussels: European Commission.

—— (2009c) COM (2009) 400 final, *Mainstreaming Sustainable Development into EU Policies: 2009 review of the European union strategy for sustainable development*, Communication from the Commission to the European parliament, the Council, the European Economic and Social Committee and the Committee of the Regions, Brussels: Commission of the European Communities.

—— (2011) *Cities of Tomorrow: Challenges, visions, ways forward*, Brussels: Commission of the European Communities.

European Environmental Agency (EEA) (2002) *Air Quality in Europe: State and trends 1990–99*, Copenhagen: EEA.

Exadaktylos, T. and Radaelli, C.M. (2009) 'Research design in European studies: the case of Europeanization', *Journal of Common Market Studies* 47(3): 507–30.

—— (2012) (eds.) *Research Design in European Studies*, Basingstoke: Palgrave Macmillan.

Falleti, T. and Lynch, G. (2009) 'Context and causal mechanisms in political analysis', *Comparative Political Studies* 20(10): 1–24.

Farrell, J. (1993) 'Meaning and credibility in cheap-talk games', Games and Economic Behaviour 5: 514–31.

Farrell, J. and Rabin, M. (1996) 'Cheap talk', *Journal of Economic Perspectives* 10(3): 103–18.

Farrell, K., Kemp, R., Hinterberger, F., Rammel, C., and Ziegler, R. (2005) 'From 'for' to governance for sustainable development in Europe', *International Journal of Sustainable Development*, 8: 127–150.

Featherstone, K. (2003) 'Introduction: in the name of "Europe"', in Featherstone, K. and Radaelli, C. M. (eds.) *The Politics of Europeanization*, Oxford: Oxford University Press, pp. 3–27.

Featherstone, K. and Radaelli, C.M. (eds.) (2003) *The Politics of Europeanization*, Oxford: Oxford University Press.

Fischer, L., Petschow, U., and Buclet, N. (2002) 'The consequences of implementing directives in the national context: the correct answer to the friction between national regimes?', in Buclet, N. (ed.) *Municipal Waste Management in Europe: European policy between harmonisation and subsidiarity*, Dordrecht: Kluwer Academic Publishers, pp. 81–110.

Franchino, F. (2005) 'The study of EU public policy – results of a survey', *European Union Politics* 6(2): 243–252.

George, A. and Bennett, A. (2005) *Case Studies and Theory Development in the Social Sciences*, MIT Press.

George, A. and McKeown, A. (1985) 'Case studies and theories of organizational decision making', *Research on Public Organisations* 2: 21–58.

Gerstenberg, O. (1997) 'Law's Polyarchy: a comment on Cohen and Sabel', *European Law Journal* 3(4): 343–58.

Gilardi, F. (2005) 'The institutional foundations of regulatory capitalism: the diffusion of independent regulatory agencies in Western Europe', *Annals of the American Academy of Political and Social Science* 598: 84–101.

Giuliani, M. (2003) 'Europeanization in comparative perspective: institutional fit and national adaptation', in Featherstone, K. and Radaelli, C. M. (eds.) *The Politics of Europeanization*, Oxford: Oxford University Press, pp. 134–59.

Goldsmith, M. (1993a) 'The Europeanization of local government', *Urban Studies* 30: 683–699.

—— (1993b) 'Local government', *Urban Studies* 29: 393–410.

—— (2003) 'Variable geometry, multilevel governance: European integration and subnational government in the new millenium', in Featherstone, K. and Radaelli, C. M. (eds.) *The Politics of Europeanization*, Oxford: Oxford University Press, pp. 112–34.

Goldsmith, M. and Klausen, K. K. (eds.) (1997) *European Integration and Local Government*, Cheltenham: Edward Elgar.

Goldsmith, M. and Larsen, H. (2004) 'Local political leadership: Nordic style', *International Journal of Urban and Regional Research* 28(1): 121–33.

Golub, J. (1996) 'State power and institutional influence in European integration: lessons from the Packaging Waste Directive', *Journal of Common Market Studies* 34(3): 313–39.

—— (2002) 'State power and institutional influence in European integration: lessons from the Packaging Waste Directive', in Jordan, A. (ed.) *Environmental Policy in the European Union: Actors, institutions and process*, London: Earthscan, pp. 218–239.

Goria, A., Sgobbi, A. and von Homeyer, I. (2010) (eds.) *Governance for the Environment: A comparative analysis of environmental policy integration*, Cheltenham-Northampton: Edward Elgar.

Gormley, W.T. Jr. (1986) 'Regulatory issue-networks in a federal system', *Polity* 18(4): 595–620.

Granovetter, M. (1973) 'The strength of weak ties', *American Journal of Sociology* 81: 1287–303.

Graziano, P. (2004) *Europeizzazione e politiche pubbliche italiane: coesione e lavoro a confronto*, Bologna: Il Mulino.

Graziano, P. and Vink, M.P. (eds.) (2007) *Europeanization: New research agendas*, Basingstoke: Palgrave/Macmillan.

Green Cowles, M., Caporaso, J. and Risse, T. (eds.) (2001) *Transforming Europe: Europeanization and domestic change*, Ithaca and London: Cornell University Press.

Green Cowles, M. and Risse, T. (2001) 'Transforming Europe: conclusions', in Green Cowles, M., Caporaso, J.A. and T. Risse (eds.) *Transforming Europe: Europeanization and domestic change*, Ithaca, NY: Cornell University Press, pp. 217–239.

Haas, E. (1958) *The Uniting of Europe*, Stanford: Stanford University Press.

Hall, P.A. (1993) 'Policy paradigms, social learning and the state: the case of economic policy making in Britain', *Comparative Politics* 25(3): 275–96.

—— (2003) 'Aligning ontology and methodology in comparative research', in Mahoney, J. and Rueschmeyer, D. (eds.) *Comparative Historical Analysis in the Social Science*, Cambridge: Cambridge University Press, pp. 373–407.

Halpern, C. (2005) 'Institutional change through innovation: the URBAN community initiative in Berlin, 1994–99', *Environment and Planning C: Government and policy* 23: 697–713.

—— (2010) 'Governing despite its instruments? Instrumentation in EU environmental policy', *West European Politics* 33(1) : 39–57.

Hassenteufel, P. and Surel, Y. (2000) 'Des politiques comme les autres? Construction de l'objet et outils d'analyse des politiques européennes', *Politique Européenne* 1: 8–23.

Haverland, M. (2000) 'National adaptation to the European union: the importance of institutional veto Points', *Journal of Public Policy* 20(1): 83–103.

Haverland, M. (2007) 'Methodology', in Graziano, P. and Vink, M.P. (eds.) *Europeanization: New research agendas*, London: Palgrave/MacMillan, pp. 59–73.

Hedström, P. (2005) *Dissecting the Social: On the principles of analytical sociology*, Cambridge: Cambridge University Press.

Hedström, P. and Swedberg, R. (1996) 'Social mechanisms', *Acta Sociologica* 39(3): 281–308.

Héritier, A. (1996) 'The accommodation of diversity in European policy making and its outcomes: regulatory policy as a patchwork', *Journal of European Public Policy* 3: 149–67

—— (2002a) 'New modes of governance in Europe: policy making without legislating?', in Héritier, A. (ed.) *The Provision of Common Goods: Governance across multiple arenas*, Boulder: Rowman and Littlefield, pp. 185–206.

—— (2002b) 'The accommodation of diversity in European policy making and its outcomes: regulatory policy as patchwork', in Jordan, A. (ed.) *Environmental Policy in the European Union: Actors, institutions and process*, London: Earthscan, pp. 180–97.

—— (2003) 'New modes of governance in Europe: increasing political efficiency and policy effectiveness', in Börzel, T. and Cichowsky, R. (eds.) *The State of the European Union: Law, politics and society*, Oxford: Oxford University Press, pp.105–27.

Héritier, A. and Lehmkuhl, D. (2008) 'The shadow of hierarchy and new modes of governance (introduction to special issue)', *Journal of European Public Policy* 28(1): 1–17.

Héritier, A. and Rhodes, M. (2011) (eds.) *New Modes of Governance in Europe: Governing in the shadow of hierarchy*, Basingstoke: Palgrave/MacMillan

Hodson, D. and Maher, I. (2001) 'The open method as a new mode of governance: the case of soft policy co-ordination', *Journal of Common Market Studies* 39(4): 719–746.

Hoeffler, C., Ledoux, C. and Prat, P. (2010) 'Temporalité et changement de politiques publiques', in Palier, B., Surel, Y. (eds.) *Quand les Politiques Changent. Temporalité et niveaux de l'action publiques*, Paris: L'Harmattan, pp. 53–79.

Hood, C. (1983) *The Tools of Government*, London and Basingstoke: The Macmillan Press.

—— (1998) *The Art of the State: Culture, rhetoric, and public management*, Oxford: Clarendon Press.

Hood, C. and Margetts, H. (2007) *The Tools of Government in the Digital Age*, London: Palgrave Macmillan.

Hooghe, L. (1995) 'Subnational mobilisation in the European Union' (special issue on the crisis of representation in Europe), *West European Politics* 18: 178–198.

—— (1996) *Cohesion Policy and European Integration: Building multi-level governance*, Oxford: Oxford University Press.

Hooghe, L. and Marks, G. (1997) 'The making of a polity. The struggle over European integration', in Kitschelt, H., Lange, P., Marks, G. and Stephens, J. (eds.) *The Politics and Political Economy of Advanced Industrial Societies*, Cambridge: Cambridge University Press, pp. 70–97.

—— (2001) *Multi-Level Governance and European Integration*, Blue Ridge Summit, PA: Rowman and Littlefield.

Hooghe, L., Marks, G. and Schakel, A. H. (2010) *The Rise of Regional Authority: A comparative study of 42 democracies*, New York: Routledge.

ISTAT (2008) *Statistiche Ambientali 2008*, Rome: Istat.

—— (2010) *Indicatori Ambientali Urbani*, Istituto Nazionale di Statistica: Roma.

Jacquot, S. and Woll, C. (2004) *Les usages de l'Europe: Acteurs et transformations européennes*, Paris: L'Harmattan.

—— (2008) 'Action publique Européenne: les acteurs stratégiques face à l'Europe', *Politique européenne* 25(2): 161–92.

Jaquier, C. (2005) 'On relationships between integrated policies for sustainable urban development and urban governance', *Tijdschrift voor Economosche en Sociale Geografie* 96: 363–376.

Jeffery, C. (1996) 'Regional information offices in Brussels and multi-level governance in the EU', *Regional and Federal Studies* 6(2): 183–203.

—— (2000) 'Sub-national mobilisation and European integration: does it make any difference?', *Journal of Common Market Studies* 38(1): 1–23.

Jobert, B. (2003) 'Europe and the recomposition of the national forums: the French case', *Journal of European Public Policy* 37(5): 463–77.

Joerges, C. and Neyer, J. (1997) 'Transforming strategic interaction into deliberative problem-solving: European comitology in the foodstuffs sector', *Journal of European Public Policy* 4(4): 609–25.

Joerges, C., Mény, Y. and Weiler, J.H.H. (2001) (eds.) *Mountain or Molehill? A critical appraisal of the Commission White Paper on governance*, Jean Monnet Working Paper 6(1). Florence: Robert Schuman Centre, European University Institute.

John, P. (2000) 'The Europeanization of sub-national governance', *Urban Studies* 37(5-6): 877–894.

—— (2001) *Local Governance in Western Europe*, London: Sage.

Jones, B. and Keating, M. (1995) *The European Union and the Regions*, Oxford: Clarendon.

Jones, P. (2003) 'Urban regeneration's poisoned chalice: is there an impasse in (community) participation-based policy?', *Urban Studies* 40(3): 581–601.

Jordan, A. and Rayners, T. (2010) 'The evolution of climate policy in the European Union: an historical overview', in Jordan, A. (eds.) *Climate Change*

Policy in the European Union Confronting the Dilemmas of Mitigation and Adaptation, Cambridge: Cambridge University Press.

Jordan, A., Wurzel, R. and Zito, A. (2005) 'The rise of 'new' policy instruments in comparative perspective: has governance eclipsed government?', *Political Studies* 33: 477–96.

Jordan, A.J., Huitema, D., van Asselt, D. H., Rayner T. and Berkhout F. (2010) (eds.) *Climate Change Policy in the European Union: Confronting the dilemmas of mitigation and adaptation*, Cambridge: Cambridge University Press.

Kassim, H. and Le Galès, P. (2010) 'Exploring governance in a multi-level polity: a policy instrument approach', *West European Politics* 33(1): 1–21.

Kazepov, J. (2005) (ed.) *Cities of Europe: Changing contexts, local arrangements, and the challenge to urban cohesion*, Malden, Mass: Blackwell Publishing.

Keating, M. (1998) *The New Regionalism in Western Europe: Territorial restructuring and political change*, London: Edward Elgar.

—— (2001) 'Governing cities and regions: territorial restructuring in a global age' in Scott, A. (ed.) *Global City-Regions: Trends, theory, policy*, Oxford: Oxford University Press, pp. 371–391.

Keohane, R. (1984) *After Hegemony: Cooperation and discord in the world political*, Princeton: Princeton University Press.

Kern, K. and Bulkeley, H. (2009) 'Cities, Europeanization and multi-level governance: governing climate change through transnational municipal networks', *Journal of Common Market Studies* 47(2): 309–32.

Knill, C. (1998) 'European policies: the impact of national administrative traditions', *Journal of Public Policy* 18(1): 1–28.

Knill, C. and Lehmkuhl, D. (1999) 'How Europe matters. Different mechanisms of Europeanization', *European Integration Online Papers (EIoP)*, No. 3(7).

—— (2002) 'The national impact of European Union regulatory policy: three Europeanization mechanisms', *European Journal of Political Research* 41(2): 255–80.

Knill, C. and Lenschow, A. (1998) 'Coping with Europe: the impact of British and German administrations on the implementation of EU environmental policy', *Journal of European Public Policy* 5(4): 595–614.

—— (2000) (eds.) *Implementing EU Environmental Policy: New directions and old problems*, Manchester and New York: Manchester University Press.

—— (2003) 'Modes of regulation in the governance of the European Union: towards a comprehensive evaluation', *European Integration online Papers* 7, http://eiop.or.at/eiop/texte/2003-001a.htm (accessed 10 November 2016).

Kohler-Koch, B. (2002) European networks and ideas: changing national policies? *European Integration Online Papers* (EioP).

Kohler-Koch, B. and Eising, R. (1999) *The Transformation of Governance in the European Union*, London: Routledge.

Kooiman, J. (1993) *Modern Governance*, London: Sage Publications.

Krasner, S. (1991) 'Global communications and national power: life on the Pareto frontier', *World Politics* 43(9): 336–66.

Kubler, D. and Piliutyte, J. (2007) 'Intergovernmental relations and international urban strategies: constraints and opportunities in multilevel polities', *Environment and Planning C-Government and Policy* 25(3): 357–73.

Ladrech, R. (1994) 'Europeanization of domestic politics and institutions: the case of France', *Journal of Common Market Studies* 32(1): 69–88.

Lascoumes, P. and Le Galès, P. (2007) 'Introduction: understanding public policy through its instruments – from the nature of instruments to the sociology of public policy instrumentation', *Governance* 20(1): 1–21.

Le Galés, P. (1998) 'Regulations and governance in European cities', *International Journal of Urban and Regional Research* 22(3): 482–506.

—— (1999) 'Is political economy still relevant to study the culturalization of cities?' *European Urban and Regional Studies* 6(4): 293–302.

—— (2001) 'Est maitre des lieux celui qui les organise: how rules change when national and European domains collide', in Stone Sweet, A., Sandholtz, W. and Fligestein, N. (eds.) *The Institutionalization of Europe*, Oxford: Oxford University Press, pp. 137–155.

—— (2002) *European Cities: Social conflict and governance*, NY: Oxford University Press.

—— (2007) *Governing Globalizing Cities, Reshaping Urban Policies: What policies for globalizing cities? Rethinking the urban policy agenda*, Madrid: OECD.

Lefevre, C. (1998) 'Metropolitan government and governance in Western countries: A critical review', *International Journal of Urban and Regional Research* 22(1): 9–25.

Legambiente (2008) *Italia 2008 – scenario 2020: le politiche energetiche dell'Italia*. Rapporto annual di Legambiente, Milano: Edizioni Ambiente.

Lenoble, J. and Maesschalck, M. (2006) 'Beyond new-institutionalist and pragmatist approaches to governance', *Synthesis Report for the REFGOV Research Project*, REFGOV Working Paper Series: REFGOV-SGI/TNU-1, 2006.

Lenschow, A. (2005) 'Europeanization of public policy', in Richardson, J.J. (ed.) *European Union: Power and policy making*, Abingdon: Routledge, pp. 55–73.

Levi-Faur, D. (2004) 'On the 'net impact' of Europeanization – the EU's telecoms and electricity regimes between the global and the national', *Comparative Political Studies* 37(1): 3–29.

Little, D. (1991) *Varieties of Social Explanations: An introduction to the philosophy of social science*, Boulder, Co: Westview Press.

Lowi, T. J. (1964) 'American business, public policy, case studies, and political theory', *World Politics* 16(4): 677–715.

—— (1972) 'Four systems of policy, politics, and choice', *Public Administration Review* 32(July/August): 292–310.

Machamer, P., Darden, L. and Craver, C. F. (2000) 'Thinking about mechanisms', *Philosophy of Science* 1: 1–25.

Mahoney, J. (2001) 'Beyond correlation analysis: recent innovations in theory and methods', *Sociological Forum* 16(3): 575–593.

Majone, G. (1975) 'Standard setting and the theory of institutional choice', *working paper 75/87*, International Institute for applied system analysis, Laxenburg (Austria).

—— (1982) 'Science and trans-science in standard setting', *Science, Technology and Human Values* 9(1): 15–22.

—— (1992) *Evidence, Arguments and Persuasion in the Policy Process*, NY: Yale University Press.

—— (1994) 'The rise of the regulatory state in Europe', *West European Politics* 17(3): 77–101.

—— (1996a) 'Which social policy for Europe', in Mény, Y., Muller, P. and Quermonne, J.L. (eds.) *Adjusting to Europe – The impact of the European Union on national institutions and policies*, London and New York: Routledge, pp. 123–37.

—— (1996b) *Regulating Europe*, London: Routledge.

—— (2005) *Dilemmas of European Integration: The ambiguities and pitfalls of integration by stealth*, Oxford: Oxford University Press.

March, J. G. and Olsen, J. (1998) 'The institutional dynamics of international political orders', *International Organization* 52(4): 943–69.

—— (1989) *Rediscovering Institutions: The organizational basis of political life*, New York: Free Press.

Marks, G. (1992) 'Structural policy in the European community', in Sbragia, A. (ed.) *Europolitics. Institutions and Policy Making in the 'New' European Community*, Washington (DC): Brookings, pp. 191–225.

—— (1993) 'Structural policy and multi-level governance in the EC', in Cafruny, A.W. and Rosenthal, G. (eds.) *The State of the European Community: the Maastricht debates and beyond*, Longman and Lynne Rienner, pp. 391–410.

Marks, G., Hooghe, L. and Blank, K. (1996) 'European integration from the 1980s: state-centric versus multi-level governance', *Journal of Common Market Studies* 34(3): 341–378.

Marks, G., Streeck, W., Schmitter, P.C. and Scharpf, F.W. (1996b) *Governance in the European Union*, London: Sage.

Marshall, A. (2003) 'Urban and local governance: the growing European dimension', *Journal of European Public Policy* 10(3): 478–85.

—— (2005) 'Europeanization at the urban level: local actors, institutions and the dynamics of multi-level interaction', *Journal of European Public Policy* 12(4): 668–86.

Martinsen, D.S. (2007) 'The Europeanization of gender equality – who controls the scope of non-discrimination?', *Journal of European Public Policy* 14(4): 544–62.

McAdams, R. (2008) 'Game theory and law: a (lack of) progress report', from the selected works of Richard H. McAdams, http://works.bepress.com/richard_mcadams/2.

McCain, R. (2009) *Game Theory and Public Policy*, Cheltenham: Edward Elgar Publishing.

McCarty, N. and Meirowitz, A. (2007) *Political Game Theory: An introduction*, Cambridge: Cambridge University Press.

Milward, A.S. (1992) *The European Rescue of the Nation State*, London: Routledge.

Moravcsik, A. (1991) 'Negotiating the Single European Act: national interests and conventional statecraft in the European community', *International Organization* 45(1): 19–56.

—— (1993) 'Preferences and power in the European community. A liberal intergovernmental approach', *Journal of Common Market Studies* 31(4): 473–524.

—— (1998) *The Choice for Europe: Social purpose and state power from Messina to Maastricht*, Ithaca: Cornell University Press.

—— (1999) 'A new statecraft? Supranational entrepreneurs and international cooperation', *International Organization* 53(2): 267–306.

Muller, P. (1995) 'Les politiques publiques comme construction d'un rapport au monde', in Faure, A., Pollet, G. and Warin, P. (eds.) *La construction du sens dans les politiques publiques, débats autour de la notion de référentiel*, Paris: L'Harmattan, pp. 153–179.

—— (2000) 'L'analyse cognitive des politiques publiques: vers une sociologie politique de l'action publique', *Revue Française de Sciences Politiques* 50(2): 189–207.

Nanetti, R. Y. (2002) 'Adding value to city planning: the European Union's urban programme in Naples', *South European Society and Politics*, 6(3): 33–57.

Neyer, J. (2006) 'The deliberative turn in integration theory', *Journal of European Public Policy* 13(5): 779–91.

Oberthür, S. and Kelly, R. C. (2008) 'EU leadership in international climate policy', *The International Spectator* 43(3): 35–50.

Oberthür, S. and Pallemaerts, M. (eds.) (2010) *The New Climate Policies of the European Union: Internal legislation and climate diplomacy*, Brussels: Brussels University Press.

OECD (2000) *The Reform of Metropolitan Governance*, Paris: OECD.

Olsen, J.P. (1995) 'Europeanization and nation-state dynamics', *Oslo: ARENA*, Vol. Working Paper No. 9.

—— (2002) 'The many faces of Europeanization', *Journal of Common Market Studies* 40(5): 921–52.

Pasquier, R. (2005) 'Cognitive Europeanization and the territorial effects of multilevel policy transfer: local development in French and Spanish regions', *Regional and Federal Studies* 15(3): 295–310.

Pasquier, R. and Weisbein, J. (2004) 'L'Europe au microscope du local. Manifeste pour une sociologie politique de l'intégration communautaire', *Politique Européenne* 12: 5–21.

Pedriana, N. (2005) 'Rational choice, structural context, and increasing returns: a strategy for analytic narratives in historical sociology', *Sociological Methods and Research* 349–82.

Peters, G. (1999) *Institutional Theory in Political Science: The new institutionalism*, London: Pinter.

Piattoni, S. and Smyrl, M. (1998) 'Regional governance in Italy: beyond the North-South divide', *ARENA*.

Pierre, J. (1998) (ed.) *Partnership in Urban Governance: European and American experience*, London: Macmillan.

—— (2000) *Debating Governance: Authority, steering, and democracy*, Oxford: Oxford University Press.

Pierson, P. (1993) 'When effects become cause: policy feedback and political change', *World Politics* 45(4): 595–628.

—— (2004) *Politics in Time: History, institutions and social analysis*: Oxford: Oxford University Press.

Pollack, M. A (1997) 'The Commission as an agent', in Nugent, N. (ed.) *At the Heart of the Union: Studies of the European Commission*, New York: Macmillan, pp. 111–31.

Powell, W. W. and. Di Maggio, P. J. (1991) *The New Institutionalism in Organizational Analysis*, Chicago: University of Chicago Press.

Putnam, R. (1988) 'Diplomacy and domestic politics: the logic of two-level games', *International Organization* 42(2): 427–60.

Radaelli, C. M. (1998) 'Game theory and institutional entrepreneurship: transfer pricing and the search for coordination international tax policy', *Political Studies Journal* 26(4): 603–19.

—— (2003) 'The Europeanization of public policy' in Featherstone, K. and Radaelli, C.M. (eds.) *The Politics of Europeanization*, Oxford: Oxford University Press, pp.27–57.

—— (2004) 'Europeanization: solution or problem?', in *European Integration on-line papers* 8:16, http://papers.ssrn.com/sol3/papers.cfm?abstract_id=601163 (accessed 10 November 2016).

—— (2008) 'Europeanization, policy learning, and new modes of governance', *Journal of Comparative Policy Analysis* 10(3): 239–254.

Radaelli, C. M. and Exadaktylos, T. (2009) 'New directions in Europeanization research', in Egan, M., Nugent, N. and Paterson, W. (eds.) *Agendas in EU studies: Stalking the elephant*, Basingstoke: Palgrave Macmillan, pp. 189–215.

Radaelli, C. M. and Kraemer, U.S. (2008) 'Governance areas in EU direct tax policy', *Journal of Common Market Studies* 46(2): 315–336.

Radaelli, C. M. and Pasquier, R. (2006) 'Encounters with Europe: concepts, definitions and research design', *Politik* 9(3): 6–14.

—— (2007) 'Conceptual issues', in Vink, M.P. and Graziano, P. (eds.) *Europeanization: New research agendas*, Basingstoke: Palgrave/ Macmillan pp. 35–46.

Radaelli, C. M. and Schmidt, V. (2004) 'Discourse and policy change in Europe – special issue', *West European Politics* 27(2): 183–210.

Ragin, C. (1989) *The Comparative Method: Moving beyond qualitative and quantitative strategies*, Berkeley, California: University of California Press.

—— (2000) *Fuzzy-set Social Science*, Chicago: University of Chicago Press.

Rasmussen, D.E. (2007) *Games and Information: An introduction to game theory*. Oxford: Blackwell Publishing.

Rhodes, R. A. W. (1986) 'Power dependence: theories of central-local relations: a critical assessment', in Goldsmith, M. (ed.) *New Research in Central-Local Relations*. Brookfield: Gower, pp. 1–33.

—— (1996) 'The new governance: governing without government', *Political Studies* 44: 652–667.

—— (1997) *Understanding Governance: Policy networks, governance, reflexivity and accountability*, Philadelphia and Buckingham: Open University Press.

Romer, T. and Rosenthal, H. (1978) 'Political resource allocation, controlled agendas, and the status quo', *Public Choice* 33(4): 27–43.

—— (1979) 'Bureaucrats versus voters: on the political economy of resource allocation by indirect democracy', *The Quarterly Journal of Economics*, 93(4): 563–87.

Roth, A. and Malouf, M.W.K. (1979) 'Game theoretic models and the role of information in bargaining', *Psychological Review* 86(6): 574–94.

Ruggie, J. G. (1998) *Constructing the World Polity: Essays on international institutionalization*, New York: Routledge.

Sabel, C. and Zeitlin, C (2008) 'Learning from difference: the new architecture of experimentalist governance in the European Union', *European Law Journal* 14(2): 271–327.

Salamon, L. K. (2002a) 'Introduction', in Salamon, L. K. (ed.) *The Tools of Government: A guide to the new governance*, Oxford: Oxford University Press, pp. 1–47.

—— (2002b) *The Tools of Government: A guide to the new governance*, Oxford: Oxford University Press.

Sandholtz, W. (1992) *High-Tech Europe: The politics of international cooperation*, Berkeley: University of California Press.

Sawicki, F. (2000) 'Les politistes et le microscope', in CURRAP, *Les méthodes au concret. Démarches, formes de l'expérience et terrains d'investigations en science politique*, Paris: PUF, pp. 143–64.

Sbragia, A.M. (2001) 'Italy pays for Europe: political leadership, political choice and institutional adaptation', in Green Cowles, M. (eds.) *Transforming Europe: Europeanization and domestic change*, Ithaca: Cornell University Press, pp. 79–97.

Scharpf, F. (1986) 'Policy failure and institutional reform: why should form follow function?', *International Social Science Journal* 38(2): 179–189.

—— (1990) 'Games real actors could play: the problem of mutual predictability', *Rationality and Society* 2: 471–94.

—— (1991) 'Games real actors could play: the challenge of complexity', *Journal of Theoretical Politics* 3(3): 277–304.

—— (1994) 'Community and autonomy. Multi-level policy making in the European Union', *Journal of European Public Policy* 1(2): 219–42.

—— (1997) *Games Real Actor Play: Actor-centred institutionalism in policy research*, Colorado: Westview Press.

—— (1999) *Governing in Europe: Effective and democratic?*, Oxford: Oxford University Press.

Schmidt, V.A. (2002a) 'Europeanization and the mechanics of economic policy adjustment', *Journal of European Public Policy* 9(6): 894–912.

—— (2002b) 'Does discourse matter in the politics of welfare state adjustment?', *Comparative Political Studies* 35(2): 168–93.

—— (2006) *Democracy in Europe: The EU and national polities*, Oxford: Oxford University Press.

—— (2007) 'Trapped by their ideas: French elites' discourses of European integration and globalization', *Journal of European Public Policy* 14(7): 992–1009.

—— (2008) 'Discursive institutionalism: the explanatory power of ideas and discourse', *Annual Review of Political Science* 11: 303–26.

Schmidt, V.A. and Radaelli, C.M. (2002) 'Europeanization, discourse, and policy change: mapping the new research agenda', *Paper presented at ECPR Joint Sessions*, Turin: Italy.

—— (2004) 'Policy change and discourse in Europe: conceptual and methodological issues', *West European Politics* 27(2): 183–210.

Schneider, A. and Ingram, H. (1990) 'Behavioural assumptions of policy tools', *The Journal of Politics* 52(2): 510–29.

—— (1993) 'Social construction of target populations: implications for politics and policy', *American Political Science Review* 87(2): 334–47.

Schon, D. and Rein, M. (1994) *Frame Reflection: Toward the resolution of intractable policy controversies*, New York: Basic Books.

Schultze, J. C. (2003) 'Cities and EU governance: policy takers or policy makers?', *Regional and Federal Studies* 13(1): 121–147.

Scotford, E. (2007) 'Trash or treasure: policy tensions in EC Waste Regulation', *Journal of Environmental Law* 19(3): 367–88.

Sheples, K. (1986) 'Institutional equilibrium and equilibrium institutions', in Weisberg, E. (ed.) *Political Science: The science of politics*, New York: Agathon, pp. 51–82.

—— (2006) 'Rational choice institutionalism', in Rhodes, R.A.W., Binder, S.A. and Rockman, B.A. (eds.) *The Oxford Handbook of Political Institutions*, Oxford: Oxford University Press, pp. 23–39.

Smith, A. (1999) 'L'espace public européen: une vue (trop) aérienne', *Critique Internationale* 2: 169–80.

—— (2000) 'Institutions et intégration européenne. Une méthode de recherche pour un objectif problématise', in CURRAP, *Les méthodes au concret. Démarches, formes de l'expérience et terrains d'investigations en science politique*, Paris: PUF, pp. 246–49.

—— (2001) *La passion du sport. Le football, le rugby et les appartenances en Europe*, Rennes: PUR.

Snidal, D. (1985) 'Coordination versus prisoner's dilemma: implications for international cooperation and regimes', *American Political Science Review* 79: 923–942.

Spitzer, R. J. (1987) 'Promoting policy theory: revising the arenas of power', *Policy Studies Journal* 15(4): 675–89.

Stinchcombe, A. L. (1991) 'The conditions of fruitfulness of theorizing about mechanisms in social science', *Philosophy of the Social Sciences* 21: 367–88.

Stoker, G. (1998) 'Public-private partnerships and urban governance', in Pierre, J. (ed.) *Partnership in urban governance, European and American experience*, London: ed. MacMillan, pp. 34–52.

Surel, Y. (2000) 'The role of cognitive and normative frames in policy-making', *Journal of European Public Policy* 7(4): 495–512.

Thatcher, M. (2004) 'Winners and losers in Europeanization: reforming the national regulation of telecommunications', *West European Politics* 27(2): 284–309.

Tofarides, M. (2003) *Urban Policy in the European Union: A multi-gatekeeper system*, Aldershot: Ashgate.

Treib, O., Bahr, H. and Falkner, G. (2005) 'Modes of Governance: Towards Conceptual Clarification', *European Governance Papers (EUROGOV)* No. N-05-02.

Tsebelis, G. (1990) *Nested Games: Rational choice in comparative politics*, Berkeley: University of California Press.

Van Boxemeer, B. and Van Beckoven, E. (2005) 'Public-Private partnership in urban regeneration: a comparison of Dutch and Spanish PPPs', *European Journal of Housing Policy* 5(1): 1–16.

Van Horn, C. E., Baumer, D. C. and Gormley, W. T. Jr. (2001) *Politics and Public Policy*, Washington, D. C.: Congressional Quarterly Inc.

Vedung, E. (1998) 'Policy instruments: typologies and theories', in Bemelmens-Videc, M. L. (eds.) *Carrots, Sticks and Sermons: Policy instruments and their evaluation*, N.Y.-London: Transaction Publisher, pp. 21–59.

Vitalis, R. (2006) 'The past is another country', in Perecman, E. and Curran, S.R. (eds.) *A Handbook for Social Science Field Research: Essays and bibliographic sources on research design and methods*, New York: Sage Publications.

Wallace, H. and Wallace, W. (2000) (eds.) *Policy Making in the European Union*, Oxford: Oxford University Press.

Weber, M. (1993) *Basic Concepts in Sociology*, New York: Carol Publishing Group/Citadel Press.

Winter, S. (2003) 'Implementation. Introduction', in Paters, G. and Pierre, J. (eds.) *Handbook of Public Administration*, London; Sage Publications, pp. 205–11.

World Commission on Environment and Development (WCED) (1987) *Our Common Future*, Oxford: Oxford University Press.

Wright, V. and Cassese, S. (1996) (eds.) *La recomposition de l'État en Europe*, Paris: La Decouverte.

Zeitlin, J. and Trubek, D. M. (2003) *Governing Work and Welfare in a New Economy: European and American experiences*, Oxford: Oxford University Press.

Zeitlin, J., Pochet, P. and Magnusson, L. (2005) *The Open Method of Coordination in Action: The European employment and social inclusion strategies*, Brussels: Peter Lang.

Zerbinati, S. (2004) 'Europeanization and EU funding in Italy and England. A comparative local perspective', *Journal of European Public Policy* 11(6): 1000–19.

Index

Note: Locators followed by '*f*' and '*t*' refer to figures and tables, respectively.

www.ingramcontent.com/pod-product-compliance
Lightning Source LLC
Chambersburg PA
CBHW021816270326
41932CB00007B/212